MAY SARTON:
AMONG THE USUAL DAYS

Books by May Sarton

Mr. et Mme. George Sarton ont le plaisir de
vous annoncer la naissance de la petite Marie.
Wondelgem, le 3 mai 1912.

MAY SARTON

AMONG THE USUAL DAYS

A PORTRAIT

UNPUBLISHED POEMS, LETTERS,
JOURNALS, AND PHOTOGRAPHS

SELECTED AND EDITED BY

SUSAN SHERMAN

PREFACE BY MAY SARTON

W. W. Norton & Company   New York   London

The text of this book is composed in 12.5/15.5 Centaur Monotype,
with the display set in Centaur.

Composition by ComCom, Inc.

Manufacturing by Courier Companies Inc.

Book design by Margaret M. Wagner.

Library of Congress Cataloging-in-Publication Data

Sarton, May, 1912–

[Selections. 1993]

May Sarton : among the usual days : a portrait : unpublished poems, letters, journals, and photographs / selected and
edited by Susan Sherman ; preface by May Sarton.

p. cm.

1. Sarton, May, 1912– —Correspondence. 2. Poets, American—20th century—Correspondence. 3. Sarton, May,
1912– —

Diaries. 4. Poets, American—20th century—Diaries. I. Sherman,
Susan. II. Title.

PS3537.A832A6 1993

811'.52—dc20

[B]

ISBN 0-393-03451-8

W. W. Norton & Company, Inc., 500 Fifth Avenue, New York, N.Y. 10110

W. W. Norton & Company Ltd., 10 Coptic Street, London WC1A 1PU

1 2 3 4 5 6 7 8 9 0

PREFACE

*W*hen Susan Sherman suggested that an interesting book could be created from unpublished poems, letters, and journals in my archive at the Berg Collection in New York and the files here in York, I was delighted. But I had no idea what an evocative work of art her selections would create, how brilliantly she would choose from the immense amount of material, nor how rich the result would prove to be.

I only knew that she had been studying the material for five years, going into the city sometimes four or five times a week from Riverdale, where she teaches at the Riverdale Country School. Her unfailing enthusiasm and faith in the work made what must have seemed an impossible task possible. She never wavered in her belief that a wonderful book could be fashioned by her and me together.

It was essential, of course, that if such a project be undertaken, the editor be of exceptional sensitivity to my way of looking at things and be able to make connections between the European in me, always near the surface, and the American, who only became rooted in the United States when she bought an old farmhouse in New Hampshire. Susan spent many summers in France and later on an island in Maine, so she had touchstones. Most of all, she knows my work better than anyone else alive, better than I do myself when it comes to unpublished material.

That is where the magic comes in, for *May Sarton: Among the Usual Days* is far more revealing and accurate than any book I could have written. For now at eighty I forget a great deal and am chiefly interested in the present, various and rich though the past has been. What I might write about the past could not have the freshness of a letter written forty years ago. So in a way Susan has given me back a self I had nearly forgotten. As an old woman I rejoice to find myself young again, to meet myself as I became myself year after year, and as I held on to a vision of life that never wavered. It is a lively story that I have greatly enjoyed reading and the best present I ever had. Thank you, Susan!

MAY SARTON
York, Maine
March 1992

ACKNOWLEDGMENTS

Grateful acknowledgment to May Sarton for permission to quote from her papers in the Henry W. and Albert A. Berg Collection of English and American Literature, New York Public Library, Astor, Lenox, and Tilden Foundations; at the Amherst College Library; at the Beinecke Rare Book and Manuscript Library at Yale University; at the Harry Ransom Humanities Research Center, University of Texas at Austin; and in her personal archives in York, Maine. Her generosity and help have been illimitable. Mostly I thank her for having produced an archive whose breadth and amplitude have sustained me through five years of work, and will sustain me for years to come as I prepare Selected and Collected Letters.

For permission to quote from the letters to Louise Bogan, grateful acknowledgment to Ruth Limmer, executor of the Bogan Estate, and to the Amherst College Library.

For the letters to Elizabeth Bowen, grateful acknowledgment to the Harry Ransom Humanities Research Center, University of Texas at Austin.

For the letters to H.D., grateful acknowledgment to the Beinecke Rare Book and Manuscript Library, Yale University.

And for permission to quote from the letters to Ethel Barrymore, Rollo Walter Brown, William Theo Brown, Marie Closset, Katharine Davis, Margaret Foote Hawley, S. S. Koteliansky, Eva Le Gallienne, Judith Matlack, Muriel Rukeyser, Eleanor Mabel Sarton, George Sarton, Basil de Sélincourt, Giorgio de Santillana, Anne Longfellow Thorp, Katharine Taylor, and Virginia Woolf, grateful acknowledgment to the Henry W. and Albert A. Berg Collection of English and American Literature, New York Public Library, Astor, Lenox, and Tilden Foundations.

The letters to all other correspondents remain at this time in Sarton's private archives in York.

Appreciation *in memoriam* to Dr. Lola Szladits of the Berg Collection. And ardent gratitude to Frank Mattson, her successor, for his kindness and staunch cooperation. Thanks to Steve Crook and Philip Milito at the Berg for their patient goodwill. To Roger Boocock and John Gulla, who helped in many indirect ways. To the Parents Association of the Riverdale Country School for summer grants. To John Hawkinson, master teacher, who gently gave me wings in the form of computer skills. To Shoji Masuzawa for his steadfast availability and knowledge. To Derek Smith for his generosity, patience, and time. To Philip Lyman at the Gotham Book Mart, who unfailingly unearthed unfindable and essential books.

Special thanks to Louise Bates, Robin Berson, Sheila Coffey, Bruce Leslie, Rhonda Rigrodsky, and Bill Pahlka.

My gratitude to Nancy Jahn Hartley can scarcely be contained in this acknowledgment. As a professional in library science she gave me a continuous private course in researching. She joined and led me in uncovering the most elusive facts and details for the footnotes. Having been secretary to May Sarton for twelve and a half years, she guided me through the archives in York, which she herself had organized and knew intimately. Her expertise, her love for and knowledge of the work, her humor and encouragement, and above all her friendship have been indispensable, and have greatly enhanced the scope and richness of this book.

The quotation on the dedication page is from "Elegy for Louise Bogan," written February 10, 1970, and published in *A Durable Fire.*

ABBREVIATIONS AND
SHORT FORMS
USED IN SOURCE NOTES

5 E 10	5 East 10th Street, New York City.
22 E 10	22 East 10th Street, New York City.
54 W 10	54 West 10th Street, New York City.
25 W 11	25 West 11th Street, New York City.
239 E 17	239 East 17th Street, New York City.
245 E 37	245 East 37th Street, New York City.
94 Macd	The McLean Club, 94 Macdougal Street, New York City. A residence for women where Sarton lived while working at the Civic Repertory Theatre.
Agnes Scott	Agnes Scott College, 134 South Candler Street, Decatur, Georgia.
AT	Anne Longfellow Thorp. Grandaughter of the poet Longfellow. May Sarton's teacher at the Shady Hill School and friend of the family. Heroine of Sarton's novel *The Magnificent Spinster.*
Austria	Sommerheim Seeblick Am Grundlsee, 700 Meereshohe, Salzkammergut, Steiermark, Austria. The summer home of Hermann Schwartzwald, Austrian director of finance in the 1930s, and his wife, Dr. Eugenie Schwartzwald, teacher and social worker; during the first four decades of this century it served as an inn for writers, intellectuals, and musicians, including Thomas Mann, Rilke, Brecht, Sinclair Lewis, Dorothy Thompson, Rudolf Serkin, the Huxleys, and May Sarton.
BB	Bill Brown (William Theo Brown). A painter living in San Francisco. Subject of Sarton's poem "Unlucky Soldier," which appeared in the *Atlantic Monthly.*
BdeS	Basil de Sélincourt. Literary critic for the *Observer* in London. Lived in Kingham, Oxfordshire.
Black Mt	Black Mountain College, Black Mountain, North Carolina.

Bread Loaf	Bread Loaf Writers' Conference, Middlebury, Vermont.
Carbondale	State Teachers College of Southern Illinois, Carbondale, Illinois. Sarton was Poet in Residence, June 8–25, 1946, and returned for frequent appearances.
CD	Cora DuBois. Anthropologist who worked under Franz Boas and Ruth Benedict, professor at Harvard and Radcliffe, author, and authority on Southeast Asia. Known particularly for her *The People of Alor.*
Chez Limbosch	The Limbosches lived in Le Pignon Rouge on Avenue Léquime in Brussels, Belgium. They had a summer home called Le Nid d'Alouettes in Knocke, Belgium. In her old age, the widowed Céline lived in an apartment on the Avenue Maréchal Joffre, also in Brussels.
Ch Pl	5 Channing Place, Cambridge, Massachusetts. Home of the Sartons.
Cornwall	Kilmarth, Par, Cornwall, England. Home of Dorothea (Waley) and Charles Singer, historians of science.
DMC	Day Mountain Camp, Temple, Maine.
Dublin	Rockbrook House, Rathfarnham, County Dublin, Ireland. Home of Lady Beatrice Glenavy.
EB	Elizabeth Bowen. Anglo-Irish novelist and critic.
EBa	Ethel Barrymore. American actress.
EBl	Eleanor Blair. Wellesley graduate, class of 1915. Taught at Dana Hall and other schools. Helped Sarton type and edit her work over many years, particularly *Plant Dreaming Deep* and *Kinds of Love.*
EFK	Edith Forbes Kennedy. Friend from Cambridge, mother of Fitzroy, Edmund, and Robert, with whom Sarton grew up. Sarton wrote "Evening Music" for her.
ELeG	Eva Le Gallienne. London-born American actress, producer, director, writer, and teacher. Daughter of the novelist and poet Richard Le Gallienne. Trained at the Royal Academy of Dramatic Arts. Founder of the Civic Repertory Theatre in New York, where Sarton worked first as an apprentice, then as a member of the First Studio, and finally as director of the Apprentice Group for four years before starting her own company.
EMS	Eleanor Mabel Sarton. Sarton's mother, artist, designer of furniture, teacher of applied design at the Shady Hill School and the Winsor School. Designer of embroidered dresses for Belgart in Washington, D.C.

	Sarton has edited selected letters from her mother in *Letters to May* (Orono, Me.: Puckerbrush Press).
Greenings	Greenings Island, Southwest Harbor, Maine. Summer home of Anne Thorp.
GdeS	Marquis Giorgio de Santillana. Historian of Science, author.
GS	George Sarton, Sarton's father, historian of science, professor at Harvard University.
GSLT	Gloucester School of the Little Theatre, Rocky Neck, East Gloucester, Massachusetts.
HC	Helen Corsa. Chairman of the English Department, Wellesley College.
HD	Hilda Doolittle. American Imagist poet, novelist, translator.
HJ	Holograph Journal.
HS	Harrison Smith. Publisher and editor at Harcourt Brace, Cape & Smith, Doubleday & Company, and the *Saturday Review*.
HW	Harvey Webster. Professor at the University of Kentucky.
Ipswich	34 High Street, Ipswich, England. Home of Eleanor Cole Elwes, mother of Eleanor Mabel Sarton.
Ireland	Bowen's Court, Kildorrery, County Kirk, Cork, Ireland. The family home of Elizabeth Bowen, and the model for Dene's Court in *A Shower of Summer Days*.
K	S(amuel) S(olomonovitch) Koteliansky. A Russian émigré living in London, reader for the Cresset Press, to which he introduced May Sarton. Translator from the Russian. Friend of D. H. Lawrence and Katherine Mansfield, as well as the Woolfs and the Julian Huxleys.
JC	Jean Clark, Friend from Shady Hill.
JH	Juliette Huxley. Widow of Sir Julian Huxley (zoologist, former secretary of the London Zoo, first secretary general of UNESCO, prolific writer), author of *Leaves of the Tulip Tree*.
JM	Judith Matlack. Quaker with whom Sarton lived for many years in Cambridge, Massachusetts. Simmons College English professor. Sarton drew her portrait in *Honey in the Hive*.
KD	Katharine Davis. Retired teacher of English.
KT	Katharine Taylor. Friend of the family and director of the Shady Hill School.

Lindenwood	Lindenwood College, St. Charles, Missouri.
Lake Erie	Lake Erie College, Painesville, Ohio.
LB	Louise Bogan. Poet and Poetry critic for the *New Yorker*.
Linkebeek	12 Longue Haie, Linkebeek, Belgium. Home of Jean and Eugénie DuBois.
London (EB)	2 Clarence Terrace, London, England. Home of Elizabeth Bowen.
London (Huxley)	In 1937 the Huxleys lived in London.
London (JS)	In London Sarton often stayed with her friend Jane Stockwood, who lived at various addresses over the years.
London (K)	5 Acacia Road, St. John's Wood, London, England. Home of S. S. Koteliansky.
London (RP)	55A Old Church Street, London, England. Home of Ruth Pitter.
MC	Marie Closset. The Belgian poet Jean Dominique. Founder and director of the Institut Belge de Culture Française in Brussels. Doro in Sarton's first novel, *The Single Hound*.
MFH	Margaret Foote Hawley. Portrait painter living in New York City.
MH	Marion Hamilton. Head of a preparatory school in New London, Connecticut.
MR	Muriel Rukeyser. Poet and woman of letters, professor at Sarah Lawrence College.
MS	May Sarton.
Myn Pl	9 Maynard Place, Cambridge, Massachusetts. Home of May Sarton and Judith Matlack.
Nelson	RFD, Munsonville, Nelson, New Hampshire. Home of May Sarton.
Oxf St	139 Oxford Street, Cambridge, Massachusetts. Home of May Sarton and Judith Matlack.
Oxon	Far End, Kingham, Oxfordshire, England. Home of Jay and Basil de Sélincourt.
Paris (Huxley)	2 Avenue Alphand, Paris, France. The apartment the Huxleys occupied in 1947. Later they lived at 38 Quai Louis-Blériot.
Paris (Mayer)	47 Vaugirard, Paris VI, France. Home of M. and Mme. André Mayer.
Paris (van L)	42 Place Jules Ferry, Montrouge (Seine), Paris, France. The apartment of Willem van Loon, son of Hendrik Willem van Loon, Dutch-born American journalist and author.

Pasadena (MT)	1150 Wotkyns Drive, Pasadena, California. Home of Marjorie Terry.
Philadelphia	The Cushman Club, Philadelphia, Pennsylvania. It was here that Sarton stayed when on tour with the Civic Repertory in Shakespeare's *Romeo and Juliet.*
Ray St	103 Raymond Street, Cambridge, Massachusetts. Home of the Sartons.
RF	Robert Francis. American poet.
RG	Rosalind Greene. Mrs. Henry Copley Greene, friend of the family, mother of Francesca, Katrine, Ernesta, and Joy. Subject of Sarton's poem "For Rosalind," in *A Grain of Mustard Seed.*
Rockport	Straitsmouth Inn, Rockport, Massachusetts.
Rowley	River Houslin, Rowley, Massachusetts. Summer house of the Henry Copley Greenes, lent to Sarton in the summer of 1934 for rehearsals of the Associated Actors Theatre.
RWB	Rollo Walter Brown. Author of many books of essays, including *Lonely Americans.* A great supporter of young poets.
Rye	Samuel Jeakes House, Rye, Sussex, England. Home of Conrad Aiken, which Sarton and three friends rented in the spring of 1937.
Santa Fe (AS)	724 Canyon Road, Santa Fe, New Mexico. Home of Agnes Sims, painter and sculptor, where Sarton was a paying guest.
Santa Fe (CF)	491 Arroyo Terrace, Santa Fe, New Mexico. Home of Catherine Farrelly, with whom Sarton stayed temporarily.
Santa Fe (DMcK)	1099 Old Pecos Road, Santa Fe, New Mexico. Home of Dorothy S. McKibbin.
Santa Fe (ER)	940 Acequia Madre, Santa Fe, New Mexico. Home of Edith Ricketson.
Santa Fe (MA)	1014 ½ Canyon Road, Santa Fe, New Mexico. Home of Marie Armengaud.
Satigny	La Roselle, Satigny, Geneva, Switzerland. Home of Marc and Meta Turian.
Stonington	Home of the Henry Copley Greenes in Stonington, Connecticut.
Sudbury	Box 128, RFD 1, Maynard (Sudbury), Massachusetts. Home of Anne Thorp.
VF	Le Petit Bois, Vouvray, France. Home of Grace Eliot Dudley.
VIT	Villa I Tatti, near Florence, Italy. Home of Bernard Berenson, American art critic and connoisseur. At Berenson's death, it became a European outpost of Harvard University.

VW	Virginia Woolf. Novelist and critic.
Wr St	14 Wright Street, Cambridge, Massachusetts. Home of May Sarton and Judith Matlack.
York	Box 99, York, Maine. Home of May Sarton.

So I am just hoping that when it is all added up, what will come through is a vision of life. And what does one mean when one says that? It is simply that every single human being sees life for himself, if he's honest, in a way that no one else sees it. And somebody like Virginia Woolf is able to project this extraordinarily original vision of life, so that when you open a page of a Virginia Woolf book you know that's Virginia Woolf speaking by the way she sees it. And I believe this is true to a not-such-a-geniusy extent in my work—that there is a vision of life which is a combination perhaps partly of my European background plus the America I know and plus the temperament, the sort of passionate temperament, which is accompanied by a rather critical mind.

—from the transcript of the film
World of Light: A Portrait of May Sarton,
Ishtar Films, 1979

Later published as:

MAY SARTON: A SELF PORTRAIT
edited by Marita Simpson & Martha Wheelock
W. W. Norton & Company
New York   London

FOREWORD

No genre is more fascinating for its daily, intimate chronicling of life, its proffering of confidence and friendship, than letters. And the richness of life—of thought, observation, and feeling—is seldom more apparent than in the letters of May Sarton. Nearly seventy years of them, together with unpublished journals and poems, are gathered in the Berg Collection at the New York Public Library, in several other special collections across the country,[1] and in her personal archives in York, Maine. These papers, including correspondences with her parents, poets, painters, and friends, all of which continue for years and most of which terminate only at death, reveal poet and woman, public and private, and illuminate her vision of life from early childhood to the bourne of her ninth decade, a life posited from its inception on primary intensity in art, work, friendship, and love.

One aspect of the power of her letters is expressed by Sarton's mother, Eleanor Mabel Sarton:

Your letters were here—one for each of us—when I came in from the lunch at Mrs. Lyman's,[2] feeling a bit depressed & lonely—the house was very still—and even the *cat* too sleepy to come to meet me & Bessie[3] out, and your

[1]All letters quoted from in this book are in May Sarton's archives at the Henry W. and Albert A. Berg Collection of English and American Literature, the New York Public Library, Astor, Lenox, and Tilden Foundations, or in her personal archives in York, Maine, with the following exceptions: the letters to Louise Bogan are in the Frost Library, Amherst College; those to H.D. in the Beinecke Rare Book and Manuscript Library, Yale University; and those to Elizabeth Bowen at the Harry Ransom Humanities Research Center at the University of Texas at Austin.

[2]Mr. and Mrs. Herbert Lyman, friends of the Sartons with homes in Milton, Massachusetts, and Northeast Harbor, Maine.

[3]The Sartons' maid.

door closed to hide the emptiness . . . & then I came down and saw your letter on the hall chair having somehow missed it? & *pounced* upon it! don't say it's not a real letter—length means nothing—but "depth" does—some word risen straight up from your heart—*that* makes a real message & somehow you attain this almost always—(it can be a gay & light word just as well as a deep thought . . . it just has to be you, your own self)— So many people seem incapable of conveying the tiniest bit of themselves by letter & that is heart-achingly disappointing—[EMS to MS, 10 Apr 36, Ch Pl]

Sarton's letters, transparent and full, convey a great part of herself—

I write often to Julian[4] of the things that happen to me because he writes to me and it is like a conversation. But with you it is a matter of essences and abstractions. [to JH, 17 Oct 37, Ch Pl]

Yet, from Beirut, Mabel Sarton appeals—

We need facts about you—outside, material facts, as well as your thoughts and reactions. [EMS to MS, 24 Oct 31, Beirut]

And so the Sarton letters give essences and abstractions, as well as a chronological ordering of events. Even the earliest of them—like the poetry and journals—adumbrate the trajectory of her life, hold seeds of future flowerings, and offer intimate glimpses of themes and images central to all that comes later.

[4]Sir Julian Huxley.

MAY SARTON:
AMONG THE USUAL DAYS

*F*rom the very beginning she seemed to know her destiny—

> Now I will beat this clumsy purpose
> Into a single keen-edged tool,
> And try to keep clear-sighted toward myself.
> I will chisel a destiny out of the hardest metal I can find
> And make it proud and cold enough
> To have been formed by iron tears . . .
> I swear it here.
>
> [from "Despair," HJ, 30 May 28, Ray St]

Her destiny to be chiseled with fierce intensity and discipline would be that of a writer—

I know that if I get as far as I want to, it will not be through genius but through intelligence, intensity of purpose, and will. Mrs. Evans[1] said that genius was having the right attitude toward a thing. There is something in that. But I don't believe it. [HJ, I Aug 29, GSLT]

Sarton may have doubted it, but her teacher Florence Evans believed absolutely in the genius that lay within Sarton's vision and attitude—

> Words are my passion
> And out of them and me
> I would create beauty.[1]
>
> [from "Creation," HJ, 20 Aug 28, Ray St]

[1]Florence Evans, teacher at the Gloucester School of the Little Theatre and director of the Boston School of Public Speaking.

And although words were her passion from the beginning, acting, too, became part of her destiny until 1935 when her own theater[2] failed—

> I have made the decision
> With heart whole.
> And if I find I am not fit
> To make beauty in this way
> I shall have strength to start again.
> That I pledge myself to do.
> This I believe:
> "I am the master of my fate,
> I am the captain of my soul."

[from "Upon Deciding to Become an Actress," HJ, 4 Jan 28, Ray St]

As early as eleven she was acting—

Class 7A is giving a French play called "Médecin Malgré Lui!" I am the doctor in spite of himself! Mary is my wife. [to EMS, 17 Mar 24, Ray St]

And at fourteen from camp—

I'm working pretty hard on studying my part in the Robin Hood play. As I am Robin Hood I have an awful lot (35 long speeches). [to EMS and GS, 28 Jun 26, DMC]

By twenty, at Glouester, acting ignited her—

But it gives me strange confidence—not exactly that, but a bright kind of hope, to be acting again. I do feel power in me, that seems to light like a dynamo when I'm playing, and which always surprises me. [to EMS, 22 Jul 32, GSLT]

[2]Associated Actors Theatre, Inc. See *I Knew a Phoenix: Sketches for an Autobiography* (W. W. Norton, 1959), pp. 180–95.

May Sarton as Robin
Hood at Day
Mountain Camp,
1926.

Norman Lloyd and
May Sarton in
Knock by Jules
Romain. Associated
Actors Theatre.
Boston, 1935.

As did the theater itself. At fifteen, after having just met her, she wrote to Eva Le Gallienne—

> I am seriously thinking of acting as a profession. I want something that I may throw my will, my whole soul into—I could certainly do that with acting. The frightening part of it is that I have no reason for thinking I have any talent. I have will enough and intelligence enough, I honestly believe, but that only means that I would make a good stenographer. [to EleG, 17 Feb 28, Poughkeepsie]

She was always an ardent theatergoer—

> Hamlet, Hamlet, Hamlet. I can do nothing but think of it and half-say over sad beautiful words. Fritz Leiber[3] is restrained, simple, deeply sincere—a great actor. I must learn some more when I have time. When? The speech about the pipe[4] I particularly love, I must ô I must know it. But instead I shall have to do Latin, Algebra, civics, faugh! The surrounding cast was so bad as to bring tears of pity and anger to my eyes. I longed to jump to the stage myself. Yes that was the only comfort. Certainly if those sticks and ranters can get positions and not be hissed off the stage I may be able to! [HJ, 6 Mar 28, Ray St]

Transported by the world of theater—

> And when I see a small figure on a gigantic stage holding thousands by the power of his mind—in the end it is a mental magnetism—I am thrilled all over again about the theatre. The actor who speaks as the critic of life—who says "Here it is. This is what it is." Oh for a Tchekov play! But I fear there won't be one this season. [to K, 24 Oct 37, Ch Pl]

---

[3]American actor (1883–1949); organized his own Shakespeare company, directed and appeared with the Chicago Civic Shakespeare Company.
[4]*Hamlet*, III, ii.

By seventeen, immediately after graduation from high school, she became an apprentice at Eva Le Gallienne's Civic Repertory Theatre. Her sense of a life in the theater, however, was always grounded in realism—

> This afternoon I went to see a small exhibition which contained the Toulouse- Lautrec of Avril[5] leaving the Moulin Rouge—a little self-contained sober figure slipping along and it looks cold—the very *essence* of the theatre—this strange fabrication of glory by strange little people who possess it so little once they have taken off their makeup. Being in the theatre is like having an endless devouring affair with a second-rate person. Oh well—[to JH, 27 Oct 36, 239 E 17]

Yet, acting notwithstanding, by sixteen she knew she had been chosen primarily as a lyric poet, for whom form would be essential—

May Sarton at graduation from Cambridge High and Latin, 1929.

SYMMETRY

They have wounded me the ancient
Rhythms of the earth:
They have sung to me and bent
My soul to feverish rebirth.

It is symmetry that haunts me
And for which I long.

---

[5]Jane Avril was a dancer and figured in several of Toulouse-Lautrec's famous posters.

> I would have the poverty
> Of pattern in my song.
>
> [HJ, 5 May 28, Ray St]

And as her song, every other aspect of her life as well would be charted and structured by pattern, discipline and strict form—her sacred order—

> My life has a definite pattern I realize more and more but I can see only one edge of it. [HJ, 23 Jul 29, GSLT]

And she would always be drawn to form in everything around her—

In society—

> The war is still on and I have some part in it because I believe it touches on a fundamental question for democracy in general as well as here—the question of obligation, the question of freedom without form, and the American fear of form and un-realization that it is only through form that one ever has any freedom. [to MFH, 31 Oct 40, Black Mt]

In music—

> I am really very ignorant about music. As in poetry I have a penchant for the 18th century—because in a world of chaos it has such pure form and form easily appreciable to the layman I expect. [to BB, 9 Apr 42, Ch Pl]

> I have a theory that in chaotic ages people long for form, the formal, the achieved—[to BB, 8 Jan 42, Ch Pl]

In literature—

> And Whitman is a tonic but the trouble is after a while one really longs for *form*, for something less diffuse, don't *you?* I always do. It's somehow tiring taken in large quantities whereas form prevents that kind of fatigue. [to BB, 26 May 43, 5 E 10]

Style is so important now, things with *form* as well as feeling keep one sane in the chaos. [to MFH, 26 Oct 42, Sudbury]

The advantage of form really is that it forces one to condense, isn't it? [to BB, 2 Feb 49, Oxf St]

In gardening—

It was wonderful to see Eugénie finally on Friday but there too I felt so sad because her garden is simply a jungle . . . grass on the paths, weeds everywhere. Now my one dream is to try to get their[6] garden in order before I go and here (you can imagine) Céline[7] is a great help and she is going to try to find a gardener. [to JM, 20 Apr 70, Chez Limbosch]

Credit: Susan Sherman.

Credit: Susan Sherman.

[6] Eugénie and Jean Dubois.

[7] Céline Limbosch (whom Sarton called Aunty Lino) and her husband, Raymond, are Mélanie and Paul Duchesne in *The Bridge of Years.* Their children are Nicole, Jacqueline, Jacques, and Claire, who became an art and theater decorator.

Credit: Susan Sherman.

*Eleanor Mabel
Sarton's desk, now in
the flower-window
room in York.
Credit: Susan
Sherman.*

I did work today, quite furiously, but work is comparatively a rest, compared to the general physical chaos and physical demands, due to the mess of the house and the garden—yesterday I did an hour's weeding, an attack on one small patch invaded by a monstrous weed, the roots of which seem to go everywhere, down and up and sideways, which I tugged at and fought against until the small wheelbarrow was full of dead bodies and I was dripping wet. The result is that I am so stiff today I can't move. But I won a small victory. [to LB, 14 Apr 54, Wr St]

And now that I've relieved the geraniums' distress by weeding out the goose grass that was devouring them, I feel much better myself! They are watered at the roots, and so am I. [to RWB, 24 Jul 43, 25 W 11]

In creativity—

But it is true that for too long I have let poetry be a luxury and come when it would and go where it would. Now it is time it was pruned and treated as a wild garden is to bear any fruit. [to K, 24 Oct 39, Ch Pl]

In gardens themselves—

We ended up at half past seven at Villandry[8] where there are simply amazing 16th-century gardens in perfect order. You go high up onto a terrace lined in lime trees to look down on the formal box cut into hearts and daggers etc. and a most enchanting immense potager[9] with the vegetables all arranged in patterns, and fountains sprouting among the cabbages. [to JM, 8 Jul 57, VF]

In lecturing—

This is quite a wonderful place, as a matter of fact, and my arduous panicky work at the lectures is paying off—if I may be arrogant among friends, my

[8]On the river Cher near Tours; has Renaissance chateau built c. 1532 by Jean le Breton.
[9]"kitchen garden."

lectures have more punch than the others because I have worked at the structure so hard and hence when it comes to give them can move around with freedom and let loose. [to BB, 15 Aug 53, Bread Loaf]

In friendship—

Whatever takes place between us takes place within a very rigid *form*, the established form of your life and the form I am trying to establish for mine. Form is always a safety. [to JH, n.d. (Jun 47), Paris (Huxley)]

Even in space—

. . . and then went on to the Chateau of Rambouillet[1] (where Napoleon kept Josephine) and I loved the Mozartian alleys of trees and formal spaces. [to JM, 3 May 48, Chez Limbosch]

In work—

The poems came and I have written 70 pages of a short novel, not an important work but it was such fun to be back in the imaginary world again where order and truth do prevail. [to RG, 21 Aug 51, Bread Loaf]

In living—

Well, I shall hate too not being able to imagine where you are. It is bad enough to have the sofa different. One wants nothing to change. Living in this chaos makes one violently conservative about all private matters, doesn't it? [to JH, 19 Sep 42, Ch Pl]

Did I tell you that I had a wonderful long talk with E. Bowen? In a strange very French room, with trees coming in the window and all very secret and quiet after this bare modern flat with its too much light. We talked about how

[1]In a forest southwest of Paris; dates from eighteenth century.

important form is in living and how with the lack of faith in God or even politics, now the only faith we have is in personal relations and so a great deal must be demanded of them. It was a fine evening. [to JM, 30 May 48, Paris (Huxley)]

I feel you are so settled, as if life had a good *form* in which you could breathe and live for a while not tossed hither and thither anymore. [to BB, 31 May 53, Wr St]

That form in living has always included for Sarton a strict routine, a disciplined daily structure—

When she was nine and a guest in the home of friends[2]—

In the morning when I get up I go downstairs and get the broom and dust-pan and brush. Then I broom the floor pick up the pile and make Joans and mine beds. Then I pick up all Hester's piles and go down stairs and help Joan broom then I pick up her piles and then we set the table then we go for the milk and then have breakfast. I always have anhourand a half rest. [to EMS and GS, 20 Jul 21, Greensboro, Vt.]

Or simply settling in to peace and work—

In Italy—

Just a word to say I am safely here—and it is wonderful to settle in for nearly two weeks—with a peaceful routine at last. [to JM, 21 May 62, VIT]

Or Nelson—

[2]The Hockings. Ernest and Agnes Hocking were the founders of the Shady Hill School. They had three daughters, Joan, Sara, and Hester, and one son, Richard. For more see "I Knew a Phoenix in My Youth" in *I Knew a Phoenix.*

I have been alone now for three days—this is the 4th—and the full sweetness of my life when I am alone comes over me. I write poems all morning—I think I sent you the first—I play records while I work—then have a glass of Metrecal and a nap. Then I go out about four and garden or stay in and write letters, then make myself a drink and supper at about six. (I often eat about 7:30, sometimes 8 as I get so absorbed in the garden.) [to KD, 23 Aug 62, Nelson]

About times to call. Eight p.m. is a good time. I let down at six and look at news (first local, then Cronkite) till seven when I eat. By eight the dishes are washed and I am longing to hear from you. [to JM, 29 Jan 69, Nelson]

But the night closes in awfully fast and I have to rearrange the rites here a little so that I do not get depressed at four when it is suddenly dark—a time when all summer I am used to being outdoors, regaining a sense of proportion after the nerve-wracking indoor struggles at my desk. [to BdeS, 3 Nov 64, Nelson]

Or Cambridge—

Typical Day in Cambridge:

6:45   Judy gets up and gets our breakfast on two trays.

7:15   breakfast in bed, Judy, me, and the two cats. (Judy comes into my room.)

I read the *New York Times* before I get up.

8:00–9:00   wash dishes, clean cat's pans, put out garbage, tidy the house, make beds etc. (Judy leaves for Simmons at 8:00.)

9:00–12:00   Three solid hours of work of one kind or another.

12:00–2:00   errands such as food for supper, very often lunch with a friend in Harvard Square.

2:00–4:00   Read and rest, usually take a nap, but sometimes have to answer mail instead. The mail comes at a bad time here, around 2 and there are often bus. matters that must be done at once.

4:00   tea time—Judy usually gets home by 4:30 and we have tea together.

5:00–6:00   read or work at my desk. A second chance to get work done.

6:00   a cocktail while one of us gets supper (we take turns).

8:00–10:00   ideally at my desk, but I am often too tired after washing up, so go to bed and read till about

11:30   Lights out.

Very little social life except on weekends.

The Nelson routine is much the same except in summer when I pick flowers right after breakfast and garden from three to six every day that is fine. [to KD, 5 Feb 6I, Wr St]

Routine and structure are her anchor and rest, and her key to creating time—

I have come to believe that one creates time very much as one creates a work of art, and that having no time (which is what makes fatigue) is all in one's own mind. This sounds quite crazy, but I'm sure you know what I mean. . . . The trick must be to learn this way with time which I believe you have—I felt it very tangibly when I walked into the room and during the hours I was there. Time, which had been boxed, began to flow. [to LB, I6 Sep 65, Nelson]

My New Year's resolutions all center around opening up the doors of time and having some real long hours for poetry and meditation. [to MFH, 6 Jan 42, Ch Pl]

We see it even in her advice to an exhausted friend—

Just be a vegetable if you can, and do the minimum of planning and thinking even about immediate responsibilities. Make beautiful neat little lists and do them quietly one by one. [to JH, 20 Aug 48, London (RP)]

Another way of creating time, and always part of the routine, is her rests—

I rest for two hours every afternoon, and if I don't the rest of the day is ruined. [to LB, 2 Feb 54, Wr St]

As well as the beautiful pauses[3] which also give freedom within the frame—

But it is all rather a rat race—what I enjoy most almost are the trolley trips in town—then I am peaceful and watch the beautiful forest[4] on my right— really a fairy forest, the trunks very slim and tall (beeches) with just a fountain of green at the very tops and the woods are beautifully clear underneath—the sun dances through the leaves and there is always a breath of coolness. [to JM, 17 May 47, Chez Limbosch]

The Sunday-morning ritual of writing letters, as it was for her father, has been part of her life's routine from the beginning—

The trouble is that Sunday is no rest as I have then to write letters that have accumulated all week. Sometimes twelve or fifteen, always at least ten long letters. [to KD, 25 Jun 64, Nelson]

As is the annual ritual of writing her Christmas poem—

My idea of the Christmas poem, by the way, is that it is a sort of letter, telling my friends where I am *in spirit* at the end of each year. The trouble is that it has to be written so far ahead of Christmas that I can rarely capture the Christmas spirit in it, but I am keeping your letter about the "otherness" (such a beautiful conception) and perhaps I'll be able to write a poem for *next* year before Christmas. [to KD, 6 Nov 60, Wr St]

And regular responsibilities—

I am happy to be here partly because there are a few little daily routines and responsibilities and after floating around for so long, that is a very good feeling. [to JM, 28 Jul 48, Chez Limbosch]

---

[3]See "The Beautiful Pauses" in *A Private Mythology*.
[4]The Forêt de Soignes, 10,400 acres extending to Waterloo, Belgium.

I am happy to be in England surrounded by good friends. I think I am in a very bad psychological state and really need to be back with you terribly and in my own life with my own responsibilities to sustain me. [to JM, 11 Aug 48, London (K)]

Five months without roots or real responsibilities is just too long even for me—[to JM, 22 Aug 48, London (RP)]

I know what your gentle routine means to you both, an airy cage which is the only kind of real freedom. [to BB, 15 Jan 75, York]

Among those responsibilities are household chores—

Yesterday I attacked my files and threw away a barrel full of old letters, a great relief. It now means that I can file things again and not just stuff them into cracks and corners. It is curious how any making of order makes one feel *mentally* ordered, ordered inside. [to LB, 15 Dec 54, Wr St]

I usually wash the breakfast dishes, water the plants in the greenhouse (a sort of glassed-in porch), set the table for some of the meals, etc. I did a big laundry when I first arrived with the utmost satisfaction. [to JM, 28 Jul 48, Chez Limbosch]

I did love all you said about your own life—and especially washing the windows! I have just been washing mine but I am not as daring as you are! But isn't it a satisfaction to make something gleam—and to see the world all bright and clear again! I have also been painting a long dark hall with Chemtone, very satisfactory stuff. [to KD, 18 Sep 49, Oxf St]

Her need to remake chaos into an intimate order is part of her need to meet and subdue challenge, a need which was strong even at twelve, and presaged the life of achievement to follow—

I am making more and more progress in climbing trees and am surprised at the trees I can climb. [to GS, 22 Nov 24, Chez Limbosch]

She found adversity exhilarating—

We went out with the Leeds for a sail and picnic to the flats those are things that at low tide are not covered made of sand where you can dig clams. We almost got caught and had to swim over a small channel to the boat. Mr. Leeds had his clothes on and had to carry his watch in his mouth. I swam with one hand and pushed a pail of clams with the other like this [drawing] [to EMS, 25 Jul 23, Woods Hole, Mass.]

And she found it valuable—

Then Aunty Lino the day after divided her collection of 1100 stamps between her four children. It was a little hard for me because I didn't get any but I guess it was good for me. [to GS, 17 Feb 25, Chez Limbosch]

And challenge was thrilling to her. At eleven—

I galloped on the pony! At first I was scared but then I sat up and held the reins tight. [to EMS, 17 Jul 23, Woods Hole, Mass.]

And throughout her life it has remained that way—

This afternoon we had a track meet. I won the running broad jump, and came in second on the high jump, and I was captain of the winning relay team! This sounds very boasting but it's all true. [to EMS, 30 Jul 26, DMC]

Tomorrow two of us we don't know which will take our Junior Life Saving Test. Isn't that exciting? The things are
    3 approaches: back, front, underwater
    4 carries: Head, hair, cross-chest, tired swimers
    3 strangle breaks: front, back, double twist
    resussitation; for efficiency, form and time.

Then we have to right a paper on resussitation, and of course the life saving stroke counts, and we have to retreive a pound weight in six feet of water. We probably won't know whether we've passed until all of us have taken it. I'm awfully afraid I won't pass. [to EMS and GS, 4 Aug 26, DMC]

It is strange that underneath everything I have so much *faith*—I do believe the things that happen to one *must* happen, that they are always a challenge, that in the end they are good. [to JH, I Sep 37, Ipswich]

Adventure is also mystery, as after her first flight in 1938 when she was almost twenty-six—

Flying is a great thing. It is all one's childish dreams of being able to sit on piles of clouds like white and golden eiderdowns—over the channel we were lost in an amethyst mist with no edges and it was all like a mystical poem by AE.[5] The roads don't look like ribbons but like little pieces of white string laid down by a little boy to find his way home. [to K, 28 Apr 38, VF]

LEFT. May Sarton at Day Mountain Camp, 1926.

RIGHT. Preparing for Junior Life Saving Test (May Sarton, first row center), Day Mountain Camp, 1926.

[5]AE or A.E. or Æ, pseudonym of George William Russell (1867–1935); Irish poet, painter and journalist. Father of Diarmuid, Sarton's literary agent.

And danger is inspiriting, always to be confronted and subdued—

We went for a lovely drive yesterday to "Swift River," Miggy[6] and I went in wading there and went across a wiggly bridge over a chasm! Don't be anxious because it was quite safe. [to EMS, 22 Jun 24, Intervale, N.H.]

There has been a terrific fire right near the theatre—frightfully thrilling! We were all woken up by the hoots and wild sighs of the fire engines rushing down to the tip of the neck. I jumped to the window and saw volcano-like huge black rolls of cloud hiding the sun, and every now and then waves of flame. It was right near the theatre. I was absolutely terrified—I couldn't think—or make my muscles work. My shoes wouldn't tie, and I kept dragging out clothes I didn't want. But finally I rushed out and saw streams of people running. I followed. The fire was eating at the most terrific rate. The sun was scorching even at a hundred yards. Finally they were able to put it out before it caught the theatre. Thank heavens! [to EMS and GS, 1 Jul 29, GSLT]

As poet she has constantly confronted the great obstacles—war, pain, aging, disappointment, loss, and death—in a way which empowers readers; indeed, "power is given to the vulnerable."[7] And even when in her teens she gentled the hardest places—

> We laughed
> And dared each other
> To farther dangerous peaks
> Where heavy water
> Shocked into salty fountains.
> The hardest places had become
> Completely safe and dull
> When at last we turned home.
>
> [from "Picnic," HJ, 30 Apr 28, Ray St]

[6]Margaret Bouton, daughter of "Aunt" Mary Bouton. Friend from Cambridge whom Sarton knew until her death in 1989.
[7]See "The Sleeping God" in *A Private Mythology*.

And always there is the sanctity of what it means to turn home. Sometimes home is merely one room, as it was at summer camp—

When mother comes back could she send me the pillow Mrs. Ekern[8] made for me, a few cakes of palm-oil and some tooth paste? You see we want to fix up our dressing room very sweetly. [to EMS and GS, Jul 27, DMC]

Or in the residence where she lived while working at Le Gallienne's Civic Repertory Theatre—

We couldn't go on the hike because it poured but I had a lovely day to myself of reading and sleeping in my blue and orange castle. [to EMS and GS, 14 Jan 30, 94 Macd]

And in the host of other rooms which followed—

Diarmuid Russell,
May Sarton's agent.

I have moved to another room on the top floor—a sweet little room looking over the roofs—My things have all found nooks for themselves—I really feel as if I fitted into this room. [to EMS and GS, 26 Jan 30, 94 Macd]

This is a charming place. Renée[9] and I have a huge room with *three* beds and a private bath, and lovely green furniture, two big windows and a quiet little street—and the most beautiful armchairs in the world—We've bought some daffodils and lavender sweet peas—the room looks adorable. O, I'm having such fun. [to EMS and GS, 7 Apr 30, Philadelphia]

[8]Alice Eckern, friend of the Sartons.
[9]Renée Orsell, member of the Civic Repertory Theatre; later stage manager of the Associated Actors Theatre.

I am in my new place, a room of my own after all these months of living here and there—it is blessed. The room itself, a big gray studio with great studio windows on one side and two ordinary windows on the other and they look out on trees on the inner part of a block, divided up into small gardens, babies sleeping on the terraces (people build tiny platforms on anything, any piece of roof in N.Y. to get the air), and I myself have such a one which I shall make into a garden with window boxes in the spring. You would, I think, like this place. It is cool and airy and light, with a great yellow armchair for guests to sit in, an emerald-covered studio couch with yellow pillows for me to lie on, a big work table, a lovely little black Chinese cabinet, and that is all except a rather nice modern striped Belgian rug with lovely greens and soft beiges in it. And lots of books up one wall. Virginia Woolf and French poets and all the things I like best from Cambridge. I feel I shall write poems here, and O I hope so! [to JH, I Oct 43, 22 E 10]

5 Channing Place.
Credit: May Sarton.

Comme j'aime mes deux chambres! De ma table je vois ma chambre à coucher, pleine de soleil avec cinq petits cactus très drôle, de tailles differentes, sur le bord de la fênetre, c'est une chambre très reposante aux murs gris presque vide, avec des rideaux blancs, et seulement le vert émeraude de la couverture du lit comme couleur. Je voudrais m'entendre là et penser longuement, mais hélas, je ne peux pas encore le faire—[1] [to MC, 18 Jan 51, Myn Pl]

But it is lovely to be home, to be in my long room which I have just had painted the most entrancing gray. It gives one a sense of peace and balance to

[1]"How I love my two rooms! From my desk I see my bedroom full of sun, with five little amusing cacti all different sizes on the windowsill—it is a restful room with almost empty gray walls, white curtains, and only the emerald green of the bedspread for color. I wish I could be at peace with myself there and think for a long while, but alas, I'm not yet able to do that."

be surrounded by one's few possessions. To be living in a place one has created for oneself. [to JH, 17 Oct 37, Ch Pl]

I must say I was *very* homesick last night and nearly cried—but I've recovered—and the queer 2 rooms begins to be a nest—[to JM, 18 Mar 62, Kyoto]

I am dismantling my room and it all looks very sad and ready to go—with the lares gone (a Japanese print and some carved animals)—[to JM, 8 Apr 62, Bhubaneswar, India]

J'aimerai que tu me vois un jour dans cette chambre qui est ma coquille où je me retire, où je fais entrer mes petites cornes sensibles d'escargot, où je travaille.[2] [to JH, 13 Jan 38, Ch Pl]

Then at Grasse we[3] found the most *perfect* little hotel, "Le Paradis" (just below the Victorio)—a KM[4] room—pretty small cretonne covers on two tiny virginal beds, a long French window opening onto a balcony—just below a perfect little terrace (huge palm trees) looking out over the dark green hills and a lazy sea or air in the distance. Such a good simple meal—delicious soup, salad, cold ham, cheese—tarte maison and a bottle of St. Émilion. [HJ, 29 Aug 54, Grasse]

Believing that a house has not really come into its own until someone in it has died, Sarton is always interested in the lives which previously inhabited her room or house—

But I have got very fond of my grim room here, because it is so dirty it is rather endearing and I feel that the people who lived in it before have had rather a hard time and often looked out of the windows over the roof and

---

[2]"I would love you to someday see me in this room which is the shell into which I retreat, into which I pull my little sensitive snail-like horns, and where I work."
[3]Sarton and Eugénie DuBois.
[4]Katherine Mansfield.

wondered what was going to happen next. All the cleaning women and eleva-
tor boys at the Albert are very kind good people. [to EMS and GS, 11 Jan 43,
Hotel Albert, NYC]

And the interior life of rooms inspired her teaching—

Je viens de finir de lire 50 thèmes décrivant une chambre—un exercise que les
élèves ont écrites en classe la semaine dernière—quelques unes avaient du
charme et de la vérité, mais la plupart sont un peu pauvres car, sans doute, elles
n'ont jamais vu une chambre pleine de vie intérieure où chaque objet à une
raison intime d'exister.[5] [to MC, 13 Jan 51, Myn Pl]

Often home is with those she loves—

Never think it was *dull* for me in England. It was like coming home. One does
not want home to be exciting—even Kot[6] seemed to think I expected some
extraordinary event. I find friendship event enough, you know! [to JH, 12 Aug
39, Ch Pl]

Or with those she wishes she could be—

. . . and I would give a great deal for a Judy-and-pussycat tea and games this
very moment! [to JM, 28 May 62, VIT]

But always it is the place to come back to, and, as well, to return to herself—

The point of a journey is to come home. I'm already dreaming nostalgically of
my study at the top of the house after the long trip next year. Isn't it awful? Of
finding a glass paperweight on a half-finished letter written six months before

---

[5]"I have just finished reading 50 themes describing a room—an exercise which my students wrote in class
last week—a few have charm and truth, but most of them are rather poor because clearly they've never
seen a room which is full of an inner life, one in which every object has an intimate reason for being there."
Sarton was teaching English A at Radcliffe.
[6]S. S. Koteliansky.

that was never sent, and finding again, after all not very changed, the person who began it. [to MFH, 29 Aug 40, Rockport]

Often it is the house of one she loves which becomes her source and haven—

On first visiting Louise Bogan's apartment in New York—

At the Straitsmouth Inn, Rockport, with Paul Dumont, a Sanskrit scholar and family friend.

It is that not since Jean Dominique[7] died two years ago have I been *in* a place *with* a person which together meant poetry to me. The first time I came I felt this so strongly that I almost burst into tears—the green walls, the peace of it, the sense of inward life, the sense that each object has been chosen with love and *means* something and of course all I have felt about you and your poetry for many years suddenly *there*. [to LB, 26 Jan 54, Wr St]

[7]Marie Closset.

Grace Dudley's house[8] in France—

Now that I am here in Vouvray it is so beautiful I can't bear to leave and am happy to come back here and work instead of going to Whipsnade.[9] It is the most utter peace, deep in the country the fruit-trees all in flower, and Grace Dudley, one of those rare people who moves in *peace*—the house itself is simply perfect (Anne[1] came here last year and will tell you about it when you see her)—a little formal garden with over the hedge soft hills and vineyards, a sense of space and grace in a not very big house that gives the feeling almost of being a chateau. [to EMS and GS, 9 Apr 38, VF]

The house is amazingly silent and yet beneficent, a real "retreat" from the world, and I long to go back for a long time, a month or even two. It is a shame that it is not used more. [to JM, 12 Jul 57, Linkebeek]

The hot spell has broken and now this house is like a still island in a sea of wind. From my window I look out on the garden, a jungle of roses and bushes, all the paths overgrown and then out beyond our high wall to a rising hillside of vines in neat rows and the old tiled roofs of houses. [to JM, 5 Jun 47, VF]

And the gentle touch of this place makes all seem possible and good. . . . I wish you could see this heavenly place—a small 17th-century house standing like a ship, with a high wall that drops down to the street all around it. There is not a sound at night except a few night birds and when we close our big gates and lock ourselves in it is like a secret world.

The house is still full of the presence of my friend Grace Eliot Dudley (a grandaughter of Pres. Eliot's),[2] who first came here and made the place what it

---

[8]Le Petit Bois, Vouvray, France; see "Grace Eliot Dudley: Le Petit Bois" in *A World of Light.*
[9]An open zoo on the Bedfordshire Downs where the Julian Huxleys kept an apartment overlooking its 500 acres and where they spent most weekends.
[1]Anne Thorp.
[2]Grace Dudley died in February 1950; she was the granddaughter of Charles William Eliot, president of Harvard University 1869–1909.

*Pencil sketch of Grace
Dudley by May
Sarton, 1938.*

is—now it is lent to her friends as a kind of memorial, and it is astonishing how much the same it feels after nearly 10 years. The countryside is very gentle and dreamy, with haystacks and stone farms (always with beautiful flowers in front and lots of beloved cats, dogs, goats etc. wandering about) looking up through the twilight and of course the long rows of vines that make a blue-green sea as one walks up the path from the house—and we have not done any sightseeing yet, content to explore the immediate foreground, but this afternoon we are going to visit an old abbey and will pass several chateaux along the way. [to KD, 22 Aug 59, VF]

LEFT. *Jean Dominique. Credit: May Sarton.*

RIGHT. *Grace Dudley with Jammy. Credit: May Sarton.*

ABOVE. *S. S. Koteliansky. Credit: May Sarton.*

RIGHT. *5 Acacia Road. Credit: May Sarton.*

Jean Dominique's in Belgium—

. . . and the rest of the time I am usually either upstairs working[3] or at the peacocks[4] . . . that is a real haven and a sort of little paradise of love and sweetness. [to JM, 10 May 48, Chez Limbosch]

Koteliansky's in London—

Jean Dominique says in her last, "J'aime ton Kot." And with each of your cigarettes I have dreamed a dream—sometimes of three tomatoes on your shelf—sometimes of James Stephens's[5] stick—or the little garden where Mansfield sat in warm days—or you and I agreeing that life is a terrible wonderful business at your Table with a graveyard of cigarette-stubs beside us. [to K, 12 Jul 37, Austria]

I am sitting in my room at Kot's which opens onto the garden and the two pear trees Katherine Mansfield loved[6] and which now in their old age lean together. I would like to write a poem about this house and about dear Kot.[7] [to JM, 11 Aug 48, London (K)]

Bowen's Court in Ireland—

This is a huge house with vast resounding halls, the old wallpaper peeling off and everything very grand and very shabby and rather *cold*—no bathrooms, the w.c. is across a large ballroom (from my room) and down three long staircases

[3]At Le Pignon Rouge, Rhodes St. Genèse, Brussels, home of Raymond and Céline Limbosch, which Sarton considered her second home and visited every summer. See "Céline Dangotte Limbosch" in *A World of Light*.

[4]Sarton's nickname for Marie Closset, Marie Gaspar, and Blanche Rousseau, who lived together on Avenue de l'Echevinage in Uccle, a suburb of Brussels. They appear as "The Little Owls" in *The Single Hound*. See "A Belgian School" in *I Knew a Phoenix*, and "Jean Dominique" in *A World of Light*.

[5]Irish poet and novelist (1882–1950); close friend of S. S. Koteliansky. See "A Letter to James Stephens" in *Inner Landscape*.

[6]See Mansfield's "Bliss" in *Bliss and Other Stories*. Mansfield was a close friend of Koteliansky.

[7]See "Kot's House" in *The Leaves of the Tree*.

and one's every step echoes—now that Elisabeth's[8] novel is to be a Literary Guild selection they are hoping to put in bathrooms. Little Colleens appear with jugs of hot water and cups of tea every morning. We eat in a simply vast room which was the front hall, looking out on the really splendid trees and meadows—one grove of oaks is called "the Lambs Drawing Room," sheep grazing everywhere. I've just been for a walk with Alan[9] to the top of the hill to look down on the house with behind it the superb gentle mountains—clouds going over and casting dark shadows. [to JM, 10 Sep 48, Ireland]

The great surprise was how inaccurately I remembered—for instance the lawn rolling up before the house is not a *steep* incline at all—the house truly vaster than I remembered—it needs *towering* personalities. The drawing room has been put to use, but I was dismayed by the decorating—lovely pale pink satin portières, but then a bright red sofa and chair, the wrong red—I felt *hurt.* [HJ, 31 Jul 54, Ireland]

The Limbosches' house in Belgium—

It is extraordinary to think of this reaching you in Belgium—and it makes me want very much to join you there in some way. I have periodic nostalgias for the country around "Pignon Rouge"—the long rolling fields under an immense sky and clouds always going over, for Brussels too and the Cranach in the museum—and most of all for the "nid d'alouettes,"[1] for Aunty Lino and Oncle Raymond and all the children. (They must have changed so much since I saw them last.) I wish I could fly over on the back of a seagull and spend Sunday with you in the garden under the apple tree. Tell Aunty Lino about what I am doing (this would surely end in a discussion of some sort!) have Oncle Raymond read "le légère Aldebaran et la lente Betelgeuse"[2] and the long late afternoon set in until we are forced to go in and build a fire in the salon. O, I wish I could be there! [to EMS and GS, 4 Aug 34, Rowley]

---

[8]Elizabeth Bowen. Sarton customarily used the French spelling "Elisabeth."

[9]Alan Cameron, Elizabeth Bowen's husband.

[1]The Limbosches' summer house in Knocke, Belgium, was called Le Nid d'Alouettes.

[2]"the airy Aldebaran and the slow Betelgeuse," referred to in poetry by Raymond Limbosch.

Sarton in the garden
at Le Pignon Rouge,
the Limbosches' house
in Belgium.

At Le Nid d'Alouettes
in Knocke, Belgium,
with the Limbosches
in 1929. (Sarton at
right.)

Le Pignon Rouge.

The de Sélincourts' in Oxfordshire—

I had a lovely week-end in Kingham with Basil and his wife[3]—it's so nice to go back to places where one has made little roots before and I get fonder and fonder of them both. I feel Basil has real faith in me and at the same time we always have long technical discussions which are pure *treasure*—we talk and then he thinks of something and goes over to the bookcase to pull out Wordsworth or Bridges and read. He reads poetry beautifully and Wordsworth with just the right mixture of love and humor—it is really very funny in places—he read "The Leech Gatherer" to us and we couldn't help laughing at the pompous and insistent—he repeats it several times—"Tell me old man, what is it that you do?" which Lewis Carroll took off in the White Knight's song:

> "What is it that you do?" I said
> And thumped him on the head.[4]

(I have misquoted.) Every morning and evening we went out and picked a huge plate of the most delicious raspberries—and then through the lovely green orchard to the barnyard to collect the eggs and feed the pigs—he is so dear with the pigs and was nursing a sick one—it is the ideal country life. They have just four acres and in that they have the most enchanting garden I have ever seen, a vegetable garden that supplies all their vegetables the year round, an orchard, a tennis court and the house—just perfect. They manage it with one man and a girl who cooks and does the cleaning. I think Wondelgem[5] must have been something like it. We didn't get any tennis as it rained on Sat. and part of Sun. but we went for a long walk between waving fields of green wheat, through flocks of sheep and cows and past hawthorne hedges,

[3]Basil de Sélincourt's first wife, Anne Douglas Sedgwick, distinguished American writer, died in 1935. This is his second wife, Jay.

[4]The White Knight's song "A-Sitting on a Gate" from Eva Le Gallienne's adaptation of *Alice in Wonderland*:
"I cried, 'come tell me how you live!'
And thumped him on the head."

[5]The town three miles outside of Ghent where Sarton was born. See "Wondelgem: The House in the Country" in *I Knew a Phoenix*.

Basil de Sélincourt.
Credit: May Sarton.

*ABOVE. May Sarton
with nurse Cécile,
Winter 1912.*

*LEFT. Nurse Cécile in
1967.*

*May Sarton at
Wondelgem at about
one and one-half
years old. Credit:
A. Harry Nevejans.*

down and up green "rises"—it is the most beautiful country, in the middle of the Cotswolds, very rich and prosperous looking. But extraordinarily primitive. There is just one well in the village from which everyone draws and carries his water—[to EMS and GS, 11 Jul 39, London (JS)]

It is beautiful here but awfully cold and damp. But we had tea outdoors (temp about 50! is my guess) yesterday and Basil and Jay are Spartan. Luckily there is lots of hot food, hot water bottles at night, and I expect it is quite healthy. They have seven dear friendly cows now and about 200 hens who dash out in a great multitude and rush toward Basil as soon as he comes into sight at the end of the orchard. . . . My window looks out onto the garden hedged in high hedges of beech, very bright green now and rippling in the wind. How nostalgic the two empty chairs and benches look on this gray day! Pink lupin, peonies, tulips, and masses of forget-me-nots are out in the flower beds. My window is framed in wisteria and sometimes a bird comes and sits there—and downstairs there are three adorable corgie puppies. It's awfully plain living here—no one smokes or drinks! [to JM, 20 May 57, Oxon]

Marc and Meta Turian at La Roselle, Satigny, Geneva.

Marc and Meta Turian's house[6] in Satigny—

Here it is really autumn—it is strange how suddenly the light changes, a very indefinable thing. Also it is cold, frosty at night which is too bad as they need

[6]La Roselle, Satigny, Geneva. See "Marc, the Vigneron" in *A World of Light.*

some golden days now if the vintage is to be saved after the rainy summer. Preparations are in full swing and the courtyard is now filled with huge barrels and bins being cleaned and filled with water so that the seams will swell and make them wine-tight when the time comes. . . . However I spend the mornings working up in my high room and am peaceful. [to GS, 6 Sep 54, Satigny]

Marc is a dear, cooks little meals, leaves me alone, drives me to town and talks in his wonderful way about J. J. Rousseau (whose 200th anniversary is being celebrated)—we are going off this afternoon to find wild flowers in the mountains. It is my kind of life and I Tatti wasn't. Also I feel Meta[7] very close, sleep in her room, and am full of thoughts and feelings again—a beneficent presence. [to JM, 5 Jun 62, Satigny]

Or the home she created in the Samuel Jeakes House in Rye, which she and three friends rented from Conrad Aiken in the spring of 1937—

. . . it is all more perfect than I had dreamed—but I am so tired from two happy days of airing mattresses, finding a char and maid (the char to clean the house first), meeting Margaret and Kap[8] and getting settled that I don't know how I can write the great fat chortling letter that you deserve. When I opened the door with John Aiken, Conrad's son, who came down with me, I ran right through the sunken dining room into the garden. So I shall begin there. It is a large, flagstoned square, steeped in sun and surrounded with borders of flowers and walled with trees and the ivy-covered side of the house full of birds' nests. There is a brilliant tuft of wall-flowers, a little quince in flower, some wood anemones, one grape hyacinth, the laburnum trees and a pear just getting ready to flower, lots of daffys and narcissus and one little bush of primroses—a garden just right for Margaret and Kap and

Elizabeth Bowen at Jeakes House in Rye. Credit: May Sarton.

[7]Meta Budry Turian died on August 21, 1959.
[8]Margaret English and Kappo Phelan were members of the Apprentice Theatre.

me. We spent the morning rearranging the drawing-room, which is a curious L shape with two big deep-sunk windows along one side—it looks quite gay already and we have unwrapped the rugs and taken the Japanese prints to be framed. The walls are gray and the colors Chinese green and gray and blue with yellow daffodils looking wonderful in a corner and some anemones. Now I am sitting in the studio which is going to be mine with a tiny bedroom off it—it is a perfect room to work in with a great view and lined with books. Kap has in exchange the nicest bedroom and a little attic room which she loves to work in. Margaret has the biggest room with lavender walls and a great bed and we are all content like the man in *Three Sisters* who goes around saying "I am content." There are two guest rooms besides and lots of possibilities of doubling up—we could have four guests quite comfortably. But the wonder is how much charm the house has even without pictures and rugs and lots of little things that his wife has taken.[9] The pictures we have are beautiful and will be ready next week. They are all Japanese or Chinese, some perfect beauties. [to EMS and GS, 14 Apr 37, Rye]

First the life of this house—a really *perfect* house for us, designed for a poet—full of silences, escapes, little stairways to nowhere—with a tiny garden containing six tulips, a quince in flower, primroses, I grape hyacinth, wall-flowers in profusion—a laburnum tree covered with cocoons getting ready to flower—and a warm (in the sun) tiled court where we had lunch today and where, later on, we can all lie in a row on our stomachs and get brown. Margaret is a *genius* and aided by a lanky, indifferent merry girl who turns out to be a wonderful cook, turns out supreme meals—we are drinking up Conrad's Spanish wine, and have a barrel of dark beer of our own (my idea of the height of luxury)—Tomorrow a German girl who was on the boat and Liz arrive and we shall be five.[1] I have never had a better place to work than this studio—[to EFK, 25 Apr 37, Rye]

But a house without love is empty for Sarton and does not nurture poetry—

[9]Aiken's first marriage ended in divorce.
[1]May Sarton met Elena Florh, a German girl, and Elizabeth Johnson, a recent Bennington graduate, while crossing on the *American Trader.*

I get rather depressed here.[2] I think it is what E. Bowen feels sometimes, "psychological discomfort"—hard to define. Partly the place is too much of a museum and the Murdocks[3] themselves not quite at home here so it all feels rather stiff. [to JM, 27 May 62, VIT]

Life here is very formal—Lady Berkeley (a former Lowell from Boston, married to Lord B. of B. Square in London) to lunch, an illiterate old woman, with houses all over Italy; tonight a dinner party. I have no proper clothes, especially as it has been v. *cold*, and find the very rich on the whole very dull. But the Murdocks are, of course old friends, and we have a few cozy evenings alone together in the vast rooms. Up here at the top of the house with a superb view over olive groves, cypresses and red roofs and the distant blue hills around Florence, I have a bedroom and study and vast bathroom across the hall. And I have tried valiantly to work. But either I am too tired (possible) or there is something in the atmosphere too alien to my inner self. Anyway I have done next to nothing, *tried* some poems (have notes for over 20), *tried* to get at rewriting Act III of the play[4] etc. [to KD, 30 May 62, VIT]

I am wildly homesick for Nelson and solitude . . . and also of course for the house in the country.[5] This is a big comfortable apartment in a rich bourgeois section of Brussels—not a tree in sight. Instead of looking down on the orchard from this familiar desk, I look out an an apartment house, and sidewalk and ladies walking their poodles. Céline, at 87, remains her remarkable self, as unconscious as ever of her possessiveness, her drive, her egotism etc. She is amazing in her avidity for life and love—but I feel a stranger in this place. I cannot really connect. [to BB, 22 Apr 70, Chez Limbosch]

And then, her own houses. At Wright Street—

---

[2]Villa I Tatti.

[3]Eleanor and Kenneth Murdock, to whom Sarton dedicated *Faithful Are the Wounds,* were the directors of I Tatti retained by the Harvard Trust.

[4]"The Music Box Bird," unpublished.

[5]*Le Pignon Rouge,* from which the widowed Céline Limbosch had moved.

As you see by address above we have moved—and really the house is quite perfect. Also we have two musical tenants (they have a wonderful machine and records) who pay us $90 a month for their suite and seem nice boys, one an Irish law student and the other a Greek (whose father teaches at Michigan) who is brilliant in grad. school physics. They have roomed together before and so far have been ideal tenants, so far being a week. We moved in about ten days ago and begin to feel fairly settled—this is much more of a house than the other, but in some ways less easy to run. The kitchen is dazzling, modern, and we find it quite difficult to feel at home in. I have two lovely rooms of my own on the top floor, but they seem a bit cold still partly from lack of *chairs*. But it's wonderful to have the books again and your montage and all the other dear things around. Unfortunately I have to be over at mother's a lot—and these last days are precious, I must say, so I want to be

LEFT. *Portrait of Céline Limbosch, now in May Sarton's bedroom in York. Credit: Susan Sherman.*

RIGHT. *14 Wright Street. Credit: Judith Matlack.*

there as much as possible.[6] I think it makes Judy feel rather lost in the grandeur here and lonely. Actually it's not a grand house at all, but very cozy and sympathique, mostly quite old with a few new additions, but it's on three floors and we are always forgetting things and having to run up or down. The cat had a psychic shock from the move and uses the whole house as a vast bathroom, much to our distress! However, he seems to be settling in and has perhaps at long last found a piece of earth outside to his liking. Anyway today we had a respite from cleaning up. [to BB, 23 Sep 50, Myn Pl]

Judy who could find no apt. finally bought a small house in desperation. I got back on Monday and have spent five frantic days getting my books off the floor, painting walls, putting in light sockets, arranging china, hanging paintings etc. also meetings at Harvard of course as the year begins Monday—also a terrific cold which seized me like a plague on landing— The house is really just right for us. It is rather ugly from the outside except from the front but has two garages so we rent one and the Austin has a shelter at last. We each have a good big study and downstairs two good-sized rooms, one formal and one where we really live, eat etc. It is just right for size and it's wonderful to think we shall never have to move again and at least are pouring our money into something. [to BB, 21 Sep 52, Wr St]

And the ambience Sarton creates around her is reflected in Elizabeth Bowen's response to visiting Maynard Place—

That *was* a most lovely weekend, so sunny and happy and restful, and I do *love* your new house.[7] I'd liked the other[8] so much that I had been sad at the idea of your moving, but here in Maynard Place you really have got a most heavenly atmosphere and setting. I shall always remember that downstairs sitting room and how cozy it was on that Saturday afternoon, coming in from my walk along the river, out of the cold wind, to sit beside the fire with you &

[6]Eleanor Mabel Sarton died of cancer on November 18, 1950.
[7]9 Maynard Place, Cambridge.
[8]139 Oxford Street, Cambridge.

Judy. And the elegance of the upstairs other parlour appeals to me too: so much style achieved with so little fuss. But of course it is what you two have done to the house which really, to begin and end with, gives it that glow. I enjoyed most vividly all my time there, and carried away in spite of the world shadow, an image of peace. [EB to MS, 18 Dec 50]

However, her real home, her cultivated space, is her work, rooted in discipline and control.

In her mid-teens she speaks of her need for control—

> These three disturb me;
> Because over these I have no control:
> Wind—wildness,
> The loneliness of sea—
> My age.
>
> [From "Miss Sullivan," HJ, 13 Jan 28, Ray St]

She was determined even then to be master of her work—

> I must not clutter my hope with impatience
> Gnawing at the ragged edge of time,
> But keep it a kind of deep set well.
> Thus may I master even fate for one day.
>
> [from "Waiting for a Day," HJ, 29 May 28, Ray St]

Wherever she was, there was her work—

The *donkey* personality of my creative self that can only do good work in the morning—and best if it is entirely alone in that strange luminous condition when *no* images have come to blur the subconscious—and *then* if it has the slightest feelings of hurry—if someone comes in and says "How about a swim when you have finished?" the "when you have finished" makes it balk completely. And of course the silly thing is that if I have the whole day in front of

)me as I did at Whipsnade I can do the day's work in three hours. [to K, 2 Aug 37, Austria]

Today it is raining soft warm rain. I have a bunch of single yellow chrysanthemums on my desk, very clear lemon yellow, and they are like sunlight, but I am depressed. After writing thirty poems in sixty days it was inevitable that there should come a pause and when I can't write I always feel as if I had fallen from grace. [to K, 28 Nov 37, Ch Pl]

I have started the new novel⁹ in trembling and with a sense of total inadequacy—but work is good—a *raison d'être*—the only one for me. [to JH, 28 Nov 37, Ch Pl]

And when I am working I immediately feel hopeful. [to JM, 29 Jul 49, Chez Limbosch]

At the outbreak of war between England and Germany—

I am working hard. If ever one stopped for an instant, allowed *nerves* to get the upper hand, one would be useless. [to JH, 10 Sep 39, Rockport]

During the war, just before leaving for Florida with her parents—

The trouble is that one is so grief-stricken inside that it is only by keeping close to work, by digging oneself a warm burrow of work and lying there, that one can keep alive at all. Florida seems so out of key. [to K, 22 Nov 39, Ch Pl]

Throughout the war—

I loved your saying "Work much—and briskly—but not with effort." Especially in poetry Pegasus¹ simply balks if you beat him but I *have* been beating

⁹"The Waterfall," unpublished. By the end of December she tears it up.
¹The winged horse of the Muses has come to represent inspiration.

him a little on a long "Letter to Americans" which is still not finished after two weeks. [to RWB, 29 Jan 41, Santa Fe (AS)]

One must have some invulnerable *structure* to one's personal life these days and work is the best. The only one as far as I am concerned. One is so vulnerable elsewhere. [to MFH, 24 Apr 41, Lake Erie]

I am brooding on the book[2] and think there must be a pause to let things come, not to force them. But I am not *suited* to pauses. When I can't work I feel miserable, a *worm*. [to RWB, 17 Jul 41, Rockport]

It is spring here and one would like to be all silent and pure and growing like a flower in oneself. But at this time in the world we carry a mass of world-birth and ache around with us and only work is the answer. I have such a hunger to be useful again. [to RWB, 23 Feb 43, 5 E 10]

It is always a leap into the dark when one hasn't written for a long time. But I long to be dealing with the permanent and deep—even the OWI[3] stuff, good and valuable as it is, is not the *final* rooted thing a good poem can be. [to RWB, 17 May 43, 5 E 10]

In times of peace—

Don't worry too much about your dead feeling—one has to absorb departures and arrivals and it all takes time. By the time you get this you will probably anyway have taken the plunge and be feeling more yourself. I lose all sense of my identity too when I am not working. I feel all scattered with no center or pride or *raison d'être*. It is really rather awful. [to BB, n.d. (1 Jan–20 Mar 50)]

What made me a bit miffed I think was that you always seem to imply that I have had a very easy life and am just now approaching a few difficulties.

[2]A proposed book of prose and poetry about America.
[3]Office of War Information, where Sarton worked writing scripts for radio and films about America.

Whereas my own view is that I've had a *sturm* and *drang* life from the time I was 17 and that I am just approaching a kind of plateau of fulfilled work and comparative peace of mind! I have always since I can remember had this queer sensation of walking on very thin ice above despair and when I get tired I get panicky about it. Where you may be right is that I shall have to fall through the ice—and maybe that is what you are really saying. At any rate I do know that work is the balancer. [to LB, 17 May 54, Wr St]

As her mother was dying—

But he[4] has a frame of work to support him, and so have I. That is the great thing. [to MFH, 14 Aug 50, Ch Pl]

At all times, and under all circumstances—

I am about to dive into a tunnel of work (I hope I shall be able), six lectures for this summer and, I hope, another story. I feel quite crazy with unwork and it is time I got back into that saving groove. [to LB, 21 May 51, Wr St]

But I wonder if a lotus eater's existence without *work* would not be rather stifling in the end. It seems to me that almost all pleasures have to do with contrast, rest after labor, waking after sleeping (or vice versa), intense love, intense solitude—also of course it happens, luckily for me, that my work is an actual joy as well as a necessity to me, that I believe in it, and that even if I were never to publish another book, or be read by a single other human being, I would still do it *because* I would wish to. Because it makes me feel fully alive. [to CD, 4 Feb 59, Nelson]

My work is my *keel*, you know, and keeps me stable. Without it I should have gone mad or committed suicide long ago. [to KD, 6 May 59, Nelson]

[4]George Sarton.

You are wise about taking time, but you see, work is in a way my rest, I mean creative work. In creative work one is *composing chaos* and that is why it is a rest, though also an effort. [to KD, 16 Apr 61, Nelson]

I suppose one has to remember that "life" is important too, though it's something I forget in some moods, everything except work seeming like an interruption or really non-life. [to LB, 27 Mar 54, Wr St]

And so, the perennial conflict between life and art—

At present there is a choice between a nun-like existence centered round emotion for one person of great intensity and a more normal existence of seeing many people, or even a few, which simply exhausts me and doesn't even produce poems. [to K, 1 Feb 38, Ch Pl]

I went to bed and read your long letter-over-several-days again and thought about it before I went to sleep. It is all questions which can't, I guess, be answered in words but only by *being*. Some of it *answered* me like a cry out of my own heart: "Time is my worst enemy, I've always known it," and the difficulty, the tiredness of living this double life of work and people and everlastingly juggling a balance somehow, while the ball falls and one is wild and desperate, for awhile and must escape. All our life is a forced escape inward I'm sure. Shutting the door—and the minute any weight of responsibility is put on the heart and spirit, yes you're right there, one becomes like the Ancient Mariner with an albatross. We are selfish and concerned with our own souls which are weight enough. We are double people, givers and receivers *within* ourselves unlike women who do not feel alive unless they are bearing the weight of a man's life. [to MFH, 15 Sep 40, Ch Pl]

It is simply democracy reduced to absurdity to believe really that the mass will ever appreciate art, I suppose. And perhaps we have become confused about the real issues. In my own life I believe the solution is to work hard politically wherever I can but write as I please. But perhaps even that is a fatal division. The thing that makes Malraux a magic name is I think just that he has managed to live without that division, that for him art and life have fused. So he towers above us all. [to JH, 5 Sep 47, Oxf St]

The difficulty with being a writer is that one is torn between life and work, all the time having to *preserve* oneself for work—then seeing that this is all wrong and work is made of life, an endless pendulum swing. [to LB, 13 Nov 53, Wr St]

I think the real problem of the woman poet, because her poetry always must come from the very center of her being, is the problem of how to keep the fire and yet mature. Millay never did. [to KD, 13 Mar 54, Wr St]

The problem seems to be how to live without dying of "living"—the novel[5] is really moving now, but I find it hard to live and write at the same time, and Elisabeth's[6] arrival, for instance, makes me tremble like a horse before a race, though we are such old friends and she knows our ways. Any sort of excitement, such as drinks and dinner Sat. night with friends, throws me off and makes me exhausted in a rather frightening way. But I can just pretend to be ill, I suppose, if all this becomes too much. The book is the real thing, but I had forgotten (luckily one always does) the extremity of strain that is involved in the first gaining of momentum, the first hundred pages or so. I am going for a checkup to my Doctor and perhaps he will provide some soothing syrup or spell so that I can live without dying of excitement. [to LB, 12 Oct 55, Wr St]

But as soon as you had left, I had to face all the accumulations here— packages of clothes to send to Belgium, books to pack for the two girls who danced, answers to teachers wanting advice about teaching poetry, endless endless letters—getting things organized for the *Times*[7] (the garden dug, window washers, new rug for front steps, tools—fetching the lawn mower—list of *things* to be crossed off). reading two long books, one for review the other for a blurb, writing a review—it is again the poison of my life here, what

[5]Probably *Birth of a Grandfather.*
[6]Elizabeth Bowen.
[7]For the *New York Times Magazine* article "There . . . Stood the House" by Lisa Hammel, published August 23, 1970.

poisons the clear stream that should be contemplative—the sheer weight of what has to be done each day—and which I do against my deepest wish. The wish is not to be lazy, believe me, but to be active in *another way*, i.e. to create, not to maintain. Probably my fear of death, of serious illness, is only a symptom or a metaphor that means that "coming to terms" means finding the means for a contemplative life—and if it means selling Nelson, then that is what I must do. [to MH, 12 May (n.y.; 1970?), Nelson]

I think what frightens me is the knowledge that whatever I may say, I *cannot* shut out and remain a poet. And that I too have a vision of life that tells me "the unexamined life is not worth living." [to MH, n.d. (1970?), Nelson]

And then the resolution of that conflict and its transcendence into art—

As for me, my darling, don't worry about me at all. It is a strange thing but you see—and I confess to you secretly—that I feel in a curious way dedicated to life—everything that happens to me *can* be transformed, and must be, *out of* life into poetry (whether it is lived or written). Because of that I don't think I shall ever be destroyed by emotion—it is my business to *build* with it. [to JH, 20 Apr 37, Rye]

You could not live in the climate I live in (where so much of the conflict is constantly translated into work), but some of the reasons why you love me are just because I am this sort of person. [to JM, 18 Jun 57, Chez Limbosch]

I am feeling most of the time very full of ideas and work and hope to do some in Ireland—but of course there are some dark hours. I so believe in the transformation of suffering into creation and I think it saves me. And also, it is only what one doesn't understand which is unbearable. [to JM, 25 Aug 48, London (RP)]

Of course the only reason for such a poem[8] is that it must touch universal springs of feeling, the private images being only images to convey a universal

---

[8]"The Captain's House," unpublished, written in April 1951 for Eleanor Mabel Sarton.

experience of the bitterness of death, the guilt and the final coming through to reconciliation with oneself and the dead through love. [to KD, 3 Feb 52, Ch Pl]

But the conflict itself is both necessary and essential, and like all challenge exhilarates—

Life does interrupt art! And I am laughing as I write this, for I don't suppose there would be very much art if it weren't so. [to LB, 27 Jun 57, Ghent]

I sometimes think that everything that makes for a good *person* really takes away from the artist. So the age-old struggle goes on in each of us between art and life. [to KD, I Sep 57, Wr St]

If you see the *New Yorker* do look at Louise Bogan's splendid and understanding review of Caitlin Thomas's book *Leftover Life to Kill.* The paragraph about innocence and violence (para 2) struck me as extremely true—the problem is that to be a good artist one has to be quite a difficult person! And the conflict for a woman is even harder than for a man. No one could have borne a woman who behaved as Dylan Thomas did! In a way I think this novel of mine[9] shows this "the victory of kindness" as the *New Yorker* review put it, but at the price perhaps of art. What is one to do? [to KD, I I Oct 57, Wr St]

My summer has been one long stream of invited and (above all) uninvited guests—cars drive up "to see the house." I wish I had never written that book![1] People are determined to see me and at once spill out their entire lives, as if I *could* be interested when I do not know them from Adam. Will I ever be a private person again? Meanwhile I plant autumn crocus—and it will be lovely to be with old friends instead of Persons from Porlock[2] who have made this summer a real Hell. [to RG, 23 Sep 68, Nelson]

[9] *The Birth of a Grandfather.*
[1] *Plant Dreaming Deep.*
[2] Legend has it that in the summer of 1797, Samuel Taylor Coleridge, who was in ill health and had retired to a lonely farmhouse between Porlock and Linton, had just been reading the words "the Khan Kubla

This continual and ineluctable conflict is the focus of perhaps her most important novel, *Mrs. Stevens Hears the Mermaids Singing*—

It is really about how life gets converted into art. [to BdeS, 7 Mar 67, Nelson]

And basic to handling that conflict is the question of balance—

The balance between work and living—

You and I are very alike in that, on the one hand a need of stimulation and on
the other paying a great price for it in fatigue. Maybe it is just being an
artist—"for," as Freya Stark[3] says, "it is his nature to avoid unpleasantness in
a degree which to normal healthy people seems extreme, and to excuse it by
explaining that things hurt him more than the uninitiate can understand. He is
born and then trained to *feel* as a thoroughbred is born and trained to race—
so that even joy 'das tiefe, Schmerzenvolle glück'[4] hurts him and pain winds
through his being like water through the arteries of the hills, wearing them
away." I think the only answer is a seesaw between periods of great outer
stimulation and then periods of almost nothingness and each is essential. [to
BB, I Nov 49, Carbondale]

I feel rather suspended, and a little sad that I did not accomplish more work,
but perhaps for all of us, at least for you and me, it was a time of inner work
on oneself—rather than outer work. I do feel more balanced, I think. [to JM,
21 Jul 57, Satigny]

The balance between emotion and intellect, between one's creative and critical
powers—

commanded a palace to be built" when he fell asleep under the influence of a drug which he had been
prescribed. While he was asleep, inspiration seized him, and he awoke confident of writing from two to
three hundred lines. However, after he had written only a few, a person on business from Porlock called
him out and detained him for an hour. When he returned to his writing, the inspiration and images had
disappeared. "A person from Porlock" has come to mean a fatal interruption of the creative flow.
[3]Dame Freya Madeline Stark (1893–?), English travel writer, poet, scholar, and author of short stories.
[4]"deep, painful joy."

Sarton, two years old.

*Embroidery done by
Eleanor Mabel
Sarton. Credit: Susan
Sherman.*

Sarton, 1922.

I think it is high time the sensuous world came back as it is doing in poetry (Dylan Thomas for instance). Louise Bogan came to Radcliffe to read the other night (more of that later) and read three poems which were a deliberate attempt to use color again in poetry as a necessary element. They are called "After the Persian"[5] and I found them beautiful. I guess the whole thing as always is a matter of balances—the balance between an emotional and intellectual concept which seems to be the essence of any art and which is well said in the review I enclose; "voluptuous yet austere" would be what I would say I want to do in poetry, for instance. It is just this paradox of formal means and anarchic sensibility which is the excitement of art, isn't it? [to BB, 21 Feb 53, Wr St]

Of course it is nonsense to imagine that evolved critical powers such as you possess decline. I should think the opposite was true. Probably, as in poetry itself, you just have higher and higher standards. It is not, I am convinced, in all this, that one's creative power diminishes but rather the danger is that one's critical power grows and at some point the balance may be upset. The critical power stops the creative flow instead of merely disciplining and shaping it. [to LB, 21 Mar 54, Wr St]

The balance between being a daughter, and being one's self—

But I am ashamed that I do not earn my living and I chafe terribly at living at home. I feel like a pear wrapped in cotton wool going sour before it ripened. I adore my family but certain elements of life are shut out living at home. I become a domesticated deer and would like to believe that I am naturally a wild one. It is not, needless to say, a love affair that I am after! But what am I after? I suppose really and fundamentally one good poem to save my soul with. Nothing else really matters. Nothing else seems quite real. But good poems are only written from the *extreme reality* of something so there is the rub. [to JH, 4 Mar 42, Ch Pl]

[5]Louise Bogan's "After the Persian" is actually one poem with five parts.

Sarton, 1926.

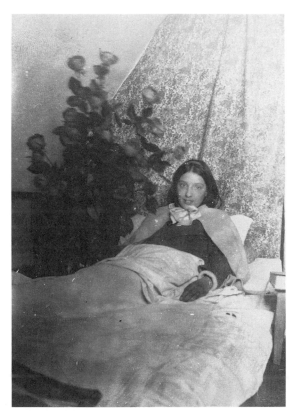

1925.

1929.

Gloucester, 1929.

With George Sarton

1934.

Assisi, June 1932.

1934.

York, Winter 1991.
Credit: Susan
Sherman.

On Thursday my darling little mother arrives here for two weeks while Daddy is in Paris. I am longing to spoil her and put her to bed and walk around in the garden with her in the evenings. But also a little afraid—as all I really want is to be left in peace to write poems and not have to be anyone's child or mother, puis-que je suis en ce moment tellement.[6] [to JH, 10 May 48, Chez Limbosch]

Thank goodness you are there, darling—I feel K[7] needs your love very much, has perhaps lately warded it off while feeling starved for it (just my own hunch, nothing she has ever *said*). Somewhere inside that heroic independence there is a little terribly sad and hungry child. Forgive me for saying this if it

[6]"since I am at the moment so much so."
[7]Katrine Greene, Rosalind's daughter, who was dying of cancer.

seems an intrusion. But there is one balm and one only in such illness—
sometimes it is like Heaven in the Hell—to feel truly cherished and loved, to
be able to *take* the love at last without warding it off or being afraid. I am so
very glad you are there, as you always are and have been through all the
ordeals, tower of radiant strength. [to RG, 29 Jul 65, Nelson]

I know what a queer kind of strain the summer must have been. That effort to
be two people at once, oneself and one's family's child—it does take it out of
one terrifically. [to BB, 25 Aug 46, Ch Pl]

Mother has had the first two of the x-rays and is hugely relieved that they
don't give her nausea and the pain is not too bad. She is getting weller every
day and the relief of having kind efficient help in the house makes an immense
difference. The peace when I go over there, the feeling of her being really
taken care of, is wonderful. Tomorrow the temporary maid goes and the
permanent one arrives so she will be well settled in by the time I leave. But of
course she can't use her arm and does have a good deal of pain at night and
sleeps badly. All this has made me realize freshly how dear my parents are.
And I go about singing their praises to myself all day. But at the same time it
has pulled me out of my own life, broken the inner current, and I find it hard
to get back where I was when I first came home—full of ideas and thoughts
and energy and that inward sort which makes all the difference between just
living and living deeply. But I expect it will come back soon. [to JH, 28 Oct
48, Oxf St]

It is so good that you can relax at Moline, play the piano and take comfort in
your family—it is so true that one can only do that when one has one's own
life apart from them. Then it is all possible and good. [to BB, 31 Dec 48, Oxf
St]

The balance between loving to teach, and deploring the academic world—

I enjoy my students but I loathe the academic atmosphere, epitomized for me
by one prof. who came up after my speech and said, "It was pleasant"—I am

a fish out of water as my father was in the petty smug world where everyone is a critic and no one, or hardly anyone, creates anything. [to JM, 27 Apr 72, Agnes Scott]

The balance between the solitary work of the poet, and the communal work of a necessary job—

But of course being a poet one is spoiled. In poetry compromise is fatal. In action of any cooperative sort it is inevitable. The thing is to find the balance. [to EMS, 19 Apr 43, 5 E 10]

The balance within love—

In love, what is so frightful is that one perhaps cannot altogether make the decisions. They are lived into. There is a point where conflict is forever settled. Only one tries and tries to maintain a balance, to find the equilibrium. [to JH, 29 Jan 43, Hotel Albert, NYC]

And always the balance between the fires of passion which ignite the work, and the secret worlds of solitude which produce the work—

> Always emotion causes fear,
> That wince before the inward blow
> As feeling tries to break its way through—
> It is disturbing when people come too near,
> Violate with strange private demands
> The entity of a pair of human hands.
> Let me tell you now. Let me explain.
> Here there is only sunlight on the quiet air,
> An open world where I can wander again
> Freely after a long imprisonment in pain.
> You need not come here. You can stay There.
> Poetry is peace for me, the always answer
> As the strict form of the dance to the dancer.
> Not a person but a piece of song breaks through

And what it always says is *thank you.*
So do not be disturbed, do not read *please*
Into those meditations or those silences.

["After Thought," undated]

Is all one's life a perilous balance between the fireworks of personality and the deep secret places that have nothing really to do with it I wonder? One longs for excitement and one *knows* that the price is usually too high, and in the end

*Eleanor Mabel
Sarton.*

*Two miniatures by
Eleanor Mabel Sarton
in Sarton's house. The
woman to the right in
the upper painting is
Melanie Altar. The
child in the lower
painting is a
grandniece of Richard
Wagner. Credit:
Susan Sherman.*

Eleanor Mabel
Sarton.

one prays for peace at any price. And yet for me at least, work is so closely allied with people, with what a person can *unlock,* the sudden stream of feeling that makes writing inevitable and necessary—the safety valve of sanity perhaps—it is difficult. I think really I am a troubadour and my business is celebration of the people I love. [to JH, 12 Mar 37, Ch Pl]

And central to her art, to that business of celebrating the people and the natural world she loves, central to her poetry, is solitude, with its inevitable companion, loneliness—

We see her at the age of ten in a tree house she built—

I have built a sort of a house in one of the trees nearby our house, I am writing in it now I get wild strawberries and other eatables and have feasts up here, or read, or draw, or write; it is lots of fun. [to GS, 26 Jun 22, Ogunquit, Me.]

And a year later—

Oh, to go to my own little nook
And lie in the tall cool grass
And take a beautiful fairy book
And see the little bugs pass
Each on his own sweet path
And see the buttercups laugh

And then to look up at the clear blue sky
through the quivering green of the leaves
That tremble and whisper and drowsily sigh
And look, see a spider that weaves
With his little round body and arms that crook
I've entirely forgotten my beautiful book.

[untitled, HJ, ? May 23]

George Sarton.

And then follow other feasts of solitude,
with their bliss and
problems—

Now for a little I have fed on loneliness
As on some strange fruit from a frost-touched vine—
Persimmon in its yellow comeliness,
Or pomegranate-juice, color of wine,
The pucker-mouth crab-apple, or late plum—
On fruit of loneliness have I fed;
But now after short absence I am come
Back from felicity to the wine and bread—
For, being mortal, this luxurious heart
Would starve for you, my dear, I must admit
If it were held another hour apart
From that food which alone can comfort it—
I am come home to you, for at the end
I find I cannot live without you, friend.

[early draft of "I have been nourished . . . " in *Encounter in April,* 13 Apr 30,
Philadelphia]

Today it is snowing, the most light Japanese snow, like an incessant soundless playing upon a musical instrument—everything is white already and the house full of that strange cold snow-light. The world in fact is a new place. [to K, 28 Dec 37, Ch Pl]

Loneliness is never a thing in itself—one is never lonely in the abstract—one is lonely for *one* person. [to K, 17 Jan 38, Ch Pl]

If you were here I would see only you and no one else and work—there are very few people here whom I want *only* to see, and sometimes I get very lonely and feel like a small bright star millions of miles from any other light. [to K, 23 Feb 40, Ch Pl]

I shall never have enough of solitude—I am so busy inside I haven't even got to the place where I may suddenly be frightfully lonely. [to MFH, 2 Oct 40, YWCA, Washington]

I look forward to being lonely in Charleston or rather to being solitary— loneliness is a physical thing, a physical need for comfort, for being given back one's physical identity through touch—but solitariness is another matter. I shall be lonely too, of course. Sometimes it is awful. [to MFH, 31 Oct 40, Black Mt]

I simply adore being alone—I find it a consuming thirst—and when that thirst is slaked, *then* I am happy. [to MFH, 9 Aug 42, Sudbury]

As she[8] said so well, in reading one still retains one's solitude—the inner life goes on—as it never does with a person. [to JM, 14 May 47, Chez Limbosch]

What you said about "solitariness" was just right. That was quoted from de Sélincourt's wonderful review[9] of *Inner Landscape* and is clearer in context. He

[8]Marie Closset.
[9]"The Blessing of Augury," *Observer*, April 2, 1939, p. 5.

goes on to say (about the poet in general): "To be the world's he must renounce the world, a spiritual center radiating light." [to BB, 11 Jun 45, Santa Fe (CF)]

After visiting Brancusi's studio in Paris—

It's time I crept back into my own darkness after all this light and had a little time to think. [to JM, 10 Jun 47, Paris (Huxley)]

Or that perennial need to "take in" experience—

I wish you had more time to yourself, not to have it takes the edge off everything—one doesn't have time to experience fully until one is alone. [to BB, 13 Jul 48, Montreux]

In the spring after her mother died, when she went away to mourn alone—

Quand j'ai mis la clef dans la porte, grande porte lourde, il me semblait ouvrir la porte d'un secret paradis, la porte de la poésie. Comme j'ai faim de cette silence, de cette solitude.[1] [to MC, 1 Apr 51, Stonington]

Je suis dans une extase de solitude, il n'y a pas d'autre mot.[2] [to MC, 3 Apr 51, Stonington]

From the Bread Loaf Writers' Conference—

Hier soir j'ai enfin pu m'échapper pendant trois heures de solitude complète, et cela m'a fait un bien immense. J'ai pu un peu me rassembler et me retrouver et te retrouver, et celles que j'aime.[3] [to MC, 21 Aug 51, Bread Loaf]

[1]"When I put the key in the door, a great heavy door, it seemed as if I were opening a secret door to heaven, the door to poetry. Oh how I am starved for this silence, this solitude."
[2]"I am in an ecstasy of solitude, there is no other word for it."
[3]"Last night I was finally able to escape for three hours of complete solitude and it did me enormous good. I was able to collect myself a little, to refind my self and to refind you, and that is what I love."

When planning to travel—

I want to get you to come to Europe, not only for selfish reasons. I would respect your hard-won freedom. I would do my best in every way and I think I could. And there would be a lot of space around us because I need solitude as much as you do, simply have to have it or die. [to LB, 30 Jan 54, Wr St]

Later, in Nelson's solitude of her own creation—

The solitude is quite wonderful—I am intoxicated with the beauty of my white world (perfectly pure snow all around without a speck of dust on it) and wander from room to room as the light changes. [to KD, 11 Jan 59, Nelson]

I do need this time even though I often feel excruciatingly lonely and dismayed. But one has to go *through* experience, not avoid it, so I know that is good. [to KD, 6 Dec 59, Nelson]

I feel calmer and more myself and am becoming accustomed to living in the dark. Perhaps the spirit develops special perceptions to deal with that sort of darkness as the eyes might for living in physical darkness. I feel often very close to the ecstasy and anguish which lie at the very heart of poetry—I am writing a lot. [to KD, 27 Dec 59, Nelson]

I want isolation, the snow, and the little flame secure within. [to BdeS, 7 Mar 64, Nelson]

Well, I realized then that Nelson does give me a kind of strength I never had before. My life is really *posited* here on solitude—the village itself will not read what I write, and takes me as I am—from here I should be able to afford to be absolutely honest. [to MR, 27 Oct 64, Nelson]

I am very much like an infant learning everything new—a good state for a poet, I expect. For instance it came upon me yesterday with the force of revelation that loneliness can be defined as missing *oneself*. Everyone but me has always known this I expect. I am still very lonely but little bits and pieces of me begin to well up. [to MH, 5 Jun 70, Nelson]

Another aspect of her solitude stems from her being torn between the Europe of her heritage and temperament and the America where she is rooted—

I told them[4] amongst other things to be aware of the pitfall of the rich (as Americans), i.e. the rich always *undervalue* the poor and we are becoming very smug about Europe because it is materially poor. Whereas actually of course we suffer from not having given enough, from emerging untouched from the war and without its death in ashes the phoenix cannot be born again. Really darling I can't tell you how I hunger and thirst for Europe. [to JH, 3 Feb 48, Oxf St]

Here in Europe one is, alas, so much more aware of American failures than of the America one loves— But on the other hand my physical self is really European—the smells, the great trees, the marvelous changing skies, the whole air and earth are what I love and ache over because I shall never live here and it's a homesickness without end. [to BB, 19 May 48, Chez Limbosch]

Mon coeur est lourd comme une pierre et je voudrais vivre et mourir en Europe.[5] [to MC, 10 Aug 51, at sea]

This brings me to some thoughts your letter induced about the whole question about Europe and pressure etc. What I miss in this land, as earth, as land, is the cherishing humanizing work of centuries which you feel everywhere in Europe. We Americans have exploited, used our land to the utmost—cut down the forests ruthlessly (even in New England almost everything is scrubby second growth uncared for, unloved), ploughed up the plains, never stopped to plant a garden, moved on to the *next* place, when they had used up

[4]An audience of students at the Beaver Country Day School in Boston.
[5]"My heart is heavy as a rock and I wish I could live and die in Europe."

a farm. Here and there in New England there are gardens, but every tiny backyard in an English slum has one—and I remember my dismay in the Midwest where you see a frame house standing in miles and miles of wheat or corn without even a tree or a hedge or a small vegetable garden near it. In the South it is even worse where the land has been exhausted, *literally*. So when I get back to Europe, what I breathe and rest in is partly this careful, patient cultivation and cherishing of the earth itself. [to LB, 18 Apr 54, Wr St]

And as she has found the emotional loam so much deeper in Europe, it is there that she has come home to her self and to poetry—

[Europe] certainly is for me a complete awakening always to true values. [to JM, 16 May 48, Chez Limbosch]

Next year you had better come to Europe, willy nilly. I shall I think have to come. It is not really any person which makes me know this, but I am just a different person here—in the sense that I feel my soul very close to the skin. Everything turns into poetry. And you had better come—there are so many things we can do together. I want you to meet Jean-Do before she dies—and there is all of England. [to JM, 5 Jun 48, VF]

I have been thinking of what you said about doing an objective job of writing. I think I know what you meant of the dangers of depending so much on feeling. But darling please remember that for nine or ten months of the year I am sober and thoughtful and give lectures and think about politics and writing technique and then when I come to Europe everything explodes, so it is not *always*. [to JH, 4 May 48, Chez Limbosch]

Well, I was pleased with "the great hunger for utter form" and with Chartres (from you) as its exemplar—and of course "old stones." They and "old trees" are what drive me back to Europe, and some quality in the air more tender and gentle than here. I doubt if the smog of Calif. will have the same effect, but it might! Travel forces the kaleidoscope of consciousness to a new pattern, don't you think? And this is sometimes as if a door that had been closed, opened again. [to LB, 12 Oct 55, Wr St]

The thing that moved me so deeply about the sheep mother was her physical tenderness (so unexpected in a sheep) and that *physical* sound she made. When I went back to Italy after World War II I was really overwhelmed by the way fathers held their children, the warmth of the physical communion in Italian families. I felt that by comparison, Americans were in some way *arid*, afraid of being whole men. Afraid of *hugging* a child. [to MH, 4 Mar 70, Nelson]

And so she is torn between both worlds—

[America] does sometimes feel like a wilderness for the spirit, but I believe that is always the failure in me, spoiled by inheriting an already created European civilization, unwilling to be a pilgrim moving painfully along the path toward a new one. [to JH, 25 Sep 44, 22 E 10]

This is the most extraordinary time of my life. A burst of poems, a great creative tide that bears me along on its stream till I almost want to cry "Enough." A real liberation after three frozen years when it seemed as if the inner eye could only look at suffering and horror, silently—look and look. But this is a holy place, the only one I know of in the States. It takes the soul out of one's body. [to JH, 15 Apr 45, Santa Fe (ER)]

And it is a terrible uprooting to me just now to leave Judy. In some ways I wish I were not going and yet I know how the poems will start again—and it is irresistible. [to BB, 29 Mar 48, Oxf St]

I am forced to *evaluate* both what the U.S. means to me and what Europe does, and hence perhaps to realize what I might try to be—such a mixture—and if it is all rather disturbing, it is not an uncreative kind of disturbance. [to LB, 22 Aug 54, Linkebeek]

From one of the frequent lecture tours on which public demands intruded—

I pine for solitude which is really my element these years. [to LB, 25 Oct 65, Lindenwood]

As her partner in solitude, there is silence: the silence she has listened to as poet, and which has nourished her—

Je sais que pour chaque chose perdu il y a une chose à *trouver*—mais il faut être très patiente et beaucoup écouter le silence pour trouver ce qui remplace l'amour quand on l'a perdu.[6] [HJ, ?Jan 38, Ch Pl]

The last months have been so full of experience and so rich in joy that I feel now I need lots of silence to be in. [to EMS and GS, 3 Aug 37, Austria]

Your letters are a great comfort for like all of us I have moments of panic— they go as soon as I have a little time and silence and can get back to poetry. [to RWB, 23 Feb 43, 5 E 10]

I suppose for anyone whose métier is words, there is a hunger for some other form of communication, for silence, and it is very hard to create or to bear silence unless there is music or passion, or one is looking at pictures. [to LB, 30 Jan 54, Wr St]

Breakfast in bed when I have written up the last week very fast—now the bubbly sound of the fire, the silence is like a *charm.* I have been lately in a state of precipitation. Now in these few moments of perfect peace it is as if all the dancing motes were gradually sifting down to the bottom, leaving clear water, clear thoughts, the sense of being myself again—[HJ, 8 May 54, Wr St]

I'll be more human when I am settled in my snow and silence. [to KD, 31 Jan 64, Nelson]

Au moins deux fois j'ai eu le sentiment, ce sentiment si immense du poèmes qui fait son silence autour de lui, du souffle retenu dans toute la salle, une fois pour mon poème de noël d'il y a deux ans sur Tilano, l'indian—et l'autre le

---

[6]"I know that for each thing lost there is a new discovery, but one must be very patient and listen well to the silence to find what replaces a lost love."

beau poème sur le chien qu'il faut que je te traduis un jour.[7] [to MC, 14 Nov 51, Myn Pl]

The silences of houses—

> This house with a brook at its feet is hers.
> She set it on this hill.
> You can see her coming up the path to greet
> it, singing—
> (Man, that will make the tears start out of your quick)
> You can see her in the early morning leaving—
> (Man, that will dazzle your eyes)
> And in case you have never seen her
> She looks like a princess out of Egypt
> With a proud walk and a face that speaks of the bone.
> If you see her stand in the door you will know
> That she chose this hill and built upon it
> For children and beasts and all wild things—
> And for her silences.
> She built it and lives there now, a blessing on the land.

[from "In Praise of Anne," 5 Mar 37, Sudbury]

Il me semble qu'il devrait avoir tout un chapitre, peut-être deux, sur l'enseignement et ta façon de le voir et d'y penser, que les poèmes entrent par la fenêtre sous la lampe dans ton bureau—et que le grand silence soit là, le silence de l'amour et de la solitude et de la poésie—qui est aussi une intègre partie de cette maison dont l'âme est *ton* silence.[8] [to MC, 26 Oct 51, Myn Pl]

---

[7]"At least twice I had the feeling, that immense response when poems create a silence around themselves, when all breath is held still within an entire room, the first time was for my Christmas poem which I wrote two years ago for Tilano, the Indian, and the second, for the beautiful poem about the dog which I must translate for you sometime." Tilano was an Indian who lived as companion with Sarton's friend Edith Warner in a pueblo in Santa Fe and is the subject of Sarton's "Letter to an Indian Friend," Christmas broadside, 1949, and also in *The Land of Silence.* The other poem is "Lament for Toby, a French Poodle," from *In Time Like Air.*

[8]"It seems to me there should be an entire chapter, perhaps two, on teaching and your way of seeing it and thinking of it, the way the poems come in through the window beneath the lamp in your study—and that

Here I come back to a great room high up in the house[9] where I have written many poems and been silent for many hours—peace, time to sort out and assemble what has happened really, and to do nothing, which is the necessity for a while. [to LB, 19 Sep 54, Satigny]

The silences within love and friendship. Even at sixteen she knew well the communion of silence[1]—

> Since I cannot gather my joys
> Into a basket
> And bring them to you
> Like many-colored fruit,
> Since I cannot blow my dreams
> Over you
> In the evening,
> And my songs will not sing
> In tune,
> Since I cannot even give you my life—
> I will sometimes give you silence.
>
> ["Gift" (to KT), HJ, 8 Oct 28, Ray St]

During the theater years—

How funny to feel as if I were encased so tightly in silence that I have to whisper to you. [to KT, 20 Apr 30, Philadelphia]

And long after—

a great silence is there, the silence of love and solitude and poetry—which is an integral part of this house whose spirit is *your* silence."
[9]Satigny.
[1]Sarton's mother, as well, was particularly sensitive to such communion: "I do so wonder what Lugné-Poë will say of your poems—I have the feeling he will be quite astonished whatever he may say or *not* say. Be sure to tell us what you think he *felt* as well as what he says." [EMS to MS, 22 Nov 31, Beirut]

How difficult it is to love *well*—to know when it is better to be silent, that even joy can *strain* the heart so frightfully—though in general everything that denies life seems to me false. [to JH, 28 Nov 37, Ch Pl]

Shall we sit in front of a little fire and talk? I am bursting with conversation really in spite of my silences (they are further down really)—or shall I only see you through a mirage of voluble Oxford, through a haze of Gladys Calthrop?[2] [to EB, 26 May 38, VF]

I wish you would send me a postcard once in a while—no, I really hear you through your silences perfectly well, so don't bother. [to EB, 13 Jul 38, VF]

I think the silence we move toward together is work apart. The other *private* silences are a luxury (and thank heavens we can afford that luxury too now). [to MFH, 16 Aug 40, Ch Pl]

I was glad of our silences—they were meetings. [to MR, 11 Dec 41, Ch Pl]

The main thing is to let you know, dearest Juliette, how much I love you and how that grows in the silence so you can expect quite a tree and perhaps even a little shade and some birds nesting by the next time we meet. [to JH, 1 Oct 43, 22 E 10]

The awful thing about a letter is that one *must* talk. But it is really—and you know this I'm sure—in the silence and in thinking about you with all my heart that I feel close to you now and always. [to JH, 26 Nov 45, Oxf St]

There was lots of mail—a long letter from Agi[3] incidentally—but so far nothing from *you*. Never mind, we are *together,* darling—I never felt it more. [to JM, ? Apr 47, aboard *Queen Elizabeth*]

[2]Scenic designer whose work included Noel Coward's *The Vortex* and Eva Le Gallienne's production of Ibsen's *The Master Builder.*
[3]Agi Sims, artist from Santa Fe, New Mexico.

The fruit is silence. Silence is our child
And very marvelous and strange she grows
And flourishes and through her now the wild
And angry loneliness more gently flows,
In trains, in the most noisy crowded places
And in the frightening forests of the night
She opens up clear distances and spaces,
She gives the poet back to his delight.
There are two faces reflected in her eyes;
Anguish and fervor shine upon her hair,
She is the ever loving, ever wise,
And we are always one when she is there—
Parted by all realities but this
Child born of two passionate silences.

[unpublished sonnet of series "These Images Remain," 1948]

Whatever sings
Has silent wings
Sleep by the moon,
The great white swan,
Cooler than snows
No lover knows.
Close, tired heart,
And rest apart,
And glad to be
Lonely and free
Keeping of this
The silences.
When words are done
Love can begin.
Sail the dark air
And find peace there.
Dear one, now rest
On the swan's breast.

["Song," unpublished, 11 Jul 48, Montreux]

Mais je ne sais pas plus écrire—tu comprendras—ô mon ange de silences.[4] [to MC, 27 Oct 51, Myn Pl]

Called Louise[5]— The quality of her voice reverberates for me in an extraordinary way—and yet I can only hear it just after we have talked on the phone. [HJ, 12 Mar 54, Wr St]

The obvious this morning which dawns (and fills me with the need to ask your forgiveness) is simply that to demand the kind of silence I mean when I talk about the composed moment is of course to demand the most absolute kind of intimacy, which if it does not presuppose passion and its exchange, does presuppose the real gift of self. [to LB, 7 Mar 54, Wr St]

The result[6] is that today I do feel a bit exhausted and I wish you were here and we could go for a walk in perfect silence. [to LB, 30 Oct 54, Linkebeek]

My little student guide[7] is blessedly silent and a great comfort. We enjoy together without words. [to KD, 17 Mar 62, Kyoto]

The need for silence even in teaching—

It couldn't have been in some ways a *worse* moment for poetry. They[8] had just beaten W&J[9] at football for the first time in 30 years—an all-day holiday was announced for Monday (when I was to have spoken), and well, I had a good dose of American football frenzy all right—ending with a grand blare in the chapel (!) with the band, cheerleaders and the President holding the football as if it were the holy ghost in his two hands—the Dean leading the band etc. I got into a panic because I thought I could never make poetry as exciting to

[4]"But I am not able to write anymore—you will understand—my angel of silences."
[5]Louise Bogan.
[6]Of having written eight poems in ten days.
[7]Kyoko Nishimura, visiting her in Nelson.
[8]Bethany College.
[9]Washington and Jefferson College.

Sarton (CENTER) on lecture tour at Bethany College, October 1940.

them as football, but also mad because all that energy can't be channeled into something else. So wrote a long poem which I shouted at them to begin my speech. They were quite stunned.

The speech was awfully hard to give because the chapel is enormous and the speech is a plea for silence, inner life, etc. It is difficult to shout about silence, or to shout poetry at all, and that is just what I had to do, and the only way to do it was to key it so high that I felt like shouting. When I'd finished I felt as if I had literally poured out two quarts of blood on the stage and also I thought (though I knew it was a good speech) that I hadn't got them at all. But afterwards I was told what a tough audience they are and that what seemed mild applause for 2 quarts of blood was really an ovation. Anyway lots of shy boys came up afterwards (it's co-ed) and said they agreed with me about silence—and then there was an informal discussion and we really got somewhere. [to MFH, 9 Oct 40, Winchester, Va.]

Il me semble que tout le problème de la vie reste dans la double nécessité de s'épandre en largeur et de s'approfondir dans l'être—solitude contre amitié, travail contre silence etc. J'ai l'impression maintenant de n'avoir plus rien à dire à mes élèves et il y a grand temps que ces cours prennent fin.[1] [to MC, 26 Apr 52, Ch Pl]

The silences within art—

The play[2] is all silences too and I love that. [to K, 23 Feb 40, Ch Pl]

I agree about *Man and Superman*. The trouble is there is never any mystery, any *silence* in Shaw. [to BB, 8 Nov 47, St. Louis, Mo.]

. . . De la Mare, too, who uses subtle variations better than anyone I think. The silence within the line—do you remember his:

> Slim cunning hands at rest, and cozening eyes—
> Under this stone one loved too wildly lies;
> How false she was, no granite could declare;
> Nor all earth's flowers, how fair.

There it seems to me the slight necessary pause between "flowers" and "how" is the very essence of poetry. [to KD, 18 Jan 53, Wr St]

The lute is rather rough and resinous—but now I have fallen in love with this instrument and its intervals of silence between the extremely vital, almost *rough* plucking. [to BdeS, 11 Nov 64, Nelson]

---

[1]"It seems to me that the greatest problem of living is based on the ironic double necessity of expanding one's breadth and amplitude, and at the same time of deepening and searching within one's own being—the necessity for solitude and the necessity for friendship; the necessity for work, and the necessity for being quiet. I have the feeling at this moment that I have nothing left to say to my students, and yet there is still a long while before this course ends."

[2]*Martine*, by J. J. Bernard.

Did I tell you that I had a lovely audience at the Harvard Summer School (they had to move the reading to a larger hall and the silence was quite moving as they listened). [to KD, 23 Aug 62, Nelson]

And then there are the problems of silence, when it is an absence of recognition, or when it must be fought for by the author who has become a public person—

I guess what moves me so much about your life as man and as poet is that it has close parallels to my own. I too have worked as poet anyway with a great silence around me as far as serious critical appraisal goes. I have had to reach my readers like a secret agent, over or under all the usual channels. I have had to battle the anger this causes, and my coming to Nelson, a small village near Dublin, and in so doing really and deliberately "leaving the world," has been of enormous help. I now believe it may be a kind of freedom to go about one's business in peace, unrecognized, as it were. In the very long run any success devours—and perhaps also corrupts. I do have a problem that perhaps you do not. The novels and autobiographies elicit huge amounts of mail and these past few years I live a sort of agony of "responding." I feel that if one has written a thing that deeply moves someone, one has no right not to answer—but then how to keep so many "friends" at bay? They know me but I do not know them. That is the real trouble. The other problem is psychological—the work of answering is the work of Sisyphus, for even when I take a whole week off to answer, by the time I have done so, a new pile is there waiting. When I get seriously overtired this leads to real depression and a wish to die. [to RF, 12 Jun (n.y.; 1971?), Nelson]

And then there is friendship. She lets Wordsworth speak for her—

> Thy friends are exultations, agonies,
> And love, and man's unconquerable mind.[3]

I read that sonnet at every lecture and it always moves me freshly. [to EMS and GS, 24 Apr 41, Lake Erie]

[3]From Wordsworth's "To Toussaint L'Ouverture."

And she has known myriad faces of friendship. While rehearsing with her company, the Apprentice Theatre—

> The last week has been full of perils and adventures which have proved to bind us up into even greater friendship. [to EMS and GS, 29 Jul 34, Rowley]

From the prewar years—

> What a darling you are to write to me—I am freshly started with surprise every time I wake up and think that there you and Julian are *suddenly* upon my horizon. It still seems preposterous. But it is true don't you think that one knows *definitely*—knows almost at once whether people are going to be of one's island or not? I fell in love with you both at first sight—Julian in a storm in Cornwall and you in a little white jacket in a green room when I was so frightened by being early that I would have read you the whole of "Testament of Beauty"[4] rather than have to talk. [to JH, 5 Dec 36, 239 E 17]

> I hated leaving everyone in London—but did leave with a lovely feeling of flowers on my head—of leaving real friends—Elisabeth, Kot, Juliette and Julian[5]—the best I have ever had. I am sorry that I didn't have time to see Virginia Woolf again but I had a very sweet note from her and feel that she is *there* and there is no need to hurry things. [to EMS and GS, 13 Jul 37, Hotel du Rhìn, Brussels]

The Apprentice Theatre rehearsing at Rosalind Greene's house in Rowley, Massachusetts, Summer 1934.

> I feel I have a real friend in Koteliansky—Jean Dominique says "nous sommes en pleine miracle"[6] thinking of his friendship for Mansfield. I had a long talk with him last week—and he said, "Whatever happens, don't worry. You are a

[4]A long philosophical poem by Robert Bridges.
[5]Elizabeth Bowen, S. S. Koteliansky, and Juliette and Julian Huxley.
[6]"we are in the midst of a miracle."

May Sarton at the
Huxleys' apartment
at the London Zoo.
Credit: Juliette
Huxley.

Julian Huxley
birdwatching. Credit:
May Sarton.

Juliette Huxley.

Julian Huxley, about
to be knighted, 1958.

writer. Just write." When the novel[7] comes out in England, he is going to get people to review it (an enormous help). [to EMS and GS, 14 Jun 37, London (EB)]

Just as war broke out—

I do think of you so often—like candles very far away burning in a storm. Do not blow out—[to JH, 10 Sep 39, Rockport]

Indeed it was a feast of friendship—

I often think what a rich cornucopia of friends you have brought me in *your* friends, darling. [to JM, 23 May 48, Chez Limbosch]

And her friends served her well during the last months of her mother's illness—

Darling, I just wanted you to *know.* At such times one's friends make a community of saints and one feels supported. [to MFH, 14 Aug 50, Ch Pl]

And she has felt supported by them throughout her life—

Il m'a semblé en le lisant que c'est assez pour toute une vie d'avoir connu *une* âme à qui on pourait parlé simplement et à coeur ouvert—comment ce fait-il que la vie me l'a donné, ma chérie? C'est miraculeux et je bénis Dieu chaque jour.[8] [to MC, 14 Apr 51, Myn Pl]

In all this your faith has sustained me and in fact and in my mind I felt my friends gather like guardian angels to save me from despair. [to KD, 26 Dec 61, Nelson]

---

[7] *The Single Hound.*

[8] "It seemed to me while reading your letter that it is sufficient for an entire life to have *one* such soul with whom one can speak simply and with an open heart. How is it that life has given me such a thing, my darling. It is miraculous, and I bless God every day."

I sometimes think that since the death of Jean Dominique you have been the only *rock*, the absolutely steadfast and extraordinary friend. Almost every day I find your hand in something I am doing—such as the files with my mother's letters, the marvelous book of Nelson you gave me for a birthday with excerpts of Pl. Dr. Deep[9] and the wonderful photographs, and this morning I used as my tray cloth at breakfast time the little handwoven cloth you gave me. But all this is nothing compared to the faith and understanding, the always-being-there, and your own great self who has taught me so much about courage and about love. [to EBl, 2 Sep 79, York]

Yet that community of saints and guardian angels has had its agonies—

We have had three French guests for the weekend (a nightmare!). I can't stand my dearest friends for more than three hours at a time but three *days!* It reminds me of a story of a very dear Boston lady— Someone asked why she looked so harassed and she said, "My best friend is coming to stay"— It is so awful and *so* true of the really farouche Sarton family. [to JH, 10 Sep 39, Rockport]

I know you have much to bear with in me, and I really do sometimes in you, but I have never looked at friendship in a deep sense as easy or entirely comfortable. [to LB, 10 Mar (n.y.)]

But we must not allow our relationship to fray out now, but do everything wise and kind to and for each other to sustain it and nourish it. Affirm, strengthen, enjoy what is real, what we truly have and face and accept what we have not—is what we must try to do. [to JM, 8 May 57, Ireland]

E.[1] keeps telling me "the whole thing is to accept oneself, and then to be oneself as fully as one can." I have been overprotective of you, and this is not good love, mature and honest. It does not do justice to our true relationship. You have allowed what we have *not* to cloud what we *have,* and that is poor

[9] *Plant Dreaming Deep.*
[1] Eugénie DuBois.

Picnic at Savannah Wood. Juliette, May Sarton, and Julian Huxley, June 1937. Credit: Alan Best.

Eleanor Blair at Nelson editing Plant Dreaming Deep. Credit: May Sarton.

love too. One can lose everything by wanting the impossible. What we have is *good,* not perfect, but that is life itself. I think there is a danger in too much outsideness and reason—i.e. one can stand *outside* and emphasize that the whole situation is a mess. One can get into a spiral of refusal and denial of what *is* and has to be accepted. But to us who are within our own relationship, it should be possible to believe that it is not a mess, because we refuse to allow it to be, and because we build on a firm foundation of mutual tenderness, trust and respect. We can look at the impossible circumstances and say, this is something we can handle because there is love and we are mature people. [to JM, 18 Jun 57, Chez Limbosch]

If you can learn not to close the door at the moment when you feel you must close it; and if I, at the same time, can learn to wait for it to open instead of trying to hammer it down, then we shall come into our peace. [to CD, 19 Aug 58, Greenings]

And so she speaks of her own continual efforts at nurturing friendships when she writes of the death of Katharine Davis's friend—

I do not believe that such a friendship between two women is easy; it had to be worked at on *both* sides, each showing true love and forbearance. *That* is the great reality and no one can take it away from you, whatever they may say or do now. [to KD, 9 Jul 62, London (JS)]

The actual volume of letters attest to another of friendship's problems—

The great thing is that I have managed to earn a decent living and support this place *and* produce a goodly number of books, as well as maintaining a hundred or more friendships by letter all over the world. This is the greatest drain, but as Judy[2] says, "if you didn't get any mail, you would mind!" So there you are. . . . [to KD, 22 Jan 66, Nelson]

And then there is love, that which waters the roots of poetry—

I have been going through a sort of salutary personal crisis—salutary because to be in love is to be alive, to feel oneself part of the sun and the moon and the day and the night and when it rains it is the earth weeping with one—and when it is a lovely day one is sharing it with all the earth—a crisis because it is founded as usual upon *impossibility*—a woman and can have no end. That does not matter. I feel quite certain and aloof when I am well. (There are moments

[2]Judith Matlack.

of illness of course.) And gravely aware that the answer is poetry, that which I can write, and there must be no other human answer at all. [to K, 17 Mar 40, Ch Pl]

But poetry and that human answer of love are inextricable for her, and both are means of communion—

When I say I love you, I am saying that I love poetry. [to LB, 26 Jan 54, Wr St]

> What other way is there than love
> To touch, to go down deeper
> Than the muffled mouth?
> To go behind
> The golden screen of eyes

*May Sarton with
Judith Matlack, York.
Credit: Eleanor Blair.*

To meet you?
What other way than love
For I am shaken with the need of knowing
Where your heart beats,
The measure of the blood in the wrist flowing.
I am drawn by what seems necessity
To find out your center
As men may utterly desire to creep back to the womb.
Their faces are carved helmets
Yet locked under the fine bone
In each this living hunger stands
Like a diviner
His whole weight struggling
Against the torments underground.

["The Diviner," HJ, ? Dec 36, Cambridge, Mass.][3]

Mais ce qui est beau c'est tous deux amènent à la fin à une même chose—la communion entre êtres humains. Le poème, puisé dans le sang du poète, rejoint finalement le coeur de tout le monde, le roman peut sembler un message intime.[4] [to MC, 10 Jan 51, Myn Pl]

Next week I give a lecture at Winsor[5] on Invisible Bridges, which is really all I have been thinking about politically and spiritually speaking in Europe—it is strange how very few poems there seem to be which talk about man's relation to man, about communion between people and so forth. I am having to write one.[6] There is some Whitman of course. [to BB, 5 Oct 48, Oxf St]

You can't imagine how rare it is to discover someone who lives in the same private world as I (not that it is good or bad but it is *special*—it is a sense of the

[3]Written in George Sarton's office, Widener Library 189, Harvard University.
[4]"But what is beautiful is that both arrive at the same conclusion, the communion between human beings. The poem, springing from the poet's blood, finally touches the heart of the world; the novel seems to be an intimate message."
[5]The Winsor School, a private girls' school in Boston.
[6]See "Invisible Bridges," a.k.a. "Innumerable Friend," in *The Land of Silence*.

colour of air, the edges of words, and the horizons of feelings—I suppose it is feminine). The minute I saw you I knew that you did. It has nothing to do with love (it is rare that one *loves* people who understand one at all) though I do love you it is obvious enough. But it is just I suppose like a solitary strange bird with a red crest suddenly meeting another. [to JH, 13 Apr 37, Rye]

Remember that when I put my head against you like a small stubborn mule what I am trying to get at is really not passion but communion. I have said this before. It is the truth. [to LB, 7 Mar 54, Wr St]

And whether through love or poetry, communion is her purpose, that which makes earth her holy place[7]—

> Help us to find Your Grace
> Not in the selfish private place
> But written on each human face.
>
> Help us to know Your Presence
> Not in the solitary trance
> But through the daily bread of sense.
>
> Help us to be more human, move
> Through the obsessive fear of love
> To where we can begin to give.
>
> There is no path away from You
> But only inward where all grow
> Deep in each other, rooted so.
>
> When the mind is lost in despair
> The arch that spans us still is there
> For pain is also what we share.
>
> When love is passionate and wild
> Your gentleness, still undefiled
> Reminds us of this church, our child.

[7]See "As Fresh as Always New," Christmas broadside, 1985, and in *The Phoenix Again*.

Help us to overcome our guilt
That all the separateness melt
And this communion may be built.

That in Your Name we build together
Through our communion with each other
This human church, our child, our mother.

["Communion," a.k.a. "This Human Church," unpublished, 18 Nov 48]

Hence, there is a purity in loving—

It is very moving and true what you say about childlikeness—it is perhaps the only sign of true love. But it is very rare in our age—in religion as well as in human love. Isn't it? [to LB, 30 Jan 54, Wr St]

And here, I must be permitted to say, love is the redeemer. At least it is for me—such a rush of humility breaks down the critical barrier, and one may become like a child again in the good sense. [to LB, 21 Mar 54, Wr St]

And love is her nourishment—

She[8] is amazing and has been for me a real renewal of the deep sources which got so muddled last year with all the mess I was in. When I first knew Jean Do I was nineteen and she was 60 and from the first moment we have just loved each other in every possible way, but without a shadow. These are the real miracles, aren't they? Love is our human miracle. [to MFH, 27 Jun 49, Chez Limbosch]

From the time I was fifteen or so I had found rejection to be my climate, a good one, because I always fell in love (and still do, it seems!) with people who had so much to teach me and before whom I felt so humble that really "rejection" was hardly the word. One can never feel rejected when one is imaginatively alive and nourished. It is just the opposite. [to LB, 30 Jan (n.y.)]

[8]Marie Closset.

[Americans] are so afraid of themselves. Human relationships seem reduced at any level of intensity or richness to just one—and that one concentrated on sex rather than on love. Now I believe that my novel[9] is *really* about the infinite variety of loves in a human life of any richness. [to BdeS, 30 Apr 64, Nelson]

But in love, as in work, conflict and tension are essential to growth and resolution. In love it is often passion which brings about such tension—

At the same time I am tired to death of the continual heights that an affair demands—how one longs for steady rhythmical unforced companionship. [to EFK, 17 Jun 37, London (Huxley)]

It makes me think of the strange immense gulf between love and passion, the gulf and at the same time the fact that it is only a *nuance*, a shade, a shutter that opens or closes in an instant no one knows why. Love really does open the world, I think; increases all one's sensibilities, generosities, flows out in all sorts of ways to all sorts of people beyond its special object. Passion is so exclusive and violent. It closes out the world. [to JH, 6 Aug 47, Oxf St]

I understand now how also perhaps [passion] should never last because it is too intense. I remember in *The Single Hound* saying "love like this is like a liqueur, one can have too much of it." It is better to be forever hungry, as I shall no doubt be, than to reach the point where the body lives more intensely than the soul. [to BB, 5 May 48, Chez Limbosch]

The question is perhaps what does passion create when it doesn't create children? For me, of course, poems. For you, it could be joy, but I wonder? Does one lose oneself to find oneself? And if the self is not found then there is something wrong. But passion itself is also a creation, a creation which creates *peace.* Sometimes there seems no other way at all to peace. [to JH, 11 Jun 48, VF]

[9]*Mrs. Stevens Hears the Mermaids Singing.*

This gift of passion, this tremendous flood,
So full of anguish, difficult and strange,
So piercing, spacious and so deeply good,
So timeless and yet always suffering change
Where every meeting startles us awake
And every glance is a discovery,
This gift of passion we both give and take,
That translates friend to dearest enemy
And love itself into a dazzling stranger,
So all between us that was safe and deep
Is made uncertain, sharpened upon danger,
This gift of torment we both lose and keep
Will it teach us beyond the fierce sensation
That discipline where love becomes
creation?

[unpublished, from sonnet sequence "These Images Remain," Jun 48]

Love makes one human—passion more *or* less human, angel or devil depending on what? How far the soul is really engaged, how far the passionate moment has been filled slowly with emotion. i.e. the end of a day of being together when everything is gathered into one great moment like an adagio. [HJ, 24 Jun 48, Paris (Huxley)]

I have sometimes imagined that the spirit only flowers when the senses flower in their own true way. There is a clear stream of physical passion in each person and if that is blocked it does somehow block everything. And yet some people can be their true selves with no lived-out passion at all in their lives— such as Jean Dominique for instance. For myself at least as I grow older sex seems less and less important and love more and more important. More than any other beauty (though it is true of all beauty except in art) passion seems to me to have the seeds of its own destruction in it. [to JH, 16 Feb 48, Oxf St]

I think that passion if really intense is always destructive if not to the two involved, always to other people. [to LB, 26 Jan 54, Wr St]

Nor do I at all think that passionate love is greatly to be desired if one has once known it. I think what I want is communion, and that the very simple and quick (though most dangerous) way to it is through passionate love. Also I think I get very exasperated with words and it is a way towards silence. These are my temptations. Because of course such a way involves responsibility and I am not an irresponsible person (no woman is about love, I think, no real woman anyway). Thus the complications. [to LB, 27 Feb 54, Wr St]

How to turn this illness into wellness? For the awful thing about passion is that it *destroys* all other values. Nothing else exists—the awful senseless agitation, chaos—[HJ, ? Dec 55, Wr St]

I am more and more convinced, aren't you? that passion is by its very nature tragic and must always end tragically—and the greater it is, the more inevitable the tragic end becomes—(as in the great love stories, Tristan, etc). It is something *outside* life and that is what makes it so tremendous and so impossible. I am more and more grateful that my relationship with Judy has never been really passionate (I understand better now that it really never was) as that is what will make it last. But how hard it is to learn these things and how much one must suffer to learn them. [to BB, 25 May 48, Paris (Huxley)]

It made me feel acutely what a lot of nonsense passion is, how unimportant on some levels, and that other things are not nonsense, such as our being able to exchange views about life and the world and write to each other. [to JH, 22 Sep 48, Oxf St]

But one cannot perhaps have both the heights and the depths, the quiet river which flows beneath all, and the ultramundane light in which I have been living lately. [to JM, 12 Jun 48, VF]

Tension is caused, too, by the difficulties of being loved—

Oh dear—ô dear—and I am so tired. I do not want to be loved, that is the truth of it. It is such a weight. One has to become the other person out of sympathy and I simply cannot do it anymore. I am too old. Sex is always a war, and all I want is peace and communion and that is that. [to JH, 8 Feb 48, Oxf St]

I am extremely unused to being loved (do not laugh). It is a fact. I don't really want to be loved very much—is that the whole truth? Not quite. It is just too devastating I suppose—I do know something of the burden that to be loved is and God knows I won't lay that on you, darling. I see some deep and flowing freedom between us. I think of you a great deal. You opened the very deep door that has not been opened for me for a long time[1] and I kiss your hands many times when I think of it. [to LB, 26 Jan 54, Wr St]

And by the difficulties of loving men—

I am realizing once and for all the difference as far as I am concerned of women and men and the necessity for both. With a man, however tender he is, one is *feeding* him—one is always and eternally understanding, mothering, supplying him with faith in himself (not in you). It is very sweet and good but for instance all the side of me that writes poems simply doesn't exist. It is given out in another way. One is creating with life itself. [to EFK, 17 Jun 37, London (Huxley)]

As by the difficulties simply of being a woman—

Of course he[2] was the most cosseted old man, surrounded by loving females and living in that glorious house above Florence—with everything done to make life as bearable as possible. It is much easier for men in every way, this life—do you agree? [to KD, 25 Jun 64, Nelson]

And that tension in love—which resolves itself into work and growth—is fed also by the need for a central person. From the beginning, she knew that both in love and in work she must serve something greater than herself—

[1]The door to poetry.
[2]Bernard Berenson.

And may not love be
The desire for complete self-expression
Through self-sacrifice.
To something or someone
Who has a quality of God?

[from "What Is Beauty," HJ, 6 Sep 28, Ray St]

And years later during the war—

So much violence is here just underneath, in everyone. And at the same time
such a desperate hunger for peace and quiet and to be left alone. Or to take
refuge somewhere. It takes courage to be part of a time that is really between
worlds where there will be no rest and no end to the struggle and where one
must fight in every possible way that the soul be not lost in the struggle. Here
coming back I feel it. Nothing but greatness is demanded. And yet who can
find greatness in himself and what do we serve great enough to pull it out of
us? I think the only question now when one meets a person is (though not to
say it), "What do you serve?" [to JH, 22 Sep 48, Oxf St]

And so from earliest childhood we see her pulled toward those who so served,
and hence those she would serve—

Why wasn't I born ten years earlier so I could have known some of these
people, Amy Lowell amongst others. Well anyway I am making brazen strides
towards meeting thrilling people that are alive.[3] Friday night I went to *Le
Jongleur de Notre Dame*[4] with Mary Garden as Jean. She is a great force! I came
away surging with admiration for her tremendous vitality and joy in life.

[3]In Sarton's interest in "thrilling people" one can see the influence of her father, who wrote to her on July
17, 1934, from Visby, Sweden: "I am myself very Carlylean in one respect at least: the cult of heroes, a
very necessary cult to lift mankind gradually above itself."

[4]*The Juggler of Notre Dame*, by French composer Jules Émile-Frédéric Massenet (1842–1912); a miracle play
with music composed originally for male voices. American operatic soprano Mary Garden (1877–1967)
persuaded Massenet to adapt the title role for soprano and sang it for many years with great success. With
her retirement, *The Juggler* vanished from the repertory.

There is a donkey in the opera and she very surreptitiously fed him! Isn't that delicious? I had to do something to let off my ardor so I wrote a special delivery to try to get to meet her. I am terrified lest it be sent back and everyone find out, though after all why shouldn't they? [HJ, 7 Feb 28, Ray St]

The worlds of theater and music offered opportunities for finding muses with that "quality of God" who brought with them the poetry which is the gift of the Muse—

KOUSSEVITSKY

It doesn't matter now
That when he smiles
He knows devoutly
That he is master here.
He bows and wheels.
Straight, still,
Sensitive as a man in anger
Or in love,
He stands, holding him taut
Then swift, the silence
Sweeps into the hum
Of many violins,
Only intensifying it.
And it is he, and he alone,
His feet, his hands, his soul
That sings here,
He, who is God for an hour!

[HJ, II Nov 27, Ray St]

And she could love many at the same time, for serving love meant serving poetry—

Lately my chief passion is Eleonora Duse. I have ordered her life by Symons and am living for that to come. How can I get pictures of her to frame? I want to have her face always where I can look on it and love. [HJ, 15 Oct 28, Ray St]

Letters, too, were an aspect of poetry, and, as love itself, a way of growing toward all that was inside her—

Dear Ethel Barrymore,

First of all don't think I'm a fan. I detest their blindness, and anyhow this is the first play I have seen you in. Until a few years ago I have been too young to take a fierce interest in the drama. I am going to pretend that you are not tired of letters like this. So—

I have been so moved by *The Kingdom of God*[5] that I long to tell you of it. The play is exquisite, so simple, so completely sincere that it hurts as a Fra Angelico painting hurts and haunts one. I was struck too by the oneness of all the acting with the play itself. I never said to myself, as I had thought I would: "Isn't Ethel Barrymore wonderful?" I forgot that you were ill and brave, that you were beautiful, and thought only of Sister Gracia. You were as clear as glass through which we saw a strange, new, marvelous Beauty and Truth. I felt the same quality in Moissi as Fedya in *Redemption*.

What is there, after all, that I can say in bare words? As I read this over I realize how barren it is. I would like to send you masses of white roses that Eleonora Duse loved, or frysias (is that how one spells it?) or a single violet. But alas! All I can do is to come as often as schoolwork will allow and to send you this with mountains of good wishes and a somersault of joy for the beauty you have made! [to EBa, 10 Dec (n.y.), Ray St.]

And the world of poetry, as well as of theater and music, was rich in heros for her—

Do you think I really will be able to meet Edna St. Vincent Millay—that is, at present the height of my ambition. It would be just heavenly! I do hope she[6]

[5]Written in 1922 by Gregorio Martínez Sierra (1881–1947); translated by Harley Granville Barker.
[6]Mary Hotson, who taught fourth grade at the Shady Hill School in its earlier days. She and her husband, Leslie, an English professor, were friends of the Sartons.

May Sarton's early
artwork.

RIGHT. Sarton's
drawing of Nils
Holgersson,
1925.

doesn't forget. Please remind her if she does. When do you suppose I can go? [to EMS and GS, summer 1927, DMC]

I met Aunt Agnes[7] the other day. For Christmas I sent her two or three of my poems. She was extremely enthusiastic and wants me to meet as many poets as I can. Next time Robert Frost comes down to Cambridge she is going to have me meet him. Isn't that exciting. [to EMS, 15 Jan 28, Ray St]

As was the world of literature in general. At twelve or thirteen—

While in bed I read the whole of Nils Holgersson in french; I enjoyed it very much even though it is the second time I have read it. I have made a picture of Nils Holgersson and I am going to send it to Selma Lagerlöf,[8] my friends at school did that last year, she answered them with a delightful letter and a photograph for each of them. [to GS, after 21 Mar 25, Chez Limbosch]

And by seventeen, she clearly understood the essence of her karma—

Is it, as K.T.[9] suggested, that I concentrate my love of life into one person who is really a symbol? All my senses respond to this one person and I live in a state of continual intoxication. Each day becomes an adventure. Love of life? Perhaps it is because I long so much to pour myself into a being or subject greater than myself. I remember that well acting Hilda.[1] I have never lived more beautifully. I seemed to see so clearly, to feel such great understanding and compassion. Spiritually I was kept sane by the tremendous release of the evening. I seemed unshackled from mortality. In the afternoon I slept like a child. [HJ, 29 Jul 29, GSLT]

[7]Agnes Hocking.
[8]Selma Lagerlöf (1858–1940), Swedish novelist and short story writer known for her romantic tales, including *The Wonderful Adventures of Nils* (1906–07). She was awarded the Nobel Prize in Literature in 1909, the first woman to be so honored.
[9]Katharine Taylor, who succeeded the Hockings as director of the Shady Hill School. See "I Knew a Phoenix in My Youth" in *I Knew a Phoenix*.
[1]In Ibsen's *The Master Builder*.

LEFT. Jean Dominique, photograph taken in the 1890s.

RIGHT. Jean Dominique with Mme. Van Rhysselberge—part of a large painting by Theo Van Rhysselberge, late 1890s, South of France. Credit: Susan Sherman.

Perhaps nowhere is that exultation, or that longing to pour herself into a being or subject greater than she, clearer than in her love for Marie Closset, the Belgian poet Jean Dominique—

> When there is no saving presence
> When even poetry does not come when I call
> When there is no answer at all
> Then I hear your voice
> At the heart of the silence.
>
> When the angels are all gone
> And the cold air empty of their wings
> When there is nothing that sings
> I meet your eyes
> That caress the bone.
>
> When there are no more cries
> When there is no one, no one to come
> From the next-door room,
> I feel your hands
> Touching my face like sighs.

When from myself I hide
Like a lost hunted animal
When there is no one to call
I know your love
And I am not afraid.

The fruitful years will come again
The animal become a human
And all the songs wrenched out of pain
Flow through an old woman
Who grows through my wild youth
Towards you and your truth.

I shall not die alone.

["For a Poet—Jean Dominique," unpublished, 1948]

Quand je pense à juillet, à te voir, j'ai des ailes un peu partout qui tâchent de m'elever tout de suite en l'air et voler dans tes bras avec des gazouillement de personne devenue oiseau par amour comme dans un conte d'Ovid.[2] [to MC, 24 Jan 52, Myn Pl]

Yesterday came a most beautiful short story by Jean Do. She has managed to write it and have it typed. I am so happy. It made me think—for it is really a memory of a strange *enfermée*,[3] savage creature she knew long ago—of that one miraculous sentence of Virginia Woolf's (which I've copied for you before I don't doubt, but never mind): "Whatever ruin may befall the map of Europe in years to come, there will still be people, it is consoling to reflect, to hang absorbed over the map of one human face." The *value* of such lives as Jean Do's has become infinitely more precious now with all the horrors, and almost unbelievable like some small tender flower which the ice age somehow did not destroy. How human beings *shine* here and there. [to JH, 10 Feb 48, Oxf St]

[2]"When I think of July and of seeing you I have wings everywhere trying to lift me suddenly into the air so I might fly into your arms chirping like a person whom love has transformed into a bird, as if from a story in Ovid."
[3]"confined woman."

I wish I could describe this afternoon because if you could see it you would know everything about Jean-Do, sitting in her tiny armchair, the great owl-eyes looking so clear and deep and straight at one through immense dark glasses as if she could see—and I really believe she must—the small dry delicate hands, warm and dry like leaves warmed in the sun, always a little fine collar and a bow at her throat and her voice which is the voice of poetry itself, *ashes* where there has been great fire. And what did we talk about? A good deal of the time about where and how she should be buried, but in *fits* of laughter, because she has discovered it is so expensive to have a permanent grave and is determined not to, and we talked about it really as if we were buying a house or renting a flat—and laughed and laughed. But I could not after all promise that there would be no plaque because of course people will want to know where she is. People will be reading her poems, you know, long after—and it mustn't be like Mozart.[4] As I explained. But it was so good to be able to talk about all this—holding hands, and so alive and laughing. I feel so sure now that she will live through the winter and I was not sure before, and that I shall see her again. There are the packages of letters, so many things to be decided about. And we talked of Camus and *La Peste*, which they are reading aloud with gratitude. Jean-Do feels it is as important to us of this time as perhaps the great Russians were at their time. And I am very relieved as I feared they would not like it. . . . And I told Jean-Do how wise she is and she said, "Je suis sage parce que je suis fou,"[5] bending her head like a bird with that indescribable half-bitter, half-gentle laugh. How I wish you could see her once before she dies, she you!

And then we went down to tea with the other two, Blanche Rousseau and Marie Gasparre[6]—Marie hurling slices of bread at me in one of her sudden gestures, always the laughter, the bouquet of their laughter, and tea with crushed red currants, whipped cream cheese, the cat's shadow appearing against the white curtains to get his saucer of milk. (He is a very ugly thin cat

[4]When Mozart died impoverished in 1791 of rheumatic fever, he was buried in accordance with Viennese custom of the time at St. Marks Churchyard in a pauper's mass plot in an unmarked grave.
[5]"I am wise because I am mad."
[6]Marie Gaspar, called Gaspari by Jean Dominique and others. See *I Knew a Phoenix*, pp. 121–35, and *A World of Light*, ch. 12.

and spoiled rotten.) Blue and white checked cloth, blue and white cups, beautiful blue plates on the wall, and pewter. Of course the trouble is that when you spread everyone's bread with so much honey, you are inundated with people who need honey and they are quite exhausted with visits. [to JH, 2 Aug 48, Chez Limbosch]

Her central person has always been her real grace, her way toward poetry; nothing else has ever mattered as much. The day she received a Guggenheim Fellowship—

This is such an incredible day I feel I shall in a moment melt into air, or become a bird and be done with it. This piece of paper is at any rate really a wing and should be bright *blue*. You see, it was not the Guggenheim, but I staggered in from a terrific heave at the garden and there on the floor was your *book*—and your wonderful letter. I could have lived without the Guggenheim, you know (not that I am not fearfully relieved to foresee clear time ahead), but your book is in another sphere of my being altogether, the event of this year. I am so glad you sent this one in its paper jacket, to be put in a pocket, read under a tree when I have been gardening, learned by heart in the car. Can you have any idea, you who know these poems so well and have labored over them in proof, what happens when they appear like this all together—what an explosive force they carry? Today for instance I can hardly read them at all. Everything blurs but that is because I am really about to melt away. Still, it is a queer feeling, isn't it, when your work suddenly, as it goes from you, finally, in a book, ceases to be yours and becomes everyone else's. Now for this day and for always it is mine. One really doesn't say thank you, I suspect, does one? It seems rather a weak locution. Just now, just today, I am reading over "To Be Sung on the Water" (this brought instant tears, not for the meaning, but the *perfect* sound), "The Daemon," and "Zone."[7] It will go with me to the Vineyard. But perhaps I shall never say very much about it, as almost every-thing I might say would be irrelevant. This, I trust, you will understand—you

[7]Louise Bogan's "To Be Sung on the Water," "The Daemon," and "Zone" are also in *Blue Estuaries*, but Sarton has an earlier volume which they are in, inscribed to her on 8 May 1954 (*Collected Poems 1923–53*. Noonday, 1954).

who so wisely do not read people's letters to discover the exact weight of each word. [to LB, 20 Apr 54, Wr St]

And yet always there is the paradox that such a pouring forth of herself both nurtures and drowns the sources of poetry. As a student at Gloucester—

I feel as if this passionate pouring of my spirit into the stream of one person would someday ruin my life. Tonight I am filled with forebodings. This morning Mrs. Evans said, "Don't become obsessed with people, become obsessed with a subject"—It is good then that I hurl myself so early into a subject[8]—but I can't escape the other thing. As I write I am intensely conscious of her[9] presence in the world and all the time. It all leads nowhere—it destroys the creative spirit in me and uses powers with which I might be changing the world simply in futile burning. [HJ, 29 Jul 29, GSLT]

And I do realize that it is this "génie de l'amour"[1] as Jean Dominique calls it which is the one thing which might keep me from doing good work. It is a terrible thing. You know me well enough and understand me to know that none of this is *light*—I do not go into these things lightly but only from a consuming need to reach the *essence* of people and to give them mine (and often, alas, this is only possible in love). [to K, 16 Jul 37, Austria]

But it was neither to be a futile burning nor to keep her from good work, and years later she addresses the same subject in a response to Bogan—

"Base not your heart on persons"—haunting phrase. I have taken it to bed with me and woken up with it in my mind, but I can come to no conclusion. I do not think one changes one's karma—and I'm afraid you have hit there the flaw in my crystal, but I do not believe it will change. I do not really say, alas, for I have learned a great deal, all I know, however little that is, from basing my heart on persons, and it seems as if there were still so much to be learned. Probably you are in a more "evolved" sphere if one believed in various

[8]The "Subject" was acting.
[9]Katherine Warren's.
[1]"genius for loving."

incarnations or spheres of spiritual wisdom, but I do not believe in them, do you? Traherne is my man, you know. "Since therefore we are born to be a burning and shining light, and whatever men learn of others, they see in the light of others' souls"—[to LB, 18 Apr 54, Wr St]

Because of all that Sarton knows and writes of love, she has become the compass thousands travel by, and is read and studied as though she were a map of the world. Her understanding and articulation of homosexual love is rare—

The great difference between men and women is that women cannot separate sex from love and men can. There are no women homosexual prostitutes, but male homosexuality (even in the case of someone as good and sensitive and honest as Auden) tends toward prostitution. The drive is primarily a *sex* drive.

Louise Bogan. Credit: Lotte Jacobi.

There is nothing wrong for a man in picking up a sailor, but a woman who would do the equivalent would be violating herself (in either a heterosexual or homosexual relationship, *bien entendu*). The drive which is back of two women who unite in passionate love is therefore, as in any love relationship for a woman, first of all and primarily emotional rather than sexual. Emotion overflows and tries to find a medium of expression. If the medium is physical, as it may be, but does not have to be, what the woman discovers is herself *in* someone else. You break out of yourself through someone else, to find yourself. The excitement—and it is very great in its way—comes from the fact that you give the *same* pleasure which you receive. This is where it is hard to pin down in words (I am not writing a handbook). It is metaphysical because the caress contains *in itself* the love and is not a pure drive towards release as it is in a man. In other words, it is exceedingly pure and intense, an exchange of souls. I don't know about homosexual men but my guess is that it's quite a different thing because there the *primal* drive remains and sex must play a more obsessive part. The chances of a complete and happy mutual response are very much greater with two women and this is why I have always felt it dangerous (and in fact I would not myself do it) to initiate a woman who might be shifted out of her center.

One never reaches the deepest place of feeling part of the almost unconscious universe, of being *lost.* Instead one reaches a place of extreme consciousness; one is *found* as an individual. Greater subtlety, less depth, a greater sense of oneself and the other as a person different from others. [to LB, 8 Mar 54, Wr St]

But actually all real love is very much alike, isn't it? And these distinctions seem in the end irrelevant. [to LB, 21 Mar 54, Wr St]

Although Sarton has loved men, the Muse has always been a woman. Yet because her work is undeniably universal, she did not as a writer in the earlier years choose to focus on that aspect of her personal life—

The *New Yorker* stuff I am doing is easy because I am making no attempt to come to grips with *any* conflict (it would not be for them if I did, and it is not for me at this time. I have to wait for that until I am much older than you because it is all so rather *queer,* you know. I do not wish to be known as a queer person until I am firmly established for central reasons, not a periphery person) and I saw how it wrecked Le Gallienne to have people know too much about her private life. They could no longer *see* her as she really is. Instead of being true in its effect, or an effect of truth, it just makes people unable to hear what you have to say. At the root of this, no doubt, is Willa Cather's denial of the right to publish any letters in her will. [to LB, 30 Jan 54, Wr St]

However, with the publication of *Mrs. Stevens Hears the Mermaids Singing* in 1965, Sarton confronted the subject of the female muse and all that it entails at a time when it was difficult for a writer to do so, and lost her job. Her old friend Basil de Sélincourt was dismayed by the novel. Her response to his letter typifies her depth of understanding and compassion, and her staunch integrity—

Dearest Basil, please look into your heart and discover whether you really believe the Almighty would have consigned Socrates and Shakespeare to the flames? Both, if you remember, wrote eloquently of the love of boys . . . and in fact long ago Julian Huxley told me when we talked about this that all through nature there is a definite regular percent of "deviants" from very low-grade creatures like slugs up to the higher mammals. So it looks as if it really were a part of this mysterious creation from the start. In human terms my guess is that the creative nature is itself and in itself a marriage between masculine and feminine (as everyone must be to some extent) so we find a great many artists, poets, painters, composers who lead lives out of the ordi-nary. The sadness is that these people have been so cruelly persecuted . . . just as cats were burned as witches in the 17th century. What has to be fought (although my novel is too special to do so in any universal way) is the tendancy to *lump* all these people as criminals. Some *are* criminals, no doubt of it. But then there are many heterosexual criminals too—pimps, prostitutes, thieves, etc. The necessity for concealment, hence for dishonesty, *leads* to criminal lives often. I simply do not believe that there is a danger to "society" or that there would ever be enough such people to tip the balance away from normality for the vast majority. (It is not a contagious disease.)

I am sure you have never considered how many people you admire are this way—Benjamin Britten comes at once to mind, for one. The writers (women) Sybille Bedford, H.D., Bryher; the composer Dame Ethel Smyth. I could make a long list but it seems pointless to do so. Not only Gide, but Julian Green in France. Proust.

Until now the literature has emphasized the criminal types—and recently there have been some horrible examples. My own feeling is that where sex is exploited (by any sex) *without love,* it is always criminal and disgusting. And in some ways my book is a reaction: what interests me is the *imagination.* And I have waited until I had a firm reputation and had written enough books which show that I understand and am *for* the normal human situation, so that this should take its place in the series of novels as one out of nine or ten. I felt it would be dishonest not to come out into the open—that this was mandatory for my own true relation with *myself*. And now it is done, I doubt if the subject will come up again in any future work. [to BdeS, 24 Jun 65, Nelson]

The muse comes and waters her roots—

Since I got here ten days ago I have been carried on a strong wave of creativity—I have written 35 pages of the novel and about a poem a day! A record as far as I am concerned; strength will not permit that it go on at this rate for long, but I feel accompanied by the angels for the moment. [to KD, 15 Feb 64, Nelson]

However I have plunged madly in and written nearly 60 pages of the novel,[2] allowing myself full speed ahead to get the big proportions down, like a cartoon for a painting. Then I may hope to enrich and deepen as I come to revise later this year . . . the book, as I perhaps told you, has to do with the angels, or the Muse or whatever the Mysterious Being may be who inspires— and what a woman does about this fem. being, a woman who is a poet. So the novel deals with crucial things in my own life—the chief character is an old famous writer and really not at all like me—except in this *one* essential problem. I have enjoyed creating her. Meanwhile—and do not say we are not all wound round in Mystery and in the hands of cycles and powers we cannot apprehend!—the Muse has come back to me—and this is something I never thought would happen again. I thought that whole part of me had been cauterized for good—and until this thing happened, I should have said "and a good thing too!" But now poetry has come back and seized me by the hair, and as well as the novel I have written 20 poems—one of the curious facts is that (as I tell my students) *intensity commands form*—that flow of lines through the head which demands formal commitment seems to be posited on a powerful human emotion, and without it, poetry goes dry. [to RG, 23 Feb 64, Nelson]

[2]*Mrs. Stevens Hears the Mermaids Singing.*

The function of the muse fascinates her—

What interested me to isolate was simply the creative process in the woman poet in relation to the muse. What has been left out has been left out deliberately to intensify and isolate that one aspect. So it is not the problems of the lesbian which interested (they are hardly touched on) but the problems of the *poet* when the poet is a woman, or perhaps the woman artist in general. It is this which narrows down the universality of the book (almost no one will be able or wish to *identify with* Hilary). What *is* revelatory and exposing of course for myself is just that the poet and the romantic lover have been so closely associated. In a strange way it seems now to be no longer so and perhaps writing the book has helped me to another phase. As you know, the new book[3] has no love poems in it. And is also a breakthrough into a new *style.* [to RH, 3 Aug 65, Greenings]

For I have been preparing for this book[4] for nearly 30 years, although I could not write it until after the episode of Margaret Clapp[5]—for it is that episode which forced me to come to terms with the Muse once and for all, and to recognize what she is—never to be "known," never really to be loved as one loves someone with whom one lives through a great deal—but the catalyzer. [to HC, 6 Aug 65, Greenings]

The muse withdraws and takes inspiration with her—

. . . the strange uplifted time is over and the muse has somewhat withdrawn, inevitable as there had been no answer to 30 poems. But I accept this *all* as a gift from the angels and expect nothing more than what it is to remember what inspiration is, perhaps for the last time. [to BdeS, 30 Apr 64, Nelson]

But Sarton, stripped down to where the world ends, continually makes nothingness a plenitude, refinds the muse within, and newly pours herself into poetry—

[3] *A Private Mythology.*
[4] *Mrs. Stevens Hears the Mermaids Singing.*
[5] President of Wellesley College 1949–66.

The whole question of to whom one writes is a complex one. In the very deepest sense, it seems to me, it is for God—whatever each poet means by God, some power outside oneself which demands the best of oneself. [to LB, 14 Apr 54, Wr St]

Just as she pours herself into all work and love—

All you say of humility is true and all great people are humble because great people have great work and are humbled by the largeness of their dreams. [to EMS and GS, 2 Oct 40, YWCA, Washington]

I have begun the new novel[6] because I thought I had better have some ground under my feet in case I didn't get the fellowship.[7] I am quite excited about it but everything always looks easy and good when one starts (luckily!) and I expect I'll end up by tearing up what I've done. The good thing is that the characters begin to live, which is always very exciting—the chief one to be an old passionate woman whom I dearly love already, violent, very alive, full of insecurity and fire. In a way the book is my political education, as I shall have in the course of writing it to discover where I really stand. The great thing is that at last I can use whole areas which I have never before used creatively and get a lot of things clear in a new way. I fear it will not be a popular or salable book, but one must do what one must and that is all. [to BB, 8 Mar 53, Wr St]

For always love means growth, and whether she is finding or losing the muse, or transcending love into work, Sarton's growth has followed a continuous and clearly marked trajectory—

Sometimes I am sad to think how many people I have loved, because it seems strange and unlike me and what I really want, but then I realize how much I have learned from each, what a great richness has poured into my life, and I cannot be sad. [to JH, 22 Aug 47, Oxf St]

[6]*Faithful Are the Wounds.*
[7]Sarton was awarded the Lucy Martin Donnelly Fellowship from Bryn Mawr College in 1953.

And I have been writing poetry furiously, a strange story, another adventure of the mind, another hopeless love,[8] but so good and so challenging I can only bless it. [to JH, 30 Oct 37, Ch Pl]

I spent the weekend cleaning out my study at Channing Pl. throwing away whole parts of my life: scripts from theatre days, packages of love letters from people long dead (it leaves a fairly ashy taste, all that accumulation of things and people), and I realize how many of my friends have died and it is sad—sad because so often people leave such a small record behind them, and because their letters tell so little of what they were—a most beautiful girl[9] I knew in Paris who died at eighteen in 1933 and whom I hurt. How cruel and exclusive love is when one is young. Narrow and piercing like the thorn of the rose. But one does learn, I think—that is comforting. One learns a lot. All my life I have been learning slowly how to deal with passion and how to love people better, to build and not to destroy. But one has so far to go. And it is never ended, is it? And a good thing, too. [to JH, 25 Jan 48, Oxf St]

My inner life in Paris was very strange with a great many ups and downs, frustrations, bafflements, little sleep, much thought, many poems. I am growing a lot. I almost feel myself growing like a tree. [to JM, 5 Jun 48, VF]

Also, it is wonderful to see Jean-Do again, always the same, so full of bitter wisdom and laughter and *douceur*. I do not think one arrives at her kind of wisdom without a great deal of suffering, which is some consolation for the Hell I have been through lately and which is probably teaching me some essential truth I don't know what. [to JM, 28 Jul 48, Chez Limbosch]

But life is always bringing unexpected gifts. The other day Jean-Do told me a story. It is this. One of her *fidèles*, the group of women who have been coming to her for 30 years for a weekly lesson and discussion about literature—one of these is a very curous difficult character called Pauline. She looks like a sullen peasant, came of the worst sort of petite bourgeoisie, and made herself,

[8]Reference to Edith Forbes Kennedy.
[9]Mary Chilton. See "That Winter in Paris" in *I Knew a Phoenix.*

climbing to the top of the teaching profession in the State Lycée, a prof. of literature. At one time when she was very depressed, Jean-Do lifted her out of it little by little, and thus saw a great deal of her for about a year. One day since J.D.'s blindness, Pauline came to her and said, "You used to be fond of me and now I feel you don't care anymore." And Jean-Do said, "I am just the same, but I am old now and have much less to give. But now I need you more than I ever did, need all of you *fidèles*, and you have much to give me." *Since that day*, Pauline is an absolutely changed character. She came to tea once when I was there and having heard how difficult she was, *rebutée, silencieuse*,[1] I was amazed at how young and gay she seemed. Hence, the story. Is it perhaps the one necessity of love, that it be needed? And the one great human tragedy that it so rarely is? [to JH, 5 Aug 48, Chez Limbosch]

How I wish someday you could see her[2] and talk with her—the point is really that she has always been like me, an impossible lover, loving too much etc. but learning to *renounce* through loving more not less. [to JH, 18 Aug 48, London (RP)]

However I am not sure that short affairs are inevitable if you do go on with men. Also there is a great difference in dignity and value between an affair like yours and Jim's and an affair of two or three nights, weeks or months. It is an entirely different thing. As long as there is real love, a real sharing for a time, then one is bound to grow from it. I feel myself that I have learned from each person so much—and could I have learned from one person? Nobody can answer that I guess. [to BB, 15 Feb 49, Oxf St]

You said something about my many love affairs. They have never been light; I have always been wholly committed. They have been spiritual rather than physical adventures, in essence, and by them I have grown. [to CD, 1 Dec 55, Wr St]

---

[1] "rejected, silent."
[2] Marie Closset.

After all, life with no controversy or reason for disagreement would also perhaps atrophy in the end. I learn a great deal, though painfully, this way. [to HC, 6 Aug 65, Greenings]

For just as she has continually grown, she has continually created her own soul, her harmony and peace—

The point about harmony (which Gide only talked about, never attained) is that it must be *re*created as new growth and disharmony arise, all the time, mustn't it? It is not something achieved once and for all. Each piece of Mozart's music is such a creation. [to LB, 26 Mar 55, Wr St]

But I am thinking about the novel. "Three Stages"[3] it is to be called and that is an allegorical title—it is perhaps an allegory of the soul, what makes and what destroys it—seen through a single man and his creation of a theatre and final destruction by it, and escape to an imaginary world. It's based really on Copeau's[4] life. [to K, 12 Mar 39, Ch Pl]

She speaks for herself in writing to a friend of his growth and selfhood—

The only word that worries me in your letter is the word "failure." That I do not believe is reasonable and probably came from your first reaction to the book. Failure would only be if you had somewhere stopped growing. As far as I can see the whole duty of the artist is to keep on growing and that you have done to an amazing extent in these last years. Don't you feel it yourself? In every way, it seems to me, you are master now of what you want to do. There seems nothing accidental about any of it. I have been so happy and proud about you—and simply won't admit "failure." That is nonsense. But I suppose one does throw off old skins like a snake and you are doing that now and will be uncomfortable in your new skin for awhile. [to BB, 15 Feb 49, Oxf St]

[3]Unpublished; a.k.a. "Fire in a Mirror."
[4]Jacques Copeau (1879–1949), French actor and director, whose work had an immense influence on the theater in Europe and America.

And even growth has its discipline and routine—

> I am aware more than ever of how exceedingly slow all real inner change is. One gets the vision first and then it is a slow daily business of discipline and deliberate directing of one's thoughts. It's rather like a poem. One is given something and then the rest has to be worked on. [to JH, 20 Aug 48, London (RP)]

And there is constantly a renewal of understanding—

> I think it is the hardest thing to accept that one can never give to those one loves best, or so very rarely, but one can give to other people and it's all part of some whole. Do you remember somewhere in Rebecca West a passage about each person being at the same time a beggar and having a rose in his hand to give, and that almost never (but I cannot say it right) is the beggar able to give his rose to the person who gives him alms. [to LB, n.d. ("Sunday morning")]

The rose in Sarton's hand has been her poetry—

> Poems like to have a destination for their flight. They are homing pigeons. [to MFH, 16 Aug 40, Ch Pl]

Yet hers have seldom reached the person for whom they were written—

> I suppose that love poems come from the tragic human fact that even passion does not and cannot completely express love, nor contain and fulfill its total reverberation and that in some peculiar way (here Eliot is so good) they are really not addressed to the beloved at all— Hence there are no mature love poems which are not tragic. At best then, love for a poet either becomes something else (religion) or simply opens the natural world so that one *sees* everything freshly as if one had been born again. It is this latter kind of poem which I know I have to write now. [to LB, n.d. ("Wed. night")]

And thus she, and poetry, are continually reborn through the natural world, her source and prime. As early as ten she wrote—

THINGS THAT I LOVE

The feeling of having accomplished something
The sound of a cat purring and rubbing against you,
The sound of bees humming,
Pleasant foods, delicious smells,
The caressing comforting touch of sheets.
Sleep.
The scarlet yellow and orange leaves
Strewn about the street before you like a wonderful carpet of rich colors.
Autumn itself with its bracing winds and colored atmosphere.
The sound of beautiful music.
Quietness.

[HJ, ? Nov 22, Ray St?]

At thirteen she is surrounded by small creatures in the woods of Belgium—

Clairette a des tritons et nous avons trouvé qu'il y a des petits dans le locale.
Nous avons aussi un microscope et nous voyons des choses très interessants.
Des ailes de mouches, des têtes de mouche et toutes sortes de choses. Nous
avons aussi fait une promènade dans le bois, qui est très beau. Nous avons
attrapé des papillons aussi, et des petits poissons à un étang.[5] [to GS, 14 May
25, Chez Limbosch]

By fourteen she is nourished on no more than air[6]—

My soul is pierced by the agony of your beauty, O sky.
You cleanse me with your infinite purity;
You strengthen me with your beautiful everlastingness;
Your immensities are one with me,
And I arise glorious, for I am yours.

["Sky," HJ, ? Nov 26, Ray St]

[5]"Clairette [Limbosch] has some newts and we've found that there are babies around. We also have a
microscope and see very interesting things in it. Wings and heads of flies and all sorts of things. We've
also taken a walk in the woods, which are very beautiful. We've caught butterflies too, and little fish in a
pond."
[6]See "Jonah," in *A Grain of Mustard Seed.*

And two years later it is the sea—

> It is good
> To have seen the moving waters
> And heard the noises of the deep.
> I had too long been wanting the sea.

[HJ, 30 Apr 28, Ray St]

As part of that natural world, animals hold a primary place—

It is wonderful here—wonderful to have no responsibilities *except* work—I am not even allowed to wash a dish, and luckily the Italian servant-girl (who is treated as family) is very efficient. All is as it always was—Franz, the goose,[7] is now 21, but as snow white and fierce as ever—the only change being that he is nearly blind and *follows* his brown wife, instead of being followed at two paces by her! We have tea in the orchard under an apple tree, as always, attended by a Noah's ark of delightful creatures—two turkeys, old maids called Julie Blanche and Julie Noire, who, having no male, become very passionate and emotional at the laying season, and lie down, begging to be stroked. So much so, that when workmen were working on the road, one came to Céline and said, "There is a dying turkey out on the road!" She was not dying, merely begging to be caressed! There are also two guinea hens, who make strange cries in the rhododendrons every morning—I thought they were being attacked by a fox the first time I heard them! A magnificent small cock and his two hens, and two ducks, one with a broken beak, and a beautiful blue Persian pussy cat. Céline herself, the Ceres of this little world, sits under the tree in her sunbonnet and dispenses pieces of bread to the assembled multitude. She is now 81, but does four hours hard gardening every day—and is exactly as she was twenty years ago. Preserved by order and hard work and peace and loving kindness, I expect.[8] [to LB, 10 Aug 64, Chez Limbosch]

And indeed Sarton always has been surrounded by a Noah's ark of animals—

[7]See "Franz, a Goose" in *A Private Mythology.*
[8]See "The Garden of Childhood" in *A Durable Fire.*

Mrs. Merriman[9] gave us 15¢ each to get ice cream cones for Molly the bear at the station, and some for ourselves, this morning. Molly was very cunning sitting on her hind legs with the ice cream cone in between her front paws. [to EMS and GS, 22 Jun 24, Intervale]

This morning Claire[1] and I washed the ducks' pond and they were delighted, all 7 of them jumped in at once and splashed about. [to EMS, 2 Mar 25, Chez Limbosch]

Nous nous amusons beaucoup ici. À côté de chez nous aux Argousiers habite Mademoiselle Baye une ancienne institutrice de l'institute. Elle nous a montré comment on attrape des crabes en attachant une ficelle à un bâton et puis en ouvrant des moules et les nouant à la ficelle. Hier nous en avons attrapée au moins quarante en comptant les tout petits. C'était gai tu n'as pas idée. Nous nous perchions sur des brises lames et la chasse commençait. Il y avait des grands et des forts crabes dont nous avions très peur; il faillait les prendre avec les mains tout le temps en danger d'être pincer. Nous les mettions dans notre seau et les rapportions à la maison pour mettre dans notre aquarium.[2] [to EMS, ? Apr 25, Chez Limbosch]

Have I told you that we have now a "pigeonnier" in the attic? Three of the four pigeons are in it. There were two babies but one has died, the other we thought dead; he was all cold but he moved a little so Aunty Lino took him in her hands and warmed him; then we gave him a little warm milk with bread in it and now he is wrapped in wadding up above the fire where he is warm. [to EMS, 23 Apr 25, Chez Limbosch]

[9]Mrs. Roger B. Merriman, whose garden on Brattle Street abutted the Sartons'. She had a home in Intervale, N.H., where Sarton spent time as a child.

[1]Claire Limbosch.

[2]"We are having a wonderful time here. Next door to us at the Argousiers lives Mademoiselle Baye, an old teacher at the institute. She showed us how to trap crabs by attaching a string to a stick and then opening mussels and they swim to the string. Yesterday we caught at least forty counting the baby ones. It was so much fun you have no idea. We perched over the breakwater, and the chase began. There were some big and some strong crabs which we were afraid of; we had to take them in our hands and there was always the danger we'd be pinched. We put them in our bucket and brought them back to the house to put in our aquarium."

With "Madelaine,"
1918. Credit:
Eleanor Mabel
Sarton.

ABOVE. Sarton and
Claire Limbosch.

BELOW RIGHT. May,
Jacqueline and Claire
Limbosch, and
Eleanor Mabel
Sarton, 1919?

Franz the Goose and
his brown wife,
Memisse, 1964.
Credit: May Sarton.

Oh! and there is the darlingest little puppy you can imagine. His name is "Cheeler," which means "little friend of all the world" in Indian. [to GS, 3 Jul 26, DMC]

I'm having a glorious time! The Fields are all dears. They are as follows: Mrs. Field, Noël the oldest who is married and his wife Herta, Elsie 20 years old and Herman 16 and lastly Letty. Then there are Timmy and Kievi [?] the cats and charming Bobby the rabbit who scampers all over the house playing with the cats. Last but not least is Topsy the Ford belonging to Herman. [to EMS and GS, 5 Sep 26, Woods Hole, Mass.]

You can't possibly guess what I've got! 2 turtles and three little goldfish! I passed a horrible animal store on Macdougal Street on the side where I very rarely go and the poor little turtles were crammed into a bowl with lots of others and almost no water—so I wanted to rescue one. Then I thought since they were only $ .25 I would get another to keep it company. The goldfish were only $ .05 and *so* pretty. One of them has a dark back. How often should I change the water? I've bought food for them. It's such fun having something alive in my room, which begins to look really charming. [to EMS and GS, 26Sep29, 94 Macd]

A family of quail has paid us several visits—a plump father, a slim mother and six tempestuous fluffy children about two inches long and as broad! They are perfectly *sweet.* [to GS, 10 Jun 34, Pebble Beach, Calif.]

Give James Stephens my warm thoughts—and listen to the duck (he is very sensible). My greatest and most *secret* passion is for *ducks*—there are six white ones in the lake with yellow bills and the most charming wagging tails—I chase them when I am swimming but they are too quick—[to K, 16 Jul 37, Austria]

I shall go down next week[3] for a few days. There is a baby giraffe and Julian says a man of theirs has found four giant pandas and they are on their way.

[3]To Whipsnade.

But last night the thing that charmed me into a state of pure joy is a little bushbaby that Julian gave Juliette for her birthday. It looks like this [drawing] only it is about twice as big and bounces about the room like a spirit, in one light hop from the table to the top of the curtains. It has huge dark eyes, the softest fur in the world and little hands that hold yours like a baby. At first he was quite shy (his name is Gulliver) but finally he climbed right into my hand and sat there. At supper he leaped onto the serving table and sat up like a tiny bear on his hind legs to lap the dessert out of little cups—he will take a beer bottle top with a little beer in it up in his hands and drink. He is really a fairy animal—I can't tell you how adorable—he has huge transparent ears like petals that move all the time, in fact he is almost never still except to fix you now and then with these huge dark eyes. He comes from Africa. [to EMS and GS, 15 Apr 38, London (JS)]

There are lots of things to learn about cows—they[4] have the radio on in the barn all the time (this keeps the cows happy and they give more milk). Also one must never argue or raise one's voice near cows because they mind and give less milk. The lore of cows is very interesting. [to EMS and GS, 11 Jan 43, Muffet Farm, Poughkeepsie, N.Y.]

On Sunday Muriel[5] and I went to the Bronx Zoo and saw the two pandas—it was quite cold but we were so ecstatic at the sight that we didn't realize we were frozen until we started home. They are incredibly charming—two great black and white sacks of fun—they push each other over, take a running start and bump into each other, and all with very slow clumsy motions like a slow-motion picture. They climb laboriously up a big tree trunk that lies across their pool and then box and shove each other off until one falls in—they lie on their backs and put their arms around each other. It is really enchanting—[to EMS and GS, 23 Mar 43, 5 E 10]

[4]Theodora (Theo) Pleadwell, sculptor, apprentice at the Civic Repertory Theatre, and later member of the Associated Actors Theatre.
[5]Muriel Rukeyser (1913–80), American poet, biographer, teacher, and fiction writer.

Yesterday evening at sunset Judy[6] and I went for a wonderful walk, first along the Acequia and then up into the hills where the Mexicans live and where for some reason it always reminds me of Greece. In an enclosure we came upon an old old man with a wrinkled face among about 100 goats and kids—he was chasing the kids like a benevolent satyr to try to put each kid to suck at the right mother! It was a fine chase as the kids bounded around, standing on the backs of the sedate cud-chewing mothers, and took it all as game. He held them in his arms with such a tender gesture, it was lovely to see. [to EMS and GS, 2 Jun 45, Santa Fe (ER)]

Muriel Rukeyser.
Credit: Lotte Jacobi.

The best thing of all was that the Mackechnies,[7] dear people who are both painters, have as a pet a sable rabbit—he is dark brown with the softest fur I've ever felt with a sort of golden sheen on it and garnet eyes, very long ears, and when I first saw him he looked exactly like Dürer's hare as he was sitting meditating in the little garden, his ears straight up, but sitting quite still. Later he came in for tea, hopping quietly about until he gets feeling rather merry and then he runs round and round in the most charming way—he loves to be petted, and then sits down, lays his ears down and shuts his eyes while you stroke him. He laps up milk like a cat, begs for his food very sweetly, and always climbs up on the bed and goes to sleep there if anyone is lying down. A perfectly angel rabbit. His name is Tino and I could hardly talk or think of anything but to watch him. [to EMS and GS, 30 Apr 47, London (JS)]

I simply love the countryside—yesterday we[8] drove into Mitchelltown to do shopping and the whole street was full of donkeys and donkey carts come to market. My heart leapt when I heard you can buy a donkey and cart and

[6]Judith Matlack.
[7]Margaret and Robert Mackechnie, who lived in Rye, Sussex.
[8]Sarton and Elizabeth Bowen.

harness for 10 pounds! That I think is the way to travel in future. [to JM, 10 Sep 48, Ireland]

The wind in the beagle's ears—he sitting on the emerald lawn with ears like souls. [HJ, 23 Apr 54, Martha's Vineyard, Mass.]

We[9] have just come back from a wonderful two days and nights away—first to Siena through the magical Tuscan landscape with great white oxen, dreamy-eyed, pulling primitive wooden ploughs through the olive orchards, and distant medieval towns on the crests of hills. [to GS, 12 Sep 54, Florence]

Just now I looked out of my window and saw my first Indian CAT, a thin white and yellow one with a very pointed face. I have a beautiful small white lizard with emerald eyes who appears on the wall now and then and a frog who seems to come out each evening—last night I worried for fear he was starving so I picked him up and he gave two dreadful cries of fear as I laid him gently outdoors. I never knew frogs had voices. But the best animals here are the cream-colored bullocks, drawing carts as in ancient drawings and paintings—they are beautiful with eloquent eyes and gentle aristocratic profiles and the whiteness is exciting amid so much dull brown and red earth. [to JM, 6 Apr 62, Bhubaneswar, India]

Today a raccoon was sitting on the wood pile in the corner of the porch when I got back—growled at me, but seemed quite unafraid, so I took out some cookies—three wild cats now come to be fed—and I saw a sad porcupine walking clumsily about under the apple trees looking for apples, so spring must be somewhere in animal hearts if not in the mountains of snow all around. [to JM, n.d., Nelson]

The poor birds wring my heart. I thought a jay was going to die on the porch this morning, he was so fluffed out and had trouble with his wing, but he revived at the sight of some sunflower seed and bread. I have given up eating

[9]Sarton and Eugénie DuBois.

bread (to try to take off ten pounds) so I give what I would have eaten to the birds. They are so brave. Today I saw a red squirrel on the barn. Otherwise, except for the constant movement of wings, it is a very silent frozen world. [to KD, 8 Feb 63, Nelson]

LEFT. May Sarton holding one of her green turtles, Nelson, in 1964.

I miss the pussies but get a lot of pleasure out of three little green turtles on my desk; they spend a lot of time lying under a lettuce leaf,[1] but when they swim their little elegant feet delight me (they eat mealworms and I do hope I can find some in Keene). [to KD, 15 Feb 64, Nelson]

RIGHT. Esmerelda, Sarton's donkey, at Nelson

You do not identify with animals—thus you never understood I think what I suffered for that poor dog your farmer had, the misery of that animal. But even in the Catholic church (which denies a soul to animals) there are saints who exemplify a tenderness toward the whole creation—St. Francis of course, St. Anthony who took a thorn from a lion's paw—I feel that you lump animals (the care of them) with *material* things, i.e. less than spiritual. But I feel that everything is or can be illuminated by the same Creative Presence if one sees it there—even a stone. In some profound way perhaps I feel that animals are one of our ways back to the primitive in the sense of *close to God.* Also in the sense of being "natural" as we, with our complexities, are no longer. So I believe they can help us to be more fully human. We are not, I think, meant to be gods—that idea seems blasphemous to me—but we are meant to become as fully human as possible, as "creaturely" as possible. [to MH, 4 Mar 70, Nelson]

[1] See "Death and the Turtle" in *A Private Mythology.*

So—to go back to the book[2]—Andy has been deprived of his power to *act* as a human being by the impossible muse, and must find some means of renewal—he rejects the contemplative if you remember (learning Russian or about mushrooms) and, instead, borrows a sick donkey and learns "donkey." There is a passage where he does not prod the beast but stands beside her and waits, that is crucial (for the author), i.e. one who has *willed* learns not to will, but to wait and to feel with a fellow creature. A donkey is the most cursed and beaten animal in the whole world—but it was on a donkey's back that Christ entered Jerusalem.

> Fools, for I also had my hour;
> One far fierce hour and sweet:
> There was a shout about my ears,
> And palms before my feet.[3]

> (G. K. Chesteron, a Catholic)

Since then, legend tells us, every donkey wears a cross on his back. And it is a fact that every donkey does. The animal world teaches us, among many other things, fidelity and patience and loving kindness. What would *you* say, for instance, about the sheep dog in Scotland who stayed with the body of his master for a *whole winter* (what did he eat? how did he survive? who knows? but it is a true story) and was found in spring still there—nearly a skeleton—when the master died in the mountains alone. Animals are often far better (gooder) than men. We can, I am sure, learn much from them. That we also exploit them is another matter. [to MH, 4 Mar 70, Nelson]

And within the animal world, it is cats—her own and those of friends—for whom Sarton has felt the greatest affinities—

The party last night[4] was peachy fun. Miss Thorp and Miss Taylor[5] came dressed as a witch and her cat. Miss Thorp was the cat—she was perfectly

[2] *The Poet and the Donkey.*
[3] From Chesterton's "The Donkey."
[4] Halloween.
[5] Anne Thorp and Katharine Taylor.

Anne Thorp. Credit:
May Sarton.

Sarton.

marvelous. The first thing she did when she came in was to rush up the banisters and spit at us from the top of the stairs! She walked exactly like a cat. When the Clarks'[6] own black pussy came in she put her back way up, and spat viciously and the real cat was absolutely terrified! [to EMS, 30 Oct 27, Ray SA]

Margaret[7] has brought two coal-black manx kittens called "Bonnet" and "Feather." They have a strange birdlike appearance in the rear and very sweet mischievous faces. [to EMS and GS, 16 Jul 34, Rowley]

Our puss[8] has four kittens—very ugly and silky all suckling in a row and she has her mother-face which is quite different from any other—pointed and saintly with very large burning deep eyes—and she has her mother-language which is a kind of purr crescendo'd into a voice. [to K, 23 Feb 40, Ch Pl]

[6]The family of Jean and Margot (Triggy) Clark.
[7]Margaret English.
[8]Cloudy.

I have just been having a hopeless conversation with a dear black cat on the roof opposite, but there is an alley between us that he can't jump over. [to JM, 18 Apr 47, London (JS)]

I loved it all about the cats but how wicked of our fat cat to catch robins however "provocante" their walk may be. The cat here is quite wild now, though very fat and well—in the morning he is completely wild and leapt into the air to the height of my shoulder and bit it this morning! I was quite frightened, but then after breakfast he comes and sleeps on my bed and is very purrful and gentle. But I am disturbed about Jean Do's cat, which was Blanchette's[9]—he is really a wicked cat. They thought that he was lonely without a friend, but what he needed, it seems, was an enemy. Il ne vit que pour se battre avec un vilain chat blanc et revient hideux et ensanglante avec de grandes touffes de fourrure arrachées—il saute sur la pauvre Jean-Do et lui mord les chevilles—et j'ai peur qu'elle tombe, mais par loyauté à Blanchette qui avait très peur que personne ne voudrait d'un si vilain chat après sa mort, il faut qu'elles le gardent! Il n'est jamais à la maison, jamais doux. C'est affreux.[1] [to EMS and GS, 20 May 49, Chez Limbosch]

Before I close I must say that I love cats passionately and have one who at the moment is quite a sorrow. He[2] is a tiger cat with a white shirt front and was until a few months ago a marvelously friendly, responsive cat, full of affection and talk and always around, sitting on my bed with his paws tucked in while I worked—until suddenly I suspect he grew up and has turned into a fierce Tom who gets into awful fights and is *never* home except to be washed with boric solution and to recover and lick his wounds! [to KD, 1 Jan 50, Oxf St]

Il ne me manque qu'un chat ou un petit hibou comme avait Florence Nightingale. Ce qui me fait penser, ma cherie, est-ce que tu ne pourrai pas maintenant

[9]Blanchette Rousseau, Clairette in *The Single Hound*, died in April 1949.

[1]"He lives solely to fight with a wretched white cat and comes home hideous and bloody with great tufts of fur torn out—he leaps up onto poor Jean-Do and bites her ankles—and I'm afraid that she will fall, but out of loyalty to Blanchette, who was very afraid that no one would want such a wretched cat after her death, they feel they must keep it. He is never at home, never sweet. It's terrible."

[2]Tom Jones of *The Fur Person*.

trouver un petit chat bien sage qui ronronnerait pour toi? Ce qui est bon avec un chat c'est justement qu'il ne sait pas trop comme on souffre, et les larmes coulent sur sa tête de velours sans qu'il s'en rend compte. Mais il fait partir de la solitude. Je voudrais tant qu'on te trouve un chat, mais je crois qu'un tout petit serait trop soudain et pourrait t'effrayer. Il vaudrait mieux un chat grand déjà et sage et rond. Quand je serai là je serai ce chat-là.[3] [to MC, 3 Apr 51, Stonington]

Le chat orange[4] est splendide comme un tigre de Rousseau parmi les fleurs.[5] [to MC, 17 Apr 51, Myn Pl]

The marmelade cat ate little pieces of bread and butter, too, in a very satisfactory way and purred and rolled over in his rococo attitudes, utterly different from our austere animal Tom Jones (whose attitudes are Anglo-Saxon). [to LB, 29 Jun 54, Wr St]

Here I am consoled by Jane[6] and her immense black and white cat, Cosmo, who is really a remarkable personality, full of gusto—he runs up and down the hall like a small wind, purrs a lot and has immense green eyes. [to GS, 6 Nov 54, London (JS)]

It is very agitating to have people reading the book.[7] A friend brought it back this morning on her way to work, so after she had left, I found it hard to settle. And the cat caught my mood or had one of his own and was frightfully

[3]"The only thing I miss is a cat, or a little owl like the one Florence Nightingale had. What I am thinking, my darling, is that couldn't you find a little well-behaved cat who would purr for you? What is wonderful with a cat is that he doesn't really understand very well how one suffers, and one's tears can drop down onto his velvet head without his understanding them. But he banishes one's loneliness. I wish so much that someone would find you a cat, but I think that a very little one would move too suddenly and might frighten you. It would be better to have a cat already grown up and well behaved and plump. When I am there I will be that cat."
[4]George Sarton's cat, Rufus.
[5]"The orange cat is splendid, like a Rousseau tiger among the flowers."
[6]Jane Stockwood, with whom Sarton often stayed in London. She worked on the staff of *Harper's Bazaar* and wrote reviews for *Queen's* magazine.
[7]*Faithful Are the Wounds.*

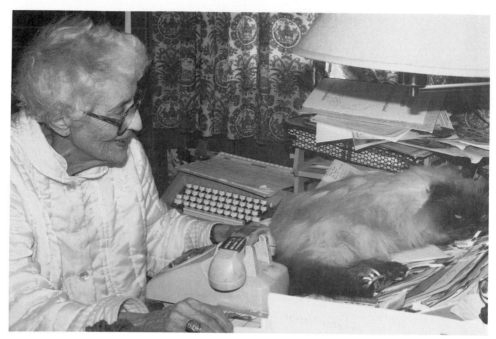

Sarton at her desk in York, February 1992. Credit: Susan Sherman.

restless, making me go down about seven times to ask for food, though his plate was full, but not approving of 1) a can of chicken cat food 2) some very good haddock and finally in my desperation *another* canned food he sometimes likes. None of these would do and I felt murderous by the time I had lost the thread of a poem half a dozen times, and put him out in the cold. Then he climbed the tree outside my window and mewed to be let in and that was one more trip. Then he insisted that what he wanted was Love, climbed all over the desk, purring and putting his tail in the way, and making starfish paws in the air. Finally I took off my sweater and gave it to him instead of me and he finally curled up on it and went to sleep. But then the morning had vanished. [to LB, 14 Feb 55, Wr St]

Then about a week later[8] a friend in Plymouth[9] announced that she had two "ravishing" kittens saved for us. We went down two weeks ago to get them— and hardly dared exchange a glance as we both felt the same: they are the ugliest little mites we ever saw! They are black and speckled, half coon

[8]After the death of the cat Union Suit.
[9]Probably Ruth Peabody Harnden.

cat—one has long fur and dear little blond paws; the other is scrawny with a very thin tail. However, we took them home and they are, of course, enchanting together at this stage. We laugh till tears run down our cheeks and have named them Ash Wednesday and Good Friday (they came just before Easter), Fuzz-Buzz and Scrabble for short. I expect we shall keep them. [to KD, 27 Apr 60, Wr St]

LEFT. With Tamas.

RIGHT. With Tamas.

Our pussies are a constant joy. While I was reading poems last night, Scrabble came past very very quietly and climbed up and got under the tree on the pile of gaywrapped packages—her little black and gold speckled face and great grave gold eyes looked out at us all evening from that nest—so sweet! Fuzz-Buzz is a show-off and with a red ribbon round her neck flirted with everyone. [to KD, 21 Dec 62, Wr St]

I am otherwise rather a wreck. I was ill on the lecture trip[1] with some bug (temp 100 a lot of the time) and dreamed only of total collapse on getting back—but one of the pussies came out of the kennel with a horrible disease

[1]Sarton had been lecturing in St. Louis and Chicago.

and I have been battling for her life for 17 days and nights. I think we have turned the corner now—but she is still very miserable. It seems absurd, I know, to have expended so much time and anguish over such a little feather of a creature, but the patience of sick animals does touch one deeply—and life is precious in all its forms. [to RG, 4 May 65, Nelson]

Poor old Scrabble is now living on the 3rd floor in my study (she has her own bathroom too) and seems quite happy. She thumps around overhead when I am reading at night in bed with Bramble and Tamas beside me—but so far she hisses at them and seems not to want to come down at all. I have brought her down at news time twice, but she just sits and *glares* at Tamas, who stares at her back until his eyes close from tension. [to BB, 2 Jul 73, York]

Bramble has become very sleek and fat and at three A.M. prowls up and begins to knead my chest with ferocity and wakes me up! But she has been such a wild cat that I have to receive these favors with joy, and I really do. She comes the whole walk through the woods nearly every day with Tamas and me. [to BB, 15 Jan 75, York]

Bramble has suddenly become quite affectionate—she is three now. The other night, very cold out, she got into a cat fight (this almost never happens). It went on and on, and I couldn't go out as I had a bad cold and it would have been fatal (below zero). Tamas was sleeping beside me and suddenly I realized he was the answer. I woke him and we trundled downstairs together. I opened the door and said, "Tamas, go and get your cat." He shot out barking furiously, and in about 5 minutes was back with Bramble, having chased the other cat and then "herded" her home! [to BB, 5 Mar 75, York]

And cats imbue her imagery—

ô Kot, write to me anyway, even if you are cross—*roar* and I will purr—[to K, 22 Sep 39, Ch Pl]

(a) Tamas's grave at
York. Credit: Susan
Sherman.

(b) Bramble's grave
at York, sculpted by
Barbara Barton.
Credit: Susan
Sherman.

Tamas.

Tamas and Bramble.
Credit: May Sarton.

Now Julian is pacing about like a restless cat and I am to go with him to the Louvre in a few minutes so I'll send this off with dear love. [to JM, 26 May 48, Paris (Huxley)]

Par moments je *suis* un petit chat sur tes genoux et comme cela me fait du bien!² [to MC, 20 Apr 51, Myn Pl]

Cet après-midi je vais dormir je crois toute l'après-midi comme un chat enroulé dans une boule, les pattes sur la figure.³ [to MC, 4 Aug 51, Hôtel Central-Monty, Paris]

Did I tell you about Mlle. Droz?⁴ We rubbed each other the wrong way like two cats. [to GS, 12 Oct 54, Linkebeek]

I feel rather like the puss whom I can hear scrabbling, leaping and thumping downstairs as he pursues a small German wool mouse with which he is madly in love—so much so that he hardly sleeps or eats, just sits with enormous eyes fixed on the drawer where it is kept until he is given it, then dances, feints forgetfulness, pounces for hours at a time in perfect bliss—we are so afraid now of losing it and Judy said ominously last night, "The mouse is at large," which made me have a fit of giggles.

My state is somewhat comparable as I have been pursuing a small American mouselike poem all day and *cannot* catch it. I feel teased out of all patience, very cross and frustrated indeed. I have just looked at it again and decided that it will have to wait till tomorrow when I shall see whether there is anything to be salvaged—such a good theme too and one I have brooded on for quite awhile. I hate to lose it. [to LB, 24 Jan 55, Wr St]

But it is before the natural world in all its aspects that she stands poised as if for revelation⁵—

²"At moments I *am* a little cat on your knees, and that does me so much good."
³"This afternoon I think I am going to sleep all afternoon like a cat rolled up in a ball, his paws on his face."
⁴Eugénie Droz, a publisher and friend of George Sarton's living in Geneva.
⁵see "Autumn Sonnets" in *Halfway to Silence*.

We[6] had supper there in a restaurant right over the shingle—in a place fitting for the "Lady Jingly-Jones sitting on her heap of stones"[7]—the loveliest calm really sapphire sea that turned to amethyst and then silver—and I use precious stones on purpose because it was really a jewel of a sea—almost unreal. [to EMS and GS, ? May 32, Genoa]

The rodeo was about fifty miles away and we tooted merrily in two cars through brown hills covered with little dark green oak trees and dotted with wild cattle—its rather like Spain south of the Pyrennes as soon as you get inland. Then orchards which are planted in the brown earth with no grass and look like those bedspreads with tufts on them. Sometimes you see them against the horizon and then they look like buttons on a giant. [to EMS and GS, 21 Jun 34, Pebble Beach, Calif.]

I have been so peaceful here, working in the big room surrounded with books and looking out on three poplar trees that are three people always talking and saying things about the weather in soft voices. [to K, 25 Sep 37, Ch Pl]

The autumn here is just beyond words—you must see it someday. One clear gold day after another—with the trees flowering into flame. All its sadness is a triumphant sadness. It is full of glory. I got up very early to get breakfast and it was absolutely still outside and gold except for the continual short broken sound of leaves falling one by one (no wind). Like music it was. [to JH, 17 Oct 37, Ch Pl]

The mountains here strip the spirit—they are plainly grand. They ask something of one. [to RWB, 18 Dec 40, Santa Fe (AS)]

---

[6]Sarton and Signora Maria Pennella.
[7]A reference to Edward Lear's "The Courtship of the Yonghy-Bonghy-Bò":

   " 'tis the Lady Jingly Jones!
   On that little heap of stones
   Sits the Lady Jingly Jones!"
   Said the Yonghy-Bonghy-Bò.

   . . .

   "I am tired of living singly,—
   On this coast so wild and shingly . . ."

Yesterday I started off early—everything glistening after a night's rain (O I forgot that on the way to Tucson in one of the canyons after miles of bare rock and scrub I saw two cherry trees in flower—my heart leapt up—there is always one moment when one *meets* the spring and this was it)— All morning I was driving through rich plains, the earth tilled and only all along the rim of the world making it a bowl, little blue pointed mountains. Then for a while the most magical stretches of desert, magical because after the great rains it was so full of life. Over and over I stopped the car to sniff the air and listen to the birds—and to look at the wild flowers, at least 12 different kinds—fields of golden poppies and little lavender flowers, and big yellow flowering bushes. Later in Cal. there were such floods of flowers but in the desert each individual one is like a jewel and one gasps with excitement. You have to see it with golden sand and then lots of low bushes, bronze-green and sage green with a background of reddish and purple jagged rocks and the giant cactus standing about like people—and the mesquite looking quite green—and wherever there is water green grass—[to EMS and GS, 19 Feb 41, Pasadena (MT)]

I feel very remote from *that* world[8] here. One of the nice things about this place is the humbleness of the houses—adobe just disappears again into the earth. The people are humble, the mountains the aristocrats. [to GS, 4 Mar 41, Santa Fe (AS)]

Yesterday on the way here (it is Rollo Brown's country by the way) I drove through many small mining towns, the men all sitting on their sills or walking with their children, as there is a strike on. But lovely still brooks and slow green rivers. On the banks of one I saw masses of violets and white and yellow adder's tongue which is most exquisite—a single peaked bell and lovely pointed gray leaves. There were hosts of these and then pale pink carpets of a flower I have never seen called "Spring Beauty"—the cherries are all out, too *lovely*. It is breathtaking and one is in a perpetual ecstasy (while another part suffers and is in anguish over the war). [to EMS and GS, 18 Apr 41, Muskingham College, New Concord, O.]

[8]The social world.

Valée du Drac.
Credit: May Sarton.

It is a most opalescent eve—a primrose-colored sky over deep blue snow, with the golden windows just lighting up in the house opposite. We have had the most beautiful snow—all at once, the kind that plumes the trees and is a glory on earth. It makes me feel high. [to MFH, 6 Jan 42, Ch Pl]

How I wish you were here and we would go for a long walk among the pale green sage on the red earth and be all surrounded with friendly mountains. Friendly is really the wrong word for these mountains because they are so austere and powerful but they do the opposite of shut in and that is what I was getting at. [to BB, 14 Mar 45, Santa Fe (ER)]

We are having marvelous Blakean thunderstorms every afternoon—like a war of angels in the air, very exciting against the purple mountains. [to BB, 24 Apr 45, Santa Fe (ER)]

. . . the marvelous, always moving skies—that, I think, is what I miss most in America. Our skies are flat by comparison. [to BB, 5 May 47, London (JS)]

All the way down to Dover we went through orchards of pink apples, white pears and cherries—like enamel, so perfectly rich and still. It was the most lovely farewell. [to EMS and GS, 10 May 47, Chez Limbosch]

I am like an *affamé*[9] getting back to Europe—just the trees in England make me new. I do miss great trees in America. [to HD, 22 Jun 47, Chez Limbosch]

Here I am! This morning I woke up to see the clouds unveiling the mountains across the lake which yesterday had been completely hidden—I looked up to the left and saw for an instant the Dents du Midi, sharp and snowy, and then they were veiled again—and now the lake is blue though there are still rather menacing clouds and fogs waiting to pounce. [to JM, 8 Jul 48, Montreux]

The best time is when I wake up and open the shutters and always my heart beats to see the mountains and what they are up to—and the lake, not my friend, but very beautiful just the same. [to JM, 14 Jul 48, Montreux]

Ah, and my great forest, the Forêt de Soignes, like a Bach fugue with its incredible tall straight beeches, making fountains of the freshest green high high up in the air. This I see on my way back from town in the trolley—a green hush which one approaches slowly and which is there half the way home. [to MFH, 7 May 48, Chez Limbosch]

The great "Bois de la Cambre," all beeches amazingly high and branchless till the top is in its full glory—a thing I have not seen for thirty years, autumn here. Quite impossible even to try to describe—the day I drove through it was raining yet even then the whole forest seems somberly on fire—such trains of gold on a bronze ground, all delicate Chinese greens and golds. I am hoping to get back for one real walk in it before Friday when I must uproot and go to London. [to LB, 30 Oct 54, Linkebeek]

[9]"a famished one."

Here, too, all the lights of the afternoon are so beautiful, deep rose and then turquoise with the leafless branches against open skies. One forgets how beautiful trees are without their leaves. [to JH, 28 Oct 48, Oxf St]

Yesterday I had my last drive in the forest, with a few sunny intervals in the middle of a very dreary depressing day of rain. But the forest is always marvelous—so endless in its variety (we found pine woods in the middle of it yesterday and wonderful opening clearings full of foxglove)—I shall miss it and the dear little fields the most. The flax field outside my window which was a lovely blue-green lake when I arrived has flowered and seeded and is now lying on the ground in sheaves, but beyond it there are green-gold fields of wheat. [to JM, 19 Jun 57, Linkebeek]

I am longing to write some poems about the country scene—just now the fireflies are so beautiful in the long grass of my meadow back of the house, and the great soft moths like small flying bears bump against the windows. [to KD, 17 Jul 60, Nelson]

. . . but the lake surrounded by *white* volcanic peaks (snow) is simply marvelous—and also the immensely high waterfall we have just seen falling through icy steep walls. I have never seen such a *variety* of beautiful landscapes in my life. [to JM, 16 Mar 62, Nikko, Japan]

Acropolis. Credit: May Sarton.

Anyway I climbed the Acropolis[1] in the early morning light of my 50th birthday—a *tremendous* experience—much more than the photos ever show, because it is the space—mountains and sea—all around *plus* the quality of the light and the marvelous reddish-gold of the weathered marble. Also *tufts* of red poppies growing up between the fallen pillars. [to KD, 7 May 62, Delos, Greece]

[1]See "Birthday on the Acropolis" in *A Private Mythology*.

It's a dazzling day after the storm which was quite wonderful here, soft thick snow like ermine, but which ended late yesterday afternoon with a terrifying black gale—really like some scourge from the skies and then a sudden drop of 20 degrees came with it. [to JM, 22 Feb 67, Nelson]

Her particular sensitivity to light has made her world a shining field, and, like Monet, she has spent a lifetime trying to undazzle that light, and pin it down[2]—

> Light is snow sifted
> To an abstraction.
>
> [from "Night of Snow," HJ, 19 Jan 29, Ray St]

Ici le lac est tout en argent avec les montagnes *noires* autour—l'orage!— Maintenant c'est déjà tout en gris mais quand j'ai commencé à t'écrire le soleil eu plutôt une lumière brillante touchait le lac *audessous* des nuages qui assombrissait les montagnes. Ce sont les lumières changeantes que j'adore ici—je n'aime vraiment pas beaucoup un paysage trop spectacle—c'est un peu trop Wagnérien—mais les lumières du ciel et le ciel-même est une merveille ici. Et cela change tout les cinq minutes. La nuit les étoiles se réflètent dans le lac et les montagnes ont l'air d'être découpés en carton![3] [to MC, 7 Jul 36, Austria]

The light[4] was simply unbelievable, soft and gold, making the trees look like green fire. [to JMS and GS, 14 Apr 37, Rye]

I've just been for a walk with Alan[5] to the top of the hill to look down on the house with behind it the superb gentle mountains—clouds going over and

[2]See "For Monet" in *Letters from Maine.*
[3]"Here the lake is entirely silver with *black* mountains around it—the storm—now it is already all gray but when I began to write to you the sun had a rather brilliant light touching the lake *below* the clouds which threw a shadow over the mountains. It is the changing lights which I adore here—I really do not like very much a too spectacular landscape—it's a little too Wagnerian—but the lights of the sky and the sky itself are really a miracle here. And it changes every five minutes. At night the stars are mirrored in the lake and the mountains look as if they were cut from cardboard."
[4]In the Kensington Gardens, London.
[5]Alan Cameron, Elizabeth Bowen's husband.

casting dark shadows. The light is the great Irish beauty as far as I'm concerned—it changes all the time and has a water-color luminosity which puts a special sheen on everything. [to JM, 10 Sep 48, Ireland]

Hier soir Judy et moi étions toutes les deux horriblement fatiguées—je crois que c'est en partie la lumière éblouissante de ces jours de printemps. Il y a *trop* a voir et tout à coup on a besoin de noir, du sommeil pour supporter encore un jour de fleurs et de soleil.[6] [to MC, 9 May 51, Myn Pl]

En regardant tout cela[7] je sentais la paix couler dans mon âme et je suis sortie toute éblouie m'asseoir pour une demie heure dans le Parc de St. James regarder la lumière magnifique parmi les arbres, et les canards, et les humains endormis sur leurs chaises dans la bonne lassitude du crépuscule.[8] [to MC, 6 Jun 51, London (JS)]

At Grundlsee, Austria.

Those are the water-color days—no shadow of a leaf falls on them. Night trembles in every petal of each daffodil, light rains through the new air—[HJ, 23 Apr 54, Martha's Vineyard, Mass.]

The way the light moves around the house and its poignant fading at five—never ceases to move me. [to RG, 4 Jun 62, Satigny]

---

[6]"Last night Judy and I were both horribly exhausted—I think it's in part the dazzling light of these spring days. There's *too much* to see and suddenly one has need of darkness, of sleep, in order to bear another day of flowers and of sun."

[7]Re a visit to the National Gallery.

[8]"Looking at all that, I felt peace stream into my soul and I left dazzled, sitting for half an hour in St. James's Park to look at the magnificent light among the trees, and the ducks, and the people sleeping in their chairs in that wonderful lassitude of twilight."

Glorious day here with brilliant sun, sparkling snow, a perfect blue sky, pale at the horizon and growing darker above. Sunlight falls on each object and lights it up—such as Scrabble, black and gold on the emerald green chair where you sat for tea—and shines through a white cyclamen—and makes Punch look very bright indeed.[9] [to BB, 25 Dec 69, Nelson]

Throughout the letters, gardens appear as characters, their forms, details and images as individual and vivid as the traits of friends. On her first visit to Grace Dudley's home in Vouvray—

She goes into the garden and gardens with Jammy the dog all morning and I can hear her singing, and then in the afternoon we go for a walk or sit in the garden and read aloud. There are great dark red peonies in the garden, strange parrot tulips and lots of pick-me-nots—it is formal with parterres with ivy instead of grass and then you look over the hedge to the vineyards, to a soft green hill and the single trees against a huge sky. This is Ronsard's country and Anatole France—it has a classic peaceful gentleness that I already adore—the pale blue Loire, rich and wide with its islands of beige sand and irregular poplars—[to EMS and GS, 29 Apr 38, VF]

Then in Belgium—

It is raining and very still with just the sound of the rain—my window looks out onto a magnificent vegetable garden—great rows of lettuce that we go out and pick for supper, the tall poles of beans and peas, the beets and even corn beginning, tomatoes onions everything you can imagine—and beyond there is a great weeping willow and borders of flowers. Such a dear human garden which the whole family and even I when I was twelve have made together. [to K, 4 Aug 39, Chez Limbosch]

And Santa Fe—

[9]The parrot in *Punch's Secret.*

. . . and every morning I take my breakfast out to the formal garden to eat it under a large chestnut tree just now in a glory of flowers. The garden is full of peonies and lupin and columbine and yellow daisies and through the leaves I can see the top of the Sangre de Cristo mountains. The dog chases butterflies and the large silky black cat with amber eyes pads secretly in and out of the jungle of flowers. It is very peaceful. [to EMS and GS, 5 Jun 45, Santa Fe (CF)]

And Penns-in-the-Rocks—

The weekend at Dorothy Wellesley's[1] was a little sad as she is so ill and could not get up at all—but we had some talks in her bedroom and I was so glad Ruth Pitter[2] was with me so I had several lively rambles round the place. It is fun to see it in a different season—what is lovely is its combination of quite wild rough landscape and formal gardens. A door opens onto a great steep hill rising to a little folly (a temple with pillars) and when I first went the whole hill was covered with daffodils—now it is covered with a sea of bracken three or four feet high, a real invasion and looks quite wild. To the right of it are The Rocks—huge boulders on which holly, beeches and mountain ash grow, all in between the stone, and there is heavenly moss underfoot—then on the other side of the house are the formal gardens, opening on into another with formal avenues of fruit trees and formal parterres—now there were masses of snapdragon and dahlias and roses and larkspur—but there is no typical English mixed border which is what I love best. One evening after supper I was allowed to go out with a basket and pick all I wanted to take back to Jane and Annie[3] it was so lovely in the evening light! And I picked a great bunch of sweet peas and a little bunch of pansies and a glorious mixed bunch of everything. The house is all *embaumée*[4] here. [to EMS and GS, 15 Jul 47, London (JS)]

[1]Dorothy Violet Ashton Wellesley (1891–1956), 4th Duchess of Wellington, lived at Penns-in-the-Rocks, Sussex.
[2]Ruth Pitter (1897–1992), English poet.
[3]Jane Stockwood and Annie Duveen Caldwell, with whom Sarton was staying in London.
[4]"embalmed."

And Rodmell[5]—

Evelyn[6] took me on a wonderful drive yesterday afternoon—then we went to Leonard Woolf's for a drink. I had never been inside the Rodmell house and was deeply moved—the garden is so lovely opening out through an intimate orchard to suddenly, a long green lawn, a pond and a big open distant view of meadows with the downs beyond. Down that field she went to commit suicide—it was much on my mind. [to JM, 30 May 57, London (JS)]

And home in Nelson—

And my real birthday present was the garden—which really is so beautiful in spring. Now the daffodils are nearly over, but tulips are in their glory and soon there will be iris, peonies, and then delphinium and poppies—it is a long grand sequence from now on and my work at it for five years is beginning to bear fruit—also all the pruning Perley has done for me. [to KD, 16 May 65, Nelson]

Flowers themselves are a universe for her, and have been since she was a child. At eight she writes of the lily-of-the-valley, the flower she later chose as her signature—

Once upon a time there was a little girl whose name was may. She was having a birthday party and all the lilys of the valley were out it was the 3erd of May And this little girl was a yearold. Im the little girl and lily of the vally is my favorite flower. And they Allways bloom in our garden on the 3 erd of May. We lived in Belgiem then. Lily of the valley are like this they are like a cup. Im going to draw a picture of One. They are white. Once they were used for drinking cups for the fairy king and queen. ["A Little Story of a Lily of the Vally," Spring 1920, Washington]

And flowers have never ceased to be at the core of her life—

[5]The village in Sussex where Leonard and Virginia Woolf's country home, Monk's House, was located.
[6]Evelyn Pember, friend of Sarton's who lived in Rodmell.

May Sarton reaching
out for a flower at
three and one-half
months with
"Grannie," Mrs.
Gervaise Elwes.

Sarton's story of a
Lily of the Valley

may Sarton

Washington
Spring 1920

A Little Story Of A
Lily Of The Vally

ONce Upon a time there was
a little girl whos name was
mary. She was having a birthday party and all the lilys
of 'the vally were out it
was the 3erd of may And
this little girl was a yearold.
I'm the little girl and lilys of
the vally is my favorite flower.
And they Allways bloom in
our garden on the 3erd of may.
We lived in Belgiem then
lily of the vally are like this they

are like a cup. I'm going to draw
a little picture of ONe. They are
white. ONce they were used
for drinking cups for the fairy
king and queen.

In the morning I had been intoxicated by the spring air. I had to do something extravagant so I bought mother a bunch of violets, they smelled earthy and wet and sweet, driving one crazy with longing for woods and peace. [HJ, 18 Mar 28, Ray St]

I can't bear to have flowers treated casually. [from "Casualness and Carnations," HJ, 27 Apr 28, Ray St]

> . . . But then I see the zinnia tempest,
> The zinnias pouring color on the air
> With autumn passion.
>
> [from "The Fatness of Fall," HJ, 10 Sep 28, Ray St]

> Give yourself blue gentians when the air
> Is deeper blue than they; and when you ache
> With autumn wind against your mouth and hair,
> Give yourself gentians for the autumn's sake.
> There was no other way to make a mind
> Windproof, against that wind who mingles leaves
> With birds and dust, who will unbind
> And loose the grain out of a thousand sheaves
> And bear it high up in a golden cloud
> To fall like golden rain across the dark,
> Who tears your petaled pride if you are proud
> And burns the bravest thought with the frost's spark—
> Give yourself blue gentians that you may
> Not wholly lose what the wind takes away.
>
> ["Give Yourself Blue Gentians," 27 Oct 29, Ray St]

I hope the pansies will be flourishing when I come—they're for "thoughts" you know, and each one that flowers is my thoughts for you. [to EMS and GS, 18 May 30, 94 Macd]

Mother's garden is a little fête against the rocks—and there are "heavenly blues" a kind of very blue morning glory that closes up every night and then burst open like trumpets in the morning. [to K, 31 Aug 39, Rockport]

The last white roses are here in a bright blue glass, that wonderful greenish white that is somehow poignant like the roses of a long time ago, like white silk found in a trunk. [to K, 8 Oct 39, Ch Pl]

In Paris it was bitter cold, October weather, *with rafales de pluie froide*,[7] but we were soon going south into blue skies with magnificent fields of poppies shot through with bluets and sometimes dark purple clover so they looked like stained glass. [to EMS and GS, 5 Jun 48, VF]

I can't tell you what a glory of wild flowers are here—yesterday I picked a magnificent bunch for Grace[8] and she was very pleased—long blue spikes like larkspur only with furry stems, brilliant poppies and daisies and pale purple bells and all sorts of little things I can't name and some fine tassled grasses. [to EMS and GS, 14 Jun 48, VF]

It was so terribly beautiful to wake up and be able to look out with a rinsed eye at the wheat field in the distance. I went often to listen to it, a sound I have never heard before, that little creeping rustling whisper, the *richest* sound. This morning the reapers were out to cut it down. Another joy was a small task of cutting every day all the seeds off of two beds of poppies, so *fragile* and winged and airy—then deprived of making their fruit, they go on flowering all summer. I liked making poets of the poppies. [to JH, 17 Aug 48, London (RP)]

Nous avons dans la maison deux gloires, deux cyclamens blanches, qui portent chacune une douzaine de fleurs ailées et ces belles feuilles vert-bleu—comme c'est beau, élancé et pur. Je pense à maman en les regardant.[9] [to MC, 10 Jan 51, Myn Pl]

Samedi—t'ai-je raconté celà? Judy et moi sommes alleés en auto à Plymouth voir des amis à la campagne et chercher un des premières fleurs sauvage qui

---

[7]"gusts of cold rain."

[8]Grace Dudley.

[9]"We have in the house two glories, two white cyclamen, each one of which has a dozen winged flowers and these beautiful blue-green leaves—oh how beautiful it is, darting forth, and pure. I think of mother when I look at them." (Sarton's mother had died a few weeks before, on November 18, 1950.)

viennent ici, c'est une petite fleur secrète et exquise avec l'odeur le plus sucré et aromatique qu'on puisse imaginer de petites étoiles roses et blanches qui poussent sous les feuilles—et c'est cela le plaisir, de se mettre à genoux où on a aperçu une toute petite feuille qui perçait l'automne de feuilles tombées, et en dessous de trouver une branche parfaite de fleurs comme une branche de corail. J'étais folle de joie comme un enfant qui cherche—et trouve—un trésor à chaque pas. Cette fleur s'appelle *Mayflower* or *Trailing Arbutus.* Je crois qu'il ne pousse pas en Belgique?[1] [to MC, 24 Apr 51, Myn Pl]

Nous revoilà dans le printemps,[2] which I suppose is another version of Madame de Sévigné's "Nous revoilà dans les lettres"[3]—it was such a good way to celebrate this entrance into spring to read all about the ranunculous—and the fritillary. The fritillary has long haunted me and I have grown them, at mother's and also in a tiny garden Judy and I had back of another house where we lived. I saw them for the first time some years ago at Dorothy Wellesley's Penns in the Rocks (where Yeats used to stay)—there they were many and magical all in the lush grass round a brookside, a carefully designed "wild garden," some white, some purple checks on greenish-gray. The whole process of their growth is so beautiful for they start by looking almost like spears of grass straight up, slightly swollen at one end, then that end bends over and becomes an octagonal lantern on which the checks show up, and finally the flower opens into childish exact points. If you come at the end of May (is it?) you will have to see the garden and perhaps I can show you a living fritillary for your poem. [to LB, 21 Mar 54, Wr St]

These last days were pure mountain ones—we had two absolutely marvelous picnics, Alpine ones. The first was just over the Simplon pass (at the pass

---

[1]"Have I told you this? Judy and I drove to Plymouth to see friends in the country and to look for one of the first wild flowers that comes up here, a very secret, exquisite flower with the sweetest most aromatic fragrance you can imagine, with little red and white stars that peek up under the leaves—and that's the great joy, to kneel down where you see a tiny leaf pushing its way up through the fallen autumn leaves, and underneath that leaf to find a perfect branch of flowers, like a branch of coral. I was wild with joy, like a child who looks for—and finds—a treasure at each step. This flower is called Mayflower or Trailing Arbutus. I don't think it grows in Belgium?"

[2]"Here we are again in spring."

[3]"Here we are again in letters."

itself I found a pale lavender gentian)—lower down we came to rich green meadows, very like those around Muzot, and sat like the people in Angelico's Paradise on a carpet of flowers, including those brilliant blue Bavarian gentians, wild orchids, autumn crocus, and everywhere the sound of water, like clear streams flowing down in the grass. [to LB, 19 Sep 54, Satigny]

Would you like an amaryllis bulb from White Flower for Christmas? They are awfully weird—that phallic symbol rising up so *slowly*, but I must say the immense radiant summery flowers in midwinter are rather glorious. [to LB, 9 Nov 65, Lindenwood]

I spent a lovely 24 hours just before she[4] came in a perfect poet's garden in Beverly at old Ellery Sedgwick's (formerly editor of the *Atlantic*). He is 85, in a wheelchair, but simply bursting with life and passionate love of beauty. He has recently bought a really wonderful El Greco of the Agony in the Garden, one of the best I ever saw (and far more beautiful than one on the same theme in the National Gallery in London)—and the house itself is all a work of love, shabby and grand and full of beautiful things, and such a relief after the rich interior-decorated houses I have seen lately. But the best was the tree peonies in the garden—have you ever seen them? They are huge single flowers, really glorious on great long leafy stems which grow four or five feet high—one sees them in Chinese paintings of course, but they do not even suggest what the light does to them, the flow of it—I wrote a poem[5] which I'll close with—[to BB, 31 May 53, Wr St]

The delphinium has been almost overpowering—almost too grand and thick and tremendous, but it is just glorious in the house with lilies and phlox, I must say. I stagger about, a drunkard of flowers these days. [to BdeS, 23 Jul 65, Nelson]

And so, the generosity she has been known for all her life, based on her belief that saving the world may be a matter of sowing a seed,[6] began with flowers—

[4]Elizabeth Bowen.
[5]"Poet of China: A Wood Peony," unpublished.
[6]See "The House of Gathering" in *The Silence Now*.

I love giving flowers. It is so deliciously unlasting and romantic. [HJ, 10 Apr 28, Ray St]

And that generosity continued with her own art work, and homemade anthologies of poetry—

After tea I came up here, took off most of my clothes and typed you very badly a little anthology. Unfortunately I have so few books here, it couldn't be what I had intended, all green and peace, but you will find one or two poems perhaps and that is all any anthology can give. It is badly typed because of the heat. It is to take on your vacation. [to JH, 28 Jul 48, Chez Limbosch]

My great joy at the moment is making Christmas presents—I am covering cigar boxes of Daddy's (he has towers of them in the attic, one of his games)—with lovely things like the *Trés Riches Heures* which *Life* produced well some years ago. Each box is different and, shellacked, they look quite fine. Anyway for me it is such a rest to be making something. The main trouble with my life is that it is all *analytic* and so, deadly in the long run. Pasting things on a box is a rather low form of creation, but it *is* wonderful fun. [to BB, 23 Nov 52, Wr St]

Her generosity has always included money, even when she did not have it herself. From the beginning she helped her mother, who received only a limited household allowance from George Sarton—

I am all right financially (!) as I asked Daddy to advance my April allowance—I sent you a money order for $20.00—it has been terribly on my conscience—I hope it will help out this month. [to EMS, 16 Mar 34, 54 W 10]

And yet despite her own financial limitations, it was Eleanor Mabel Sarton who taught her daughter generosity—

Mother has been worried about all sorts of things, the old question of money which hangs over our heads, partly because she entirely supports three exiled

Russians in Florence, a grandmother, her daughter and granddaughter.[7] [to K, 17 Oct 37, Ch Pl]

And there follows a host of people to whom Sarton has committed herself—

Often with money—

I had quite a wild day yesterday because Mrs. Ulich wrote to ask me to help Gerhart[8] raise $500 for his brother to come over and after *wracking* my brains and deciding that I couldn't ask any more of Boston friends I called up Mrs. Meem,[9] the wife of the architect—she is a very delicate shy and discriminating person who has taken in 4 English children for the duration of the war! Anyway she gave me a check for $100, which is what I had hoped to raise. [to EMS and GS, 14 Feb 41, Santa Fe (AS)]

The one nice thing that has happened is that I have managed to raise the money to send the little Missouri girl[1] on to Northwestern for a year. That is a thrill. [to MFH, 23 Jul 43, Rockport]

As godmother—

Today looked like a great stretch of peace and I wanted to go and pay a visit to the Wilton Triptych,[2] but then Amélie Hanbury-Sparrow called. She is my German friend and I am godmother of her adopted twins (adopted after her own adored child was killed by a flying bomb here in England). She brings with her her astonishing German son who held out as a boy against Nazism, alone, and with a terrible Nazi father. His disillusion now had been one of her problems and I am glad to know him. I lunch with them today. [to JH, 19 Aug 48, London (RP)]

[7]The Baranovitch family.
[8]Gerhart Speyer, a German refugee friend.
[9]Faith, wife of the architect John Gaw Meem (1894– ?).
[1]Hazel Gohn.
[2]Probably the Wilton Diptych, once owned by Charles I.

As friend—

My father gave me a long lecture about my extravagances—which have been chiefly this year sending packages to Europe and also, I was really forced to lend $200 to an old man who is more desperate than I and has a wife to support—Rollo Walter Brown. He promised to pay it back and now can't do so. It is not his fault but it is something like the straw that broke the camel, I must admit! I expect this kind of giving when one can't afford it is a sin. But I feel that if you borrow as I often have to, then you almost must also *lend* when you can afford it. And as Mélanie's mother used to say, *"Je ne regrette rien!"* [to MFH, ? Mar 47, Oxf St]

Only one dismaying thing—just *after* I sent off a check for $100 to the Greek family[3] (the little girl had an appendicitis op. so the money I sent for a vacation went for that) I heard from the Foster Parents Plan at long last about the washing machine which Angeliki had told me she needed more than a holiday. They found one for $250 and were waiting for my reply, so I sent it. But it is clear that I must now pull in *every* horn and lie low as far as giving for awhile. Anyway Angeliki will have what she most wants and she does work terribly hard, poor dear. I figured that I used the *Va. Quarterly*[4] for that gift—nice to turn poems into washing machines! [to EBl, 21 Jun 66, Nelson]

It is good that you will have all that money—it really is a lot. It means that you are free to paint as you will, and also perhaps to help some young painters along the way. Isn't being rich being 1) able to have in a simple way whatever one wants from a tweed jacket to a bottle of wine, *nothing* to the very rich, but luxury to you and me, and 2) to be able to *give.* I am earning about $20,000 a year—how long will it last? But for the moment I feel very rich and blest. [to BB, 31 Oct 71, Nelson]

Often she gives materials, as for a school of seven hundred girls in Germany—

[3]Angeliki, Dinoula, and Mando Vassiliou, her Greek Foster Parent family.
[4]The *Virginia Quarterly Review* had published the Emily Clark Balch Prize winners, vol. 42, No. 3 (Summer 1966). May Sarton was one of them.

Polly and Rollo
Walter Brown.

May Sarton's Greek
foster parent family.
From left to right;
Dinoula, Angeliki,
and Mando
Vassilliou.

Some of my week has gone into trying to find a school here to adopt the school: they do their homework on the margins of newspapers, have nothing in the way of drawing materials or paints or sewing materials . . . [to BB, 7 Dec 47, Oxf St]

Or blood—

Hier, je suis allée donner une demie-litre de sang au Croix Rouge (en Korée les pauvres soldats en ont grand besoin). C'est toujours une expérience très émouvante car voilà une des seules choses que chacun peut donner et c'est beau de voir tous ces êtres réunis par le besoin de donner un peu de leur essence pour aider les autres. J'étais entourée par des jeunes gens de Harvard aplatis sur les lits, blaguant pour cacher leur peur (car je crois que nous avons tous un fort instinct *contre* l'idée de donner du sang et un peu peur aussi). Je me sentais très bien après et pas plus fatiguée qu'avant, et je suis contente de l'avoir fait.[5] [to MC, 26 Apr 52, Ch Pl]

Always she gives herself—

Who cares about money anyway? I mean, if you have it you give it away—if you don't have money you give everything you have instead. [to JH, 17 Sep 47, Oxf St]

I can imagine what a nightmare your aunt must have seemed after the feasts you had been having but I feel more and more that we must give back in every possible way all that we are given—and so bear the dull and loving because we can give to them, even when we can't give to the people *we* love or take from. [to BB, 1 Sep 48, Dublin]

[5]"Yesterday I went to give a half liter of blood at the Red Cross (the soldiers in Korea have great need of it). It's always a very moving experience because there is something that everyone can give and it's beautiful to see all these people joined by the need to give a little of themselves to help others. I was surrounded by young men from Harvard, flat on their cots, joking in order to hide their fear (because I think all of us feel a strong instinct *against* the idea of giving blood, and a certain fear also). I felt very well afterward and not any more tired than before, and I was happy to have done it."

Way down deep inside me now there is such a well of happiness and trust and
love—and someday I shall be able to draw all that there is up from it and give
it to you. So all is well. [to LB, 14 Apr 54, Wr St]

As We Are Now has had splendid reviews in London, really surprising—and of
course an ancient lady of 86 whose name is Elsa Spencer wrote me at once to
say, "I *am* Miss Spencer"—she is in a nursing home and I hope to see her
when I'm there—though it is Aldershot and God knows how I can make the
time. She is in a posh home, only 18 people, all rich and all neglected by their
families. She was Inspector of Schools and is perfectly lucid and has a rich
sister who *never* goes to see her. So I guess I am going to adopt her. [to BB, 13
Sep 74, York]

I must say some letters are wonderful—I mean, letters from strangers. I got
one from a widow in Alamogordo, N.M., a semi-invalid who lives on $105
welfare a month—she had seen the excerpts from *Journal of a Solitude* in the
Aug. *Reader's Digest*—and wrote a very sensitive letter, recommending various
books she liked and that I might enjoy (she was right. I had read them all and
they were my sort of thing). Anyway she let fall that she saved (on $105)
enough to buy a book she wanted and the social worker cursed her for wasting
money! It is really so appalling one shudders. Beer or cigarettes, she said,
would have caused no scolding! But a BOOK! Of course I sent her a couple of
books—I keep thinking about her. [to BB, 26 Aug 75, York]

And as poet to poet she has been generous and supportive—

The great news is that I have managed to get Betty Middlebrook a scholarship
at Breadloaf (where I spent that lovely weekend where the waterfalls are)
Writers Conference! She has never been on a train before and is awfully
excited and I think it will be so good for her to meet other writers and have a
chance to communicate with people who are struggling with writing problems. I am delighted. [to EMS and GS, 9 Jun 43, 5 E 10]

Here[6] I was deeply moved by the perfect marriage of devotion and scholarship. The professors are nuns, most of whom had degrees from Oxford! Among them is Sister Maris Stella, a really good religious poet, the rarest of beings. She is 58, and I observed at once how tired she looked—they never get a sabbatical year off or even proper holidays—and she has not been able to write poems for years. So I took my courage in both hands and wrote a letter after I left enclosing a check for $1000 (all I made on those six weeks of lectures) and said that I wanted to give it to provide a year off for Sister Maris Stella, if they would double it. Of course I was afraid the hierarchy would object, but I had a charming letter back from the President, Sister William Mary, and she is to have her year. Now I hear from all sides that she looks ten years younger. I have much more feeling about helping an older person get some time, than a young one—there are so many fellowships for the young—and she has given a lifetime to her students. So this made me very happy. It is to be called the George Sarton Fellowship. [to KD, 29 Jun 58, Wr St]

Not being a critic, I want always to be receptive and affectionate toward poets. [to LB, 16 Sep 65, Nelson]

Everywhere we find her humor, imagination, and healing laughter—

So be prepared! When you see an assortment of odd bags with a nose peering from beneath them, it will be the return of the prodigal. (I think I'll have to take a cab all the way from Boston, as a matter of fact, because of the mirror—unless God sends me an extra three arms then, which is possible.) [to EMS and GS, 25 May 30, 94 Macd]

But time is a snark[7] here—and I have succeeded neither in charming it with smiles and soup nor capturing it by more drastic methods. [to AT, 15 Jul 32, GSLT]

[6]At College of St. Catherine, St. Paul, Minn.
[7]Ref. to Lewis Carroll's mock-heroic nonsense poem "The Hunting of the Snark."

But no work and no love is for me a kind of illness (double pneumonia).
. . . [to K, 7 May 39, Ch Pl]

I don't know if I told you that we are here for the "purr-poase of seeing
porpoyses" (phonetic sp. to show you how Daddy says it in English). . . . [to
K, 21 Dec 39, St. Petersburg, Fla.]

I knocked them out with my speech—they are not used to *conviction* nor *energy*
in these parts. Vitality knocks them over—I'm afraid it is a physical rather
than a spiritual victory! [to MFH, 18 Oct 40, Sweet Briar College, Va.]

Don't laugh at my style. It is grotesque what reading Henry James does to
one's style. I'm sure I don't mean to sound like a bishop but there is a hint of
unintended purple gaiters in the above as I reread! [to JH, 10 Sep 42, prob.
Ch. Pl]

I spent the morning with great satisfaction cleaning Muriel's[8] apartment from
top to bottom to thank her for letting me use it all this time—it was fun and
I must say it looks better now! Then I went out and got her a pail and mop
and other uninteresting things like Dutch Cleanser which she needs and
carried them back triumphantly through all the slush with everyone smiling at
me (felt like Don Quixote as if I should rush at a windmill with my mop). [to
EMS and GS, 1 Feb 43, Hotel Albert, NYC]

I've just had a sweet letter from Ruth Pitter the poet, saying that my package
of food to Dorothy Wellesley (now Duchess of Wellington) got there
safely—it gives me a peculiar pleasure to be feeding SPAM to a Duchess!
Especially to a Duchess-poet. [to BB, 25 Jun 46, Carbondale]

I cashed my last check for ten bucks about 5 days ago and am now living on
the land and on my friends. Soon we will fry the last zinnias out of the garden
and dig up the petunia root. [to MR, 19 Oct 48, Oxf St]

[8]Muriel Rukeyser's.

But there is one good thing about bad luck, it is endearing—and friends do rally round. It really should be "Cry and the world cries with you—laugh and you laugh alone." [to BB, 6 Feb 47, Chez Limbosch]

I was kept awake half the night by a rather loud inexperienced nightingale, and finally took a sedative (the first time I've used one). [to JM, 10 May 47, Chez Limbosch]

I have named my hot water bottle Mr. le Duc and shall soon decorate it with a medal for its admirable good work. [to JH, 8 Feb 48, Oxf St]

I feel I was rather mean above about the cocktails. Do not believe a word of this letter. It was not written by May Sarton but by Sinus Sarton, another person altogether! [to JH, 8 Feb 48, Oxf St]

But when I saw her[9] on Monday we really laughed till we cried about how she should be buried—it seems that a "perpetually kept grave" is fearfully expensive—and so she doesn't want one and wants me to be sure that her wishes are carried out. It sounds unbelievable that we could laugh about this but we did, and for some reason it made me feel that she would live for a long time and that I should see her again. [to JM, 28 Jul 48, Chez Limbosch]

However like the dormouse in the treacle I am "well in"[1] now and have done 60 pages, quite a lot I must say. [to EMS and GS, 25 May 49, Chez Limbosch]

I wish you could see the house which is a lovely Christmas house—such a beautiful tree—I really cannot believe it is ours, the house, the garage—the only sadness is that Tom Jones is in the hospital. A cat bit the base of his tail and then it got infected—I have begun a poem which goes:

[9]Marie Closset.

[1]Ref. to *Alice in Wonderland*. The dormouse tells a story about three little sisters who live in a treacle-well. The Mad Hatter says, "You can draw water out of a water-well so I should think you could draw treacle out of a treacle-well." Alice replies, "But they were *in* the well," and the Dormouse says, "Of course they were, well in."

He's Tom at home,
Jones is his hospital name

but that is all so far. [to BB, 22 Dec 52, Wr St]

My musical genius reached its apex thirty years ago when I played the triangle in Haydn's children's symphony, so I could not play unless you needed someone to make one sustained note! [to BB, 31 May 53, Wr St]

You will then have the pleasure of seeing Judy eat a lobster (as well as eating one yourself) which is one of my chief though rare pleasures, as she does it so beautifully and systematically like a Euclidean problem. [to LB, 10 Feb 54, Wr St]

I am getting quite used to a diet of chiefly fish (mostly raw) and rice—it is all very *elegantly* presented so we are surrounded by about ten small bowls and dishes each containing one *small* mouthful of something—I even managed to swallow what looked like a large black beetle with whiskers the other day! [to JM, 25 Mar 62, Kyoto]

I am getting lockjaw with trying to exercise silence for a change. [to MH, 5 Jun 70, Nelson]

. . . and I am enjoying the teaching though the students are not exciting. They are too genteel for words—the class president is called *Tinseley Swann* and that about says it. One of my students is called *Blue Argo*, if you can believe it! [to JM, 19 Apr 72, Agnes Scott]

The Sunday *Times* gave a hilarious review to *Punch*,[2] treating it as though it were *The Waste Land.* Having brushed *Kinds of Love* aside, and sneered at *As We Are Now* and the journal,[3] they appear at last to be taking me v. seriously indeed as *viz* this sentence: "but as I read this simple and touching tale a

[2] *Punch's Secret.*
[3] *Journal of a Solitude.*

second and third time, I wondered why, like one of Miss Sarton's fine poems, it yielded increasingly complex and disturbing resonances. The book's final sentence, 'it is good to have a secret friend in the dark,' was not comforting but a cause for anxiety, suggesting that darkness is a more fundamental condition of life than friendship." (!) I laughed so much over this it blew away all resentment about reviewers in general. Why worry? [to BB, 13 Sep 74, York]

We see her as teacher—

I have been reading till I can't see out of my eyes and writing the first lesson in detail on "Words as Meaning," a subject which began simply but ends by turning into a history of English literature as one examines why and how word-values changed from the precise intellectual image-compressed Donne school to the vague atmospheric 19th century, which is perfectly summed up in these two brief verses by Shakespeare and by Tennyson:

> The bright day is done
> And we are for the dark.[4]

> Sunset, and evening bell
> And after that—the dark.[5]

I really have too much material and haven't had time to digest it properly but I think I can make it provocative and send them chasing after the ends of ideas, which is something. The plan is to deliver a series of talks on the Elements of Poetry—dry and definite, ending with a detailed analysis of one poem, then plunge them into writing themselves with simple exercises in class, and end with something about poetry as a way of *being*, as essence forgetting about technique altogether. [to K, 9 Oct 38, Ch Pl]

I have had a good week of business—my first week of teaching. My first day of meeting the acting class my heart sank into the soles of my feet, it was so awful to think of teaching *theatre* to these fat dull or pretty, silly girls who

[4]From *Antony and Cleopatra*, V, ii.
[5]From "Crossing the Bar," misquoted.

giggled and whispered a great deal out of shyness—and it was intensified by the fact that I was going on to sup with Katharine Cornell and her manager Gert Macy, an old friend—and this comparison of the *real* thing (Kit Cornell is our greatest actress) with what I was doing seemed pretty awful. But now I have realized that after all as they know nothing about anything (they have never heard of Tchekov, with whom I am beginning) then they can learn a great deal. On second sight they are not quite so dull nor quite so silly. And yesterday I saw them from total incomprehension move toward understanding and even love of Tchekov, so I feel better. It is a small thing to be doing, but it is a human thing and so has a value that one mustn't try to measure. They can be taught to think if not to act—the first term I am giving them "Plays of Ideas" to read and discuss and act scenes from. [to K, 8 Oct 39, Ch Pl]

Such a lovely thing happened—of course I made roots at Bethany right away and had rather painfully to wrench them up this morning—and drive off through the mist and down the mountains. The head of the English department[6] whose name is on the left upper corner of this paper is a big, generous, relaxed, discriminating creature with a lovely head and that childishness of face with very clear eyes that teachers get if they don't marry and become gifts to the world (in the sense that they are always pouring out themselves on people who go away)—and when I left she said that she was going to be able to teach much better now (I am sure she's a wonderful teacher)—but I was so touched and happy I almost burst. Not a spark of jealousy—I'd been afraid of that, it would be so natural and it's so easy to come glamorously from the outside, stay two days, and make an impression on the fickle facile young— but everyone there was really happy—and though there are certainly no geniuses I think I got them going. [to MFH, 9 Oct 40, Southern Inn, Winchester, Va.]

I cannot stand much more of these open intense child faces, these eyes asking for the heart of the mystery. And I do not want to have to pour any more faith into anyone for a long time. [to MFH, 31 Oct 40, Black Mt]

[6]Florence Hoagland.

I am very tired of innocence and polite pretty girls already! One spends one's *blood* and all they say is "Thank you so much, Miss Sarton" as if you had given them a light for a cigarette. [to BB, 11 Apr 46, DePauw University, Ind.]

I am really very tired of teaching, tired and dried up. I don't see how people do it for long periods of time without withering away. But I guess some people enjoy being analytic and intellectual whereas I know more and more that I am not an intellectual. The values which interest me passionately have to do with feeling; intellect is only useful for criticizing form in my own work, not for analyzing that of other people. [to BB, 31 Jan 53, Wr St]

I almost cried when I said goodbye to my 50 students[7]—losing them all at a blow. For they go on and one goes on and real friendships are rare out of teaching. But the relief of being free to be my real self makes up for everything. [to BB, 31 May 53, Wr St]

It is rather fun getting the Briarcliff lecture ready, "Novelist versus Poet," as it has made me think of all the others who have worked a double stream from Hardy, Meredith and De la Mare down to Elinor Wylie, Cummings etc. and what the kinds of experience are which are involved. One is forced to make dangerous general statements (but they can easily be qualified of course) such as that the writing of poetry is self-discovery and the writing of a novel the discovery of other people. [to LB, 9 Feb 55, Wr St]

I am hugely relieved to be through with the seminars at last—I realized when I laid down the burden of 32 women's psyches what the weight had been! Creative writing classes mean just that. . . . [to KD, 22 Mar 58, Wr St]

Very odd how similar my experience with W.[8] and my father's at Harvard—for the powers sneered at History of Science just as the powers at W. sneer at poetry-writing. Both are primarily *humanizing* disciplines. I feel strongly that

[7]At Radcliffe.
[8]Wellesley.

bringing thought and feeling together (as is so rare in college courses in general) is of primary importance if one is hoping to make whole women, and not just wry bluestockings and rugged encyclopedists. [to RG, 12 Dec 64, Nelson]

But as you say we live in a frightful society. I went into a black rage and depression in one class of freshmen whom I scolded for giving such a small part of themselves to their classes (as opposed to sports) and one slouching boy raised his hand to say, "I pay $4000 for a year here—why should I work?" This view is so twisted in so many directions that I was *speechless*. The professors are considered servants or dancing bears who are paid to "do their stuff," I suppose. [to BB, 24 Apr 75, Ohio Wesleyan]

What depresses me about teaching is the complete lack of any standards— how do you criticize when things far worse than those perpetrated by students are published? It is all such a welter of overblown "personalities" these days. [to BB, I Feb 76, York]

We travel with the richest of companions, and with her lucid observation and depth of understanding she virtually transports the places she visits, always seeing a country's marrow—

The Mardi Gras in Binche when she was not yet thirteen—

The "Mardi Gras" we went to the carnaval of Binche! It is one of the most wonderful things I have ever seen. I wish you had been there it was such fun. The "Gilles"[9] dance from 6 or 7 o'clock in the morning until I o'clock the following morning! They stop 3 seconds every time the music has played 5 times and only eat a very little. They drink only Champagne because they could not support anything else.

All the morning they dance until the "rondeau" of the afternoon and then they put on great high hats made of ostrich plumes. None of the gilles own

[9]Clowns.

their costumes but they rent them. All the year round they save to be able to pay the necessary money. The "gilles" march around in a great cercle in the market place, they try to make their cercle complete but it is very difficult with the crowd.

Each gille has a basket of a strange shape made for that; It is filled with oranges and they throw these everywhere on the windows, on the people. The windows are luckily all barred so there are none broken.

The morning the "gilles" have a kind of stick made of faggots like this [sketch] and they have masks, they are all the same with the same smile the same eyes and the same colors.

The "rondeau" at night was even more lovely, although they don't wear their hats the evening. It is done by torchlight and fireworks. And is perfectly beautiful, it is like a medieval picture. The fireworks throw their blue light on the white kind of bonnet that the "Gilles" wear and makes a curious effect.

All day the city is as if it was crazy everyone dances and everyone laughs, I did not hear anything cross or "énervé"[1] said and it was a lovely day. [to GS, 4 Mar 25, Chez Limbosch]

A rodeo in California—

Finally we arrived in the mad rodeo town full of cowboys in scarlet and blue satin shirts, their horses in silver trappings with gallon hats (sometimes a cowboy on his horse fully clothed—if the horse is a good one—is worth thousands of dollars!). The women are extraordinary and all look like moiré platinum blondes very much made-up. I have never seen such fantastic people and felt I was at a really American spectacle for the first time. We made our way through the mob to the grandstand where we sat in the top row of bleachers on perilous and very hard benches—and the rodeo was quite thrill-ing—bareback bull-riding in which some of the bulls are so pleasant and nonchalant that the cowboy has to spur them to make them buck—they have funny endearing faces and lumber off after they have thrown the man in a sad apologetic way. Sometimes when it is a wicked red bull it is quite exciting and

[1]"irritating."

I don't know how the cowboys stick as long as they do. The crowd gets up and yells "Ride 'em cowboy!" when it is a good one. No one gets hurt, to my great satisfaction. But I learned afterwards that they are terribly shaken up and those who go from rodeo to rodeo only have about 8 years of life. They did bronco-riding, bull lassoing, bull-dozing in which a man jumps from a horse to a running bull holding him by the horns and slips a rubber band around his nose. He used to throw the bull but this is now forbidden by law and old-timers consider rubber banding nothing at all. Then there were races, including a *wild* horse race—trick riding—trick lassooing by professionals. It went on for about six hours and we consumed a great many hot dogs, ice cream pies and peanuts and popcorn. [to EMS and GS, 21 Jun 34, Pebble Beach, Calif.]

A boat trip on the Lys—

The great event was last week when Aunty Lino, Claire and I spent the day on the Lys—I thought of you two on your engagement day. I must begin at the beginning—first I asked to be taken to see Daddy's house so we went on a pilgrimage along the quay and I took a picture of it which I hope comes out for posterity! We rang the bell and a very fat Flemish man with a little hat on smoking a cigar came to the door and let us go through the long passage that Aunty Lino remembered so well—after a time he told us, "Ah, mais Sarton, l'ancien ingénieur des chemins de fer—Mon père était Chef de Gare, il en parlait souvent!"[2] Then we went back via Catherine Spek[3] to get a little bag of "boules"[4] and so to our sumptuous boat. One of the lovely things is that with all their terrific personal economy they can enjoy spending and do it with an air—the boat flew the Belgian flag and was huge. Lino had ordered through people she knew a lunch packed with spécialitiés de Gand[5]—sandwiches to eat in the middle of the morning for we were already starved by the time we

[2]"Ah, Sarton, the former railroad engineer— My father was station master and spoke of him often."
[3]A woman famous for the candy she made.
[4]From an undated holograph note: "I—peppermint—dark brown striped with white—II—soft brown tasting of burnt sugar."
[5]"specialities of Ghent."

went aboard, fruit, a chicken and a bottle of wine! It was lovely being so few as we really sat silently for hours in the sun watching the incredibly lovely paysage[6] change like a dream before our eyes—I sat at the prow, Claire on the roof full length and Mamie[7] beside the man who ran it. If ever there is time we *must* do this once together. We stopped at Madame de Waert's, the painter on the way. The boat drew up to a tiny pier at the foot of an orchard, all green and luminous in the sunlight with a white farm and a delicious blue and white house seen under the trees. Madame saw us from a window and though she has been ill insisted on showing us all over the house, which is quite exquisite, one room painted pervenche-blue with a great deal of brass and painted china (a lovely combination)—a marvelous kitchen with a warm tiled floor leading out onto a great flower garden. I would have liked to settle right down and live there. One of the pleasures of such a journey is that one imagines a thousand lives one might live connected with each charming house. We passed the little pink café where Lino said you used to stop in her father's boat to have coffee—and then on and on through fields with lines of trees in the distance and the rich waterfalls of trees in the parcs, the small delicate chateaux—and then of course some hideous modern chalets. Our objective was the painter Klaus'[8] house, which has been turned into a museum. There we feasted, slept a little while on the bank and then looked at the Klaus paintings, some very beautiful but many I thought too *pretty* in color. But it is a lovely idea to go by boat to pay homage to a painter in the very landscape he painted so often. On the way home we stopped at Maurice Van der Noo's for a minute and there was Mathilde from "Les Asselles,"[9] who remembered Mother very well. Everyone of course asked after you both and was delighted to have news. It was really a fairy-tale of a day, absolutely perfect—great gray clouds that covered and then uncovered the sun—a wonderful changing light, and the whole thing so peaceful and lovely. Mamie said she felt when we came back that she had been round the world. It was really a great success and I am so grateful that

[6]"scenery."
[7]A nickname for Céline Limbosch.
[8]Émile Claus (1849–1924), Flemish impressionist painter.
[9]Les Assels, along the Lys near Ghent, country house of the Dangottes (parents of Céline Limbosch). See *I Knew a Phoenix*, p. 58.

you were able to do it as I couldn't have afforded it. [to EMS and GS, 12 Aug 39, Chez Limbosch]

A pueblo in New Mexico—

. . . I got warmly dressed and went off on a picnic to see some more Indian dances—the sun came out in a glory of cloud, clouds that seem like mountains, snowy mountains that seemed like cloud—incredible blues and reds on the cliffs as we turned off the roads and got into wide open country, with the Pueblo off in the distance looking like a legend up on a cliff across a wide dry river bed, golden in the sun. The air is crystalline, with that clarity that aches in your chest. The colors are really intoxicating. I am exhausted with excitement every time I go out. And when we got to the pueblo after eating our lunch against an adobe wall in the sun taking off coats it was so warm—then seeing hundreds of Indians sit in the plaza in every red and purple you have ever dreamed I thought I would burst! It was the corn dance, one of the most beautiful, the men half naked painted a strange green and yellow with long fox tails waving behind them, bright feathers, a shoulder band (like a cartridge belt) of bells around them, soft leather boots, wonderful heavy silver jewelry on their chests, *long* straight black hair falling down their backs. The women as usual hardly move but their small white feet, bound in white leather, are exquisite. The dance is slow, formal, repetitive, cumulative with a big chorus of old men who sing the chant and of course the drum never missing a beat, like the beat of life itself. These dances are grave and virile and so close to earth the excitement they provoke is not a theatrical excitement but a seasonal one, the sort of inner bursting that spring makes. They are really a great experience and what I had not expected with all the exploitation absolutely done for *themselves* as a Catholic might go to Church. We were the only white people at the dance that day. [to MFH, 4 Jan 41, Santa Fe (MA)]

A New England village—

I wish you could see a town like Newcastle[1]—it must be so different from your ideas of this rude country! It has a simple gravity and dignity that makes

[1]New Hampshire.

one believe in human beings again. And all is so light, the lovely wooden houses painted white and receiving the flowing shadows of great fountain-elms, the open emerald lawns with no fences going down to the water or to the road, and the people themselves, extreme individualists and anarchists. [to JH, I Oct 43, 22 E 10]

The city of Charleston—

Charleston is a wonderful romantic city, a woman like Venice or Paris, a city that seems to gather up in itself some nostalgia in everyman for a hidden secret part of himself. It is a compound of nostalgias—of the West Indies, the soft voices of the darkies and their laughing birdlike screams, and their bright dresses (a certain pink and a certain blue-green, and purple), mysterious courts and gardens just glimpsed behind iron grilles and high houses with balconies and curved flights of stairs leading to the doors. Some of the houses are painted pink and have *pignons.*[2] They look Dutch. Some of the streets are bare, sad and formal like an Utrillo. Some are elegant, patrician, and almost English. Charleston reminds one of many pasts and of other places and yet is entirely and always itself (as a beautiful woman evokes legends, Helen, Deirdre—and yet is unique and irreplaceable). And when you approach the city it's like entering a legend, for you enter by jungle-swamps, "the low country" with long gray mosses hanging from the trees and vivid evil green Virginia creeper and grapevines—something *primeval* and very soft—[HJ; Quoted in letter to BB, 15 Feb 42, Ch Pl]

A beach at Ogunquit—

The three days of the sea were like heaven. Oh that you had been there! I thought of you very much. It is the most beautiful place and years and years ago I was there as a small child, running about naked on the dunes and "gathering the wind" in my hands. It was wonderful to find it unchanged. There are great *falaises*[3] of red and black and gray rock with a carpet of laurel

[2]"gables."
[3]"cliffs."

Sarton at Ogunquit, 1916.

and asters and goldenrod and little white roses on top and below delicious sandy coves, hard-packed sand where the waves deliver their webs of lace— and then the incredible blue and green sea—great green waves rolling up and curving over into white white foam, like a dream of waves. One can dive into them and ride them like a dolphin. We explored all the little rocky pools looking for sea anemones and lay in the sand soaking in sun—and I persuaded Mother to come down for two of the three days which was a real fête, her first vacation for years. She was just like a child, her eyes so open to all wonders from the small purple asters to the *innombrable sourire*[4] of the sea. It was a very happy time and reminded me of old summers before the world became quite such a fearful place. [to JH, 5 Sep 47, Oxf St]

A pilgrimage to Rilke's chateau—

We aimed for Sion—do you know it?—with its two steep hills, one crested by a mediaeval castle in ruins and one with a 13th-century church? It looks exactly like the magical scenes one glimpses through the windows of 15th-century portraits. The town itself below rather grand and Catholic, sumptuous houses with tiers of iron balconies and large courts, a bishop's town, you know, with I am sure a small jealous aristocracy. We stopped for coffee while I went to ask the police where Muzot, Rilke's little chateau, could be found and they didn't know, so on we went to Sierre where there might be hope. Here the valley opens and smiles and there is room on the gentle slopes for innumerable villages and church towers. This is La Noble Contrée:[5]

> Chemins qui ne mènent nulle parts
> entre deux prés,
> que l'on dirait avec art
> de leur but détournés,
>
> chemins qui souvent n'ont
> devant eux rien d'autre en face
> que le pur espace
> et la saison.[6]

---

[4]"innumerable smile," a phrase used by Homer.
[5]"The Noble Region."
[6]"Roads which lead nowhere between two meadows, of which one speaks with art of their sequestered end, roads which often do not have anything before them other than pure space and the season." Quatrain #31 of Rilke's "Les Quatrains Valaisans."

I ran into a hotel to ask again, and everyone was so apologetic explaining they had only been there a year. The old Italian porter beamed and said he himself wrote poems but had never heard of Rilke—and then a little maid came and said, "But it is just up the hill, the next on the left." It seemed like a miracle and off we went, winding round and round, panting and coughing and the engine steaming like a train engine, higher and higher till we came to a most beautiful ancient village gathered round a church and what looked like Rilke's house—a steep rectangular forbidding stone building—and looking down into the valley, to the Rhône and the most luminous mountains. But it was not. It was Venthone instead and we had gone too far and missed a turning, so we crept down again and into gentler pastures and saw the little house in the distance. Here, after a terrible long silence, years, Rilke wrote the *Sonnets to Orpheus* and the great Elegies all *in three weeks.*

It is an adorable place. We wandered all around it, through thick grass fairly springing with water, so you felt a fountain might jet up under each footstep, streams running down on every side, channeled very carefully and here and there bursting into tiny waterfalls over a rock. We looked through the fence into the very much loved and cared-for garden, just careless enough, just secret enough—and then we lay down in the grass for awhile and ate our lunch and waited hoping the guardian would come back, the "demoiselle" a little boy told us lived there. But she never did and so we left the magic place and drove back to Sion, where Daddy was determined to climb one of the mounts and see the Museums—Mother and I now hot and tired—but it was worth the climb to be once more in these airy places, les pentes remplies de vignes, les grands aperçus adoucis par tous les travaux de la terre, une ampleur, une douceur partout.[7] [to JH, 13 Jul 48, Montreux]

A visit in France—

It is all like a dream—it was marvelous staying at the de Lestanville's—and Judy was delighted by all of it—they have a great dilapidated house full of charm and dirt—but we slept in pure linen sheets with a crown and the de

[7]"the slopes full of vines, the great vistas softened by all the worked land, an amplitude and sweetness everywhere."

Mlle. Penautot.
Credit: May Sarton.

Lestanville arms on them, were fed like kings—there is so much to tell I don't know where to begin. For instance they have a magnificent library, books all in wonderful bindings to the ceiling on all four walls, in a large case a crimson and gold saddle which was given to Madame's grandfather in Constantinople, and in Sweden—but the rugs looked as if they had never been beaten and everywhere a wonderful livable disorder reigns, punctuated by the exits and entrances, often through the windows, of *three* dogs, a huge black police who looks like a wolf but is so timid that he runs if you look at him, a griffon and a little fox terrier who yapped all night, chasing rats in the kitchen. After dinner we sat in the salon, a most elegant and beautiful room with much white, vermilion and gold, and an alabaster lamp lit from within. Marie de L. is a very Catholic woman, a most sweet and endearing character who works herself nearly to death taking care of a place which needs many servants and they have a few odd old retainers but nothing like what they need. There is a boy who takes the goats out every morn and they toll a great bell when it's time to bring them back. There is a Mlle. Penautot, an old friend of mine, who comes to help in the kitchen, and speaks the purest French I have ever heard though she is dressed in rags, and there is the former governess of the children who has come back to live with them and help out. There is also a cook, though she left the day before we came, and they had not yet got another. Marie milks the five goats herself and makes cheese to make a little pocket-money. Monsieur is a very witty original old man who teased us all the time and seemed the epitome of Gallic wit—white moustaches, brilliant black eyes, was a cavalry officer in World War I. We had lunch, a good contrast, at Madame Javarry's stone farm—she is a vigneronne[8]—her son, in overalls, with a beautiful lean dark face, and her daughter were there. They had just brought in the last of the hay and we had a wonderful meal in celebration with lamb chops grilled

[8]"winegrower."

over a wood fire, delicious—and of course Vouvray, 1948. In history they think there have been only three years as good as this. It will be a great wine. [to EMS and GS, 29 Jul 49, Pontivy, France]

The Hawaiian island of Maui—

I must say I enjoyed getting to Maui, which is like a dream of what a tropical island should be, very much. It is less sophisticated than here[9] and much less urban. We[1] stayed at a simply wonderful old hotel, now being refurbished, but still very "plain," over the lee side of the island where the whalers (as many as 600) used to put in for the winter. The whole town was like something in a Somerset Maugham novel—the first evening we sat out having drinks on the upper porch that surveys the town's main square and watched "life." Life was one person usually barefooted wandering across as slowly as is possible and still to move forward! For instance, a girl, barefooted, in a close-fitting pink kimono and nothing else went back and forth twice. Then a very old tattered man. That was about it. Below us in the bar three native Hawaiians played on their guitars, more for themselves than for anyone else. We looked out on a silken sea, a small harbor, and behind us pointed volcanic peaks dropped down to emerald green sugar plantations. Palms, banyans everywhere and huge hibiscus flowers. The island has long stretches without any human habitation—on one of these along the coast we saw a huge whale suddenly loom out of the perfectly calm sea—quite a sight. The next day we went on a grueling but fascinating drive around hairpin dirt roads, at every bend a deep declivity, narrow steep waterfalls and very lush tropical forests, dripping orchids, giant ferns, bamboo forests etc. The next day we climbed 10,000 feet (by car needless to say!) to peer into a series of extinct volcanos. What was beautiful was to look down on the island through the clouds, and wonderful clouds reflected in the water on all sides. Cora drove alternating with me, which was a help, and has given her confidence in her driving at last. [to JM, I Apr 57, Honolulu]

[9]Honolulu.
[1]Sarton was on a lecture tour, accompanied by Cora DuBois.

Farms in Belgium—

I took a five-o'clock train back and everywhere families were cutting and bringing in hay. It looked like a Brueghel—sometimes a man alone in a field with a scythe, sometimes a man cutting and a woman raking and spreading, sometimes a while family helping to load a cart. There was a wonderful sky with big white clouds shot through with blue. I did enjoy it all. [to EMS and GS, 15 Jun 49, Chez Limbosch]

In Linkebeek I looked out yesterday all morning at a man with two huge horses ploughing a field. There is nothing more beautiful than this. The slowness of it, and the look of earth, almost purple, as it is thrown over by the plough. The way the horses stand still, so patiently, while the man heaves the plough round for the turn, and shake their harness, and you can see the sweat on their rumps. They will be sowing winter wheat now the turnips are in. [to LB, 24 Oct 54, Chez Limbosch]

Nelson itself—

First about practical matters about the Nelson house. It is really very comfortable and I do have a telephone (one asks for Sullivan then Victor 7-3480). Nelson was once the center of all these villages, but they have separated off in the 19th century—so Sullivan is the telephone headquarters, Munsonville is the P.O. etc. It is quite confusing! It was all given in a grant as Monadnock No. 6 back in the 17th century. Nelson was then called Packersfield and renamed when Mr. Packer reneged on his promise to give the town 300 acres! The plumbers have now put in a "bypass" pipe and suction thing that keeps a little water flowing constantly from well to pump and I think that problem is now solved for good. I shall find out when I go back tomorrow as I imagine it went down to zero last night—am simply incredibly happy up at Nelson alone—each day seems like a great wonder and the absence of immediate pressures is of real help in my work, as I knew it would be. I often, for instance, do not have my supper till eight. And when I get up (around eight) and the sun pours in and I have a fire lit in my study and feel the whole day opening out, it is a wonderful feeling of release—I am learning an awful lot already, but of course must wait some years before I shall feel sure enough to use any of this material. I simply love all my neighbors—who are chiefly two retired missionary ladies who live in the parsonage back of the church (my least favorite, but they come to tea and to listen to records now and then and bring me news of Turkey—a wonderful description of a plague of locusts, for instance!). The lights I see from my house at night across the green are the Quigleys,[2] simply dear people and quite characters: he is a very good painter especially of portraits (was an intimate friend of Alec James, the painter, son of William James, now dead), and he also makes violins—his wife supports the family, I gather, by doing all sorts of odd jobs, including taking care each morning of the bedridden wife of 80-year-old Horace Upton, who delivers the mail. He is a whole legend in himself. Then there is the dilapidated farm full of cherished animals about two miles away along a primitive dirt road. They come and cut my meadow and store the hay in my barn—they have an angelic donkey whom I feed sugar to, many rabbits, a herd of cows, a goat, innumerable dogs, cats, kittens, birds in cages, goldfish, Heaven knows what! So you see I am surrounded by life, even up here.

I am sure that for a poet all these country images are very rich because they are immemorial and universal. [to KD, 7 Feb 59, Nelson]

Ruins in England—

. . . but I think the single most moving experience was Fountains Abbey—we were there after dinner, driving about three miles to the gates of a large estate, then through the park to another gate where one leaves the car. No one told us we had a three-mile walk ahead (fortunately as we might not have had the courage and it was worth it)—one walks first along a most ravishing 18th-century water garden, with a lovely Greek temple reflected in half-moon-shaped pools with long emerald strips of grass between, statuary, etc. No flowers, just marvelous great trees. A poem. Finally after this quiet walk for

[2]Albert and Mildred Quigley, neighbors in Nelson. See "Neighbors Happen" and "Death and the Maple" in *Plant Dreaming Deep*. Also "Death of a Painter" in *As Does New Hampshire*.

about a mile one sees the ruins of the abbey, immense and still. It is the most beautiful ruin I have ever seen and there is something very poignant about the complete great empty windows, sky instead of stained glass, and the swifts flying in and out among the broken arches. [to KD, 20 Jul 59, Cornwall]

An expedition in India—

Just back from my first expedition here—we left at 6:30 A.M. (you have to get going early before the heat) in two bicycle rickshaws to 3 temples off in the country—at that hour the whole scene is *Biblical*—low-lying lands, and dark, and the people walking barefoot wrapped in cloths of lovely colors, often violet or blue, some orange and yellow— They look quite Gothic (in *line*), long and thin and walk beautifully—everywhere cows and goats—we saw one jackal—the general color is reddish brown with some exquisite pale *bright* green rice fields and the temples standing up, surrounded by open *space* so they look very handsome from afar [drawing]—inside they are filled with squeaking *bats*. I love it here because everything takes place with a lot of *space* around it—a long line of bullock carts against the horizon, groups of women walking with loads on their heads. It is very ample and quiet like a scene in the Bible— So different from Calcutta! [to JM, 3 Apr 62, Bhubaneswar, India]

She also transports the people she meets and we live the notable encounters of her life. Whether it is her first meeting with Eva Le Gallienne—

On Wednesday afternoon we went to *Cradle Song*.[3] Mrs. Hotson sent round a card between the acts to ask if we might speak to Eva Le Gallienne after the play. The next act began. I couldn't pay any attention but only hope, hope, hope. At last the usher came back and whispered that we might. There were crowds of people or it seemed crowds—a whole group of flapperish high school students waiting for a chance. Once when the door opened I saw the back of her head.

---

[3]*Canción de Cuna* (1911) by Gregorio Martinez Sierra, translated by J.G. Underhill (1917).

At last she came, still in her nun's white robe but with the hood taken off. A funny little shirt showed over the top, and she was smoking. She was exactly as I have thought of her always: about my height, with fair boyish cut hair brushed back, a quiet willed mouth, roguish nose, fine forehead, beautifully molded strong hands. Her eyes are quite large and grey, straight clear eyes full of vision and sensibility. She was extremely cordial with a certain warm dignity. First she talked with Mrs. Hotson about a mutual friend. I hardly listened; I was trying to dig an ineffaceable memory of her in my mind. It seems, and this I did hear, that she is studying Russian in odd moments. Then she turned to me to ask about my acting. She was glad that I am still young. I got up courage to ask her what she thought about college. "No, don't go to college, you would be much too old to make a start. It takes ten years to get a real start. Get as much culture as you can by yourself—hear beautiful music, learn languages, and read, read, read." She is perfectly decided and clear cut in her way of speaking. Her voice in its tones and accents is exactly the same as her stage voice. [HJ, 17 Feb 28, Vassar College]

Or hearing Millay read her poetry in Cambridge—

I have now passed the gates of heaven and gone down into the dark week.

E. St. V. Millay! I was glad to have seen this creature whom A.L.T. and K.T.[4] always speak of with a subdued smile. I expected her to be pitiless and harsh and gay; I found her whimsical, very young; she made me think of a princess in a fairy story at first, later of Mélisande. She wore a dull green loosely falling dress, absolutely plain. It looked medieval. She came out carrying a bulky load of books and proceeded to sit down in a huge armchair, glaring at the latecomers. At last, after a gentle and very amusing fuss about the amplifier she began to read. First "My heart being hungry." I was terribly disappointed. I think because she was trying so hard to make the people in the back hear that she said it in a very distinct, rhythmical way without much sense. Then gradually she lost that quality (or I became used to it). She read "The Fall of the Year"[5] that one ends

---

[4]Anne Longfellow Thorp and Katharine Taylor.
[5]"The Spring and the Fall."

> Tis not love's going hurts my days
> But that it went in little ways.

That most beautifully. Later on she read the whole group of poems to D.C.,[6] Persephone not half as well as Jean! Anyway by the end we were all enchanted. The last glimpse was of her furiously scribbling E. St. V. Millay's on countless books. On the whole she gave me the impression of being a delightful but slightly spoiled child. [HJ, 19 Nov 28, Ray St]

Or the extraordinary summer of 1937—

At Elisabeth's[7] in her cool underwatery drawing room on Monday I met Virginia Woolf. This is something I have dreamed of for so long that the hugeness of transition into reality has been *terrific!* But good. I am going to see her again. In the middle of the evening she discovered that it was *I* who had brought the poems and was very nice about them. She will read the novel I think—en garde, Cresset![8] [to K, 16 Jun 37, Whipsnade]

I met him[9] there the other night but he was completely eclipsed by the presence of Virginia Woolf. Elisabeth has a very high cool drawing-room with great windows looking out onto the green trees of Regent's Park and the lake full of boats—the long pink curtains blow in and out. There are usually white peonies very open in a rococo shell on the mantelpiece. It is a formal room with a curious atmosphere of its own—into this stepped Woolf looking like a seahorse, delicate and fabulous and *exactly* as she should be. She went right over to the window and stood looking out until dinner was announced—the room affected her as being underwater and the rest of the evening was *Waves*-ian. She sat eating lettuce with her fingers and drinking white wine and talked about poplars to Elisabeth's fat cheerful husband, Alan.

[6]Dorothy Coleman, a close college friend whose untimely death moved the poet to immortalize her glorious singing voice in the elegies she called "Memorial to D.C."

[7]Elizabeth Bowen's.

[8]Cresset Press, the English publisher of *Inner Landscape*, for which Koteliansky was a reader.

[9]Sir Cecil Maurice Bowra (1898–1971), British classical scholar and literary historian.

I talked to Bowra as well as I could being constantly distracted by the presence opposite. In her own house Elisabeth brings people together and observes them happily, making no effort once they are gathered—she sits like a cat in a corner and watches. Finally dinner was over and (thank God for the British custom) E., Woolf and I had the submarine drawing room to ourselves. It was really most extraordinary because one couldn't help falling into this stream of consciousness conversation. I remember eating two little white pinks in the course of it and thinking it sounded so like a parody of *The Waves* that she would notice it and be horror-stricken. Well, the evening went on until I finally went and sat down on the floor very rudely and then Woolf turned to me and said, "Are you professional." When I first came to London I left my book[1] with some primroses at 52 Tavistock Sq. and had had a short note from her about them. I stammered something about it and then she said, "Oh it was you. It was you"—apparently they had come when she had no flowers and she likes the poems. I'm glad she only found out in the middle of the evening—it meant that one was exploring without introduction, so to speak. I'm going there to tea on Monday. [to EFK, 17 Jun 37, London (Huxley)]

Friday I came to London, staying at Elisabeth's. A *most* thrilling night. The Huxleys and I alone dined at H.G. Wells'—and went on to the ballet at Covent Garden. H.G. has a beautiful house on Regents Park full of flowers, of Chinese objets d'art (few and *good*), really an atmosphere of light and taste which astonished me. A delicious dinner. Then on to the ballet—the new Berlioz ballet, which is magnificent. Clemence Dane[2] was there and I had quite a good talk with Col. de Basil, who speaks English and French equally badly. Then we went back to H.G.'s for a drink—the whole evening had so much *glamour*, I can't tell you, really the most exciting and perfect I have ever had. [to EMS and GS, 8 Jul 37, London (EB)]

Or in Santa Fe—

[1]*Encounter in April.*
[2]Pseudonym of Winifred Ashton, English playwright.

We had brought a picnic—but finally landed with it in Brett's[3] studio—one room with a magnificent window on the Taos mountain—a little iron stove (as in N.E. railway stations) set up on a platform under a sort of pavilion, a lot of couches and beds, a bench for making the tin frames she cuts for her paintings which are incredibly bad— Lots of color and bright pieces of material, Indian rugs, jars full of crushed Christmas tree ornaments looking so magical—she uses them for appliqué decorative panels of fish and angels. There she was, deaf as a post, bright as a robin, *very* bright quick eyes and then her face falls away—but she is real and honest and simple, not at all like the legend. I always have a picture of her in my mind trying to wrest Lawrence's ashes from Frieda[4] or Mabel D.[5] [to MFH, 13 Feb 41, Santa Fe (AS)]

Or in the Weald of Kent—

I spent a heavenly day at Sissinghurst[6] in 1938, talking poetry. It is quite a fabulous place and seems like the very remote past when aristocrats lived in the country and really ran their estates. V. does a lot of gardening and farming—inside the big room when I walked in out of the sun (that smell of sunned grass!) my eye lit first on a lapis-lazuli table about six feet by four with a huge bowl of larkspur on it—and the whole place is like that, extreme luxury and perfect taste. There is a lake with swans, and also a moat where they swim among crimson water lilies. V.S.W. herself looked like Orlando,[7] for she wore riding trousers, rather peculiar old-fashioned boots, and then from the waist up was very feminine in an orange silk blouse with long earrings! It sounds awful but was queer and rather attractive. She looked very Spanish, and is as liberal as that great tradition behind her will allow. There is a certain noblesse oblige about her. But of course she could never quite escape and be a real writer. [to BB, 15 Feb 42, Ch Pl]

[3]Dorothy Eugénie Brett (1883–1977), painter, and author of books about D. H. Lawrence.

[4]Frieda von Richthofen Lawrence, wife of D. H. Lawrence.

[5]Mabel (Ganson) Dodge Luhan (1879–1962), American heiress and patron of the arts.

[6]Sissinghurst Castle, a large 12th-century manor-farm in Kent with lavish gardens, home of Vita Sack-ville-West and Harold Nicolson.

[7]The protagonist who is first a man, then a woman in Virginia Woolf's novel *Orlando*, dealing with three centuries of English history presented symbolically through the family heritage of Vita Sackville-West.

Or in Greenwich Village—

I intended to[8] last night but Giorgio[9] took me out and then up to St. Exupéry's (and I was too curious to say no). It was the end of a dinner party composed of André Maurois and his la-di-da wife who is Madame Cail-lavet's[1] daughter—and St. Ex and his extraordinary tough little South American wife who has no chic but lots of vitality—but something a little disorganized and cheap—and an unknown girl whose name I never caught and a Mr. Le Roy, who is a famous flutist. Giorgio and I arrived much too early at 9:30—they were just at dessert—there was no conversation to speak of though I tried to get Maurois to talk about his American college experiences but he is just tired and urbane and charming and a little vain. Both St. Ex and Maurois are really Vichy people it seems—I did not like what they said about France. Madame Maurois said she would never go back but they are so un-American and so smugly French that they will never be part of what is going on here. The whole thing made me sad—it was somehow shabby and an awful picture of the refugées—St. Ex started playing card tricks (he is really a magician at it) and I got more and more tired and finally left very rudely at 11:00. [to EMS and GS, 25 Jun 43, Hotel Albert, NYC]

Or Paris—

Yesterday was my big day. In the morning I dashed over to the Madeleine to cash some money, leave flowers at Grace Dudley's hotel to welcome her, and then to try to fix up my unfashionable clothes for the big UNESCO lunch[2] —I paid 1400 francs for a stunning blue belt which makes my little pink and white dress (which I bought for half that sum!) look suddenly quite dressy, then found a hat for 2200 (cheap it seems!) at a little place on this street—a piece of luck! It is a very French hat with a big blue bow, very much on one side of my head—really rather handsome but I doubt if I ever wear it outside

[8]Have dinner with Katrine Greene.
[9]Marquis Giorgio D(iaz) de Santillana (1902–), professor of philosophy and history of science, Harvard University.
[1]Mme. Arman de Caillavet, whose *salon* was a center of French literary life.
[2]Sarton's friend Sir Julian Huxley was first Secretary General of UNESCO.

Lugné-Poë, April 20, 1940.

of Paris! Then I felt more or less armed and went off to the Hotel Majestic—I sat between Malraux and Hill[3] (who edits *Fontaine*) with Stephen Spender on the other side of Malraux—it was simply marvelous to have a chance to talk long and seriously with Malraux and I fear I was rather rude to Hill in consequence. Malraux is feverishly intense and talked a blue streak, but so beautifully about the Resistance, France, the future, everything. It all poured out before me while I tried desperately to remember and have written most of it down. He is a Gaullist and believes there will be trouble here in November and that then de Gaulle will get in. "It is a matter of whether democracy can be made to work in France. The alternative is communism." We spoke of Spain and when I told him how rare I thought his combination of man of action and really great writer is, he said it was partly luck and quoted T. E. Lawrence as another instance of that kind of luck. Malraux is one of the few great men I have ever met—so pure and deep and so utterly without pretense of any kind. One sad thing he said about France today, "Il n'y a pas de foi. Il n'y a que colère."[4] After 1943 a great many people got on the Resistance bandwagon but before that it was pure, a "mouvement désespéré"[5] and so, pure. He spoke wonderfully about the Spanish anarchists and said he would love to go back to Spain—"except that I'm second on the death list." And he told me a beautiful story about his experiences in the Resistance—I've written all this down and will tell you when I can read it out of my diary. [to JM, 29 May 47, Paris (Mayer)]

Or remembering Lugné-Poë[6]—

---

[3]Henri Hill, critic, worked at UNESCO, was editor of *Fontaine*.
[4]"There is no faith. There is only anger."
[5]"hopeless movement."
[6]Aurélien-François Lugné-Poë (1869–1940), French actor, director, and theater manager.

I have been thinking (because of the book) very much of Lugné-Poë, rereading his heartbreaking notes all through the years up to Munich and then the gradual dark. He died luckily before the fall of France but not before his heart was broken: "Se verra-t-on jamais avec ses heures folles qui me *font si mal*,"[7] and this which finding again meant so much to me today (1938): "Mais ta lettre a l'air (assez?) filtrant la lassitude. Ah non! Pas ça de ta part—si toi tu manquais d'enthousiasme où irions nous? Tu comprends ce n'est pas pour jeter le manche après la cognée qu'un bon destin m'a dit à moi: tu laisseras tes armes en dépot aux mains de cet enfant qui poursuivra ici où là,"[8] and "ce qui me rend furieux c'est qu'il y a des heures de lumière où ce qui se passe dans l'humanité me parait *ignoble* et que j'enrage d'avoir été inscrit sur la liste des passageurs de ce monde!"[9] and finally, "Les forces me manquent et le mal va vite. J'en suis à m'interroger si je pourrai atteindre mai et aller jusqu'à Paris. Tu es arrivée à temps dans ma vie pour que j'ai pu t'entrevoir mais la vie des hommes d'aujourd'hui à fait du mal à l'idiot sensible que je suis resté et les nouvelles de chaque jour me tuent."[1]

Some of this you will find in the poem for Lugné,[2] but now I feel I must write another. It takes a long time fully to understand, darling, what any relationship holds, doesn't it? And now the riches of Lugné pour over me and I think it is a miracle that we met, he so old, I so young. I was nineteen, he was over sixty when we first knew each other and then he stopped writing suddenly and only much later told me that it was because he had been warned about his heart and couldn't bear to become attached to another human being he would have to leave. He was always such a violent angry man. You would have loved him. He would have loved you. [to JH, 24 Feb 48, Oxf St]

[7]"Will we ever see one another again in these mad times which cause me *so much pain?*
[8]"But your letter has a rather pervasive tone of weariness. Ah no, not that! If you lacked enthusiasm, where would we be? You know, it isn't just so that we could give up that a kind of fate told me, "You will entrust your weapons to the hands of this child who will carry on here or there.' "
[9]"what makes me furious is that there are moments of clarity when what is happening to humanity seems *ignoble* and when I rage to have been listed player on this stage."
[1]"My strength is failing me and the evil progresses quickly. At this point, I wonder whether I will be able to make it to May and to go as far as Paris. You arrived in my life just in time for me to be able to catch a glimpse of you, but the life of people today has hurt the sensitive fool that I have remained and each day's news kills me."
[2]"What the Old Man Said" in *The Lion and the Rose.*

Or on board the *Queen Mary*—

On the first day I saw that Rebecca West was in first class and in a burst of courage sent her up a note with a copy of my poems. She didn't answer for two days and I had given up when a very candid note arrived, saying she loved the poems (especially the American Landscapes) and would be down at my cabin at 8:15 that night to arrange for me to come up. They have very severe laws on this boat and she couldn't get permission, actually, but we had a drink in *our* bar that night and she came back for another at 5:00 the following afternoon with a rather dull woman friend. Anyway she was *awfully* nice—so eager and simple and gay, quite plain looking with kind bright brown eyes and a rather ugly arid mouth, the mouth of a great *talker*—I wish you had been here! When she left she said "but I haven't given you my address" as if she wanted me to call her, and as I didn't have a piece of paper wrote the following inscription in the enormous war book[3] Rinehart had given me:

> "From
> Rebecca West
> (who gives you this book,
> which it took her 11 years
> 6 weeks & 5 days to write)"

and then the address which I *can't* read! [to JM, 10 Apr 48, aboard *Queen Mary*]

Or her first meeting with Dorothy Wellesley—

Ruth[4] and I went down together in the train. We were met at the station by D.W.'s "man" who to my surprise shook hands with us and then ushered us into a sumptuous car, with all sorts of gadgets such as you never see in America anymore—a sliding panel between chauffeur and passengers, black silk curtains that could be pulled down to shut out the world entirely, very comfortable cushions, and so on. The village of Withyam is nothing and we

[3] *The Naked and the Dead* by Norman Mailer (Rinehart, 1948).
[4] Ruth Pitter.

soon climbed out of it across rolling not very fertile country and turned in to an unpretentious drive. Ruth suggested that we be dropped and walk up as I was so eager to get my feet on the ground and near to the primroses and violets that line all the roads. So we walked up to the house past a pasture full of baa-ing sheep and lambs (I think I would like to be a shepherd) to the warm brick house in the distance. It's a Queen Anne house, one which D.W. bought when she separated from the Duke many years ago and it is not "a great house," though very lovely and richly furnished with marvelous books, paintings etc. We went right up to an upstairs sitting room to meet the Duchess, escorted by an old butler who rules the house and is a dear. I was horrified by my first sight of D.W. She looked rather like the White Queen,[5] a bloated red-faced old woman with scraggly fair hair and messy lipstick, walking with great difficulty. She is crippled by neuritis and in continual pain and was having a bad day. We had tea (with no sugar), thin bread and butter, and a cake Ruth had brought. I soon found out that if anything duchesses in the country eat less well than modest working girls like Jane![6] And it is quite a shock and makes you feel what a Labor Gov. means and what the war has done, as the surroundings were really rather grand. D.W. is a rabid Tory, and no wonder, as the life she stands for and represents is finished and being quite deliberately killed off. But there was an uncomfortable moment when I said I was a socialist. However she is a rather hearty big tempestuous woman who likes character and honesty and we got on very well. She is an awful snob and continually teased Ruth about being "nobody" which I would have found very hard to take myself. As an American I escape all that. After tea we went for a long very slow walk all around the gardens with D.W. First there is a lovely wild garden built round a brook and a pool with cress growing in it and primroses and violets and forget-me-nots along its banks and lots of flowering bushes, almond and things like that, a fairy place. I saw my first fritillary, a most lovely white flower, a bell, octagonal shaped, very delicate and stately. Some are purple. Then into a large walled garden with fruit trees and beds of

[5]In Lewis Carroll's *Through the Looking Glass*. In Eva Le Gallienne's stage adaptation of *Alice in Wonderland and Through the Looking Glass*, produced in 1932 at the Civic Repertory Theatre, the White Queen was played by Le Gallienne; in January 1933 Sarton took the role while Le Gallienne was ill.
[6]Jane Stockwood.

grape hyacinth and lots of *blue* primroses, too lovely. Then out of that into the kitchen gardens and greenhouses where we sat down for a while as D.W. was tired. But all the gardens are seedy for lack of labor. The place required seven gardeners and she has one old man now. That is the way things are.

We talked of Yeats and other poets sitting on an old sack on a bench.

When we had got the old girl back into the house safely Ruth and I still had an hour before dinner (which was at eight) to explore the Rocks for which the house is named. They are a small hill of great decorative boulders, some with trees growing on them, holly and oak and mountain ash, with rhododendrons between them, a sort of wild island in the middle of the green meadows (with lakes of daffodils strewn across them). It must be a wonderful place for children. Under a giant cedar on our way in we found a dead jackdaw, his eye still bright and so living looking that it was quite startling to feel him stiff, poor dear. His feathers purple and deep blue were very lovely. We took him into the heart of the rocks and buried him under some bracken and then climbed a big rock and sat where we could see the house—it reminded me of the house in V. Woolf's *Between the Acts* as it is also set in a dell with hills all around. It must be melancholy and damp in winter. But it looked very lovely in the late afternoon sun. Double summer time means it's light till ten now.

We had a little drink before dinner, Ruth and I, and it was the last liquor I saw alas, as D. is not supposed to drink and so drinks secretly and doesn't remember to offer her guests anything. We went in to dinner in a formal dining room designed by Duncan Grant and Vanessa Bell, light gay colors, lots of mirrors, a huge table. There were three wineglasses at each place, but no wine (!), only a bottle of orange pop which looked very incongruous. For dinner we had some horrible carrotlike vegetable served as a first course, watery creamed chicken, potato and onions with cloves (ugh) and lastly a savory which was delicious of mushrooms on toast. It was the worst meal I've had. And the table was covered with ornate silver and everything served very formally.

After dinner we went up to the upstairs sitting room for coffee and Dorothy read her poems—she is really a great poet so one can forgive her eccentricity and snobbism and she was really awfully kind and so grateful. I fear very few people go down to see her anymore—she is like a great ruin of what was beauty and power and it is sad. [to JM, 28 Apr 47, London (JS)]

Or hearing Marianne Moore read in Cambridge—

I had a wonderful letter from a woman I don't know in Cal. about the *Atlantic* poem.[7] It ends "The least I can do is absorb your poem and live it." That is how I felt after we heard Marianne Moore speak at Harvard the other day. I simply ached with delight and a desire to laugh all the time, just because she is so marvelously original and unexpected in all she says. And is so humble, Bill, it made me feel very humble and ashamed. I went up to speak to her afterward and she looked at me with a stricken face and said, "Miss Sarton," then when I mumbled something about pure delight she said in a most tragic voice, "I know. I know that not one of my poems can really stand." In anyone else it would have seemed false modesty, but one had to believe she believed it. And she said, "I am gay, being of a melancholy turn of mind." And she said, "Revision is its own reward." [to BB, 12 Dec 48, Oxf St]

Or an unexpected encounter at the Huxleys'—

I was dispatched in the UNESCO shiny gray Dodge and chauffeur to meet the Golden Arrow from London at six and kidnap Freya Stark passing through on her way to Asolo. It was nightmarish trying to sort her out of the crowd as I have only seen her once, but there she was, all in stripes and reds and blues (she dresses fantastically) with a very tall slim elegant blonde who turned out to be the Vicountess Ruthven (pronounced Riven), who had also come to meet Freya. They disappeared in a taxi while I went back for Juliette with the car full of their bags and turned up here an hour later for dinner. We were just sitting down with a drink when the doorbell rang. There is no chambermaid now and it was the new cook's first night so I rushed to open, only to be confronted by two fabulous women. One about sixty looked like a greatly exaggerated and ancient Le Gallienne—she had on a skirt to the floor;

[7]Probably "Now I Become Myself," which the *Atlantic Monthly* bought in September.

a very 18th-century red brown corduroy coat with the légion d'honneur in the buttonhole and a jabot and looked rather like the White Queen. Her companion had blue hair, was much made up, very tailored. They asked for Mrs. Huxley and I was so sure they had come to the wrong house that I made them repeat the name. They insisted they were invited and then murmured "the Duchesse de Clermont-Tonnerre."[8] I had an immediate brainstorm as I had written a lot of the cards for the cocktail party and apparently no one could read the date (I was not meant to be a private sec.) so they thought it was yesterday! Nothing to do but invite them in. Well, they came and sat and exuded charm and interest, having no idea who Freya was and making one gaffe after another. At one point the duchess turned to me and whispered in stentorian tones, "You are American so you don't mind if I'm anti-British." I hastily replied "Don't, not here," and I still don't know who heard and whether she herself got the point. However the French of this kind are quite unbelievably provincial, look at everything from France's point of view etc. Finally when they had been there three quarters of an hour, Freya got up and they left and we gobbled our dinner and she made her train by a split second! [to JM, 29 Jun 48, Paris (Huxley)]

Or meeting Frank O'Connor at Bread Loaf—

But this is nothing compared to what Frank O'Connor does—he came up for three days with no lectures prepared, but gave two marvelous ones—one felt just "ripeness is all" and all the wisdom and craft he has distilled over the years was just there in his hands. I learned a great deal from him—and such a wonderful face too, a long bony head with black bushy eyebrows and white hair, growing far back on an El Greco forehead. He has the quality one imagines Tchekov must have that it is something beyond what he says, just sheer humanity on a gigantic scale.[9] [to BB, 15 Aug 53, Bread Loaf]

Or a dinner with Le Gallienne—

[8]Title of Elisabeth de Gramont, the author of several volumes of memoirs and biographies.
[9]See "Der Abscheid" in *Cloud, Stone, Sun, Vine.*

Last night was a continuation of my birthday as Le Gallienne was here and we had a bang-up supper in her room at the Ritz and a long very good talk, looking down on the public gardens, a red umbrella, empty benches, the round soft umbrella shapes of the trees just in leaf, the little formal parterres of pansies, and rain. I was happy to see her this time at her very best, the true glory and greatness. This is something absolutely *pure* which she possesses and which I have never seen in another theatre person. The tragic thing is that it is not being used— though she has made a good life without the theatre now. She has just designed and added a guest wing to her house and wants me to come in June so maybe I could drive you back (though maybe the train is more restful, I don't know)—we talked about the possibility of a novel on the subject of women or should I say "Extraordinary Women"?—a project for my extreme old age I think. And about Virginia Woolf. And about various things Le G. is writing herself. Today I went to hear her read Shakespearian scenes and really play the whole of the Happy Prince at Simmons—a performance of the most subtle and perfect *control*. I wish you had been there. She looked very tired and—alas—very old the night before, and then it was exciting to see the stage presence, so radiantly alive, beauty put on from the inside, so to speak, and the amazing sapphire eyes, a *different* person. [to LB, 5 May 54, Wr St]

Eva Le Gallienne.
Credit: Albert
Petersen.

Or a visit to Isabel Fry[1]—

This can hardly be a letter. The physical circumstances are too uncomfortable, for I am sitting under the eaves of a 16th century farmhouse which is in a dell and *totally* unheated. I do have a small electric heater which roasts one side while the other freezes (this induces a split personality I fear), but the temp must be under forty. Luckily I bought some wonderful fur-lined boots in London and I have on two sweaters and a leather jacket. This is Isabel Fry's

[1]Isabel Fry (1868–1957), sister of Roger Fry, founded the Farmhouse School. Close friend of Eugénie DuBois.

Isabel Fry. Credit: May Sarton.

house—it is inhabited by her, 84, and so British in the good eccentric way that I am all the time trying to keep from laughing because it is so like an invented character in fiction. She has a high pointed head like an El Greco, straight white hair like a man's only a bit longer, very keen bright brown eyes, a hawk nose, heavy tweeds, thick sweaters, huge silver brooches etc. She has been a great lover of women in an unconscious Victorian way (though perhaps I underestimate her there), but at any rate passionate and jealous. She flew to Turkey last year, in spite of bad arthritis and a bad back that goes back to a cricket accident when she was a girl ("I was very keen"), and here she lives now with three geese, a cat and an endless stream of people of every race, color and belief flowing in and out. The permanents are an Estonian woman and her two daughters and an Estonian Gardener-Chauffeur, all members of the family in that they eat with us, and are read aloud to periodically by Isabel. Last night we unfortunately embarked on politics and I was horribly distressed (as well as violent) to discover that they think we should make war with Russia *now*. It opened up all the horror of this responsibility we all have, I expect, inwardly at least to make up our minds, to throw our psychic weight in one direction or another. I cried for hours afterwards—really these abysses which open up are terrifying. However, all is peaceful this morning and I can hear Isabel coughing downstairs which means that she wishes to talk. I forgot to say that she paints wild flowers ("I am only interested in weeds") really very well and brings out portfolios of these. It is a great thing to see someone so old, so alive, passionate, humble and torn. Blessèd are the sinners for they never grow smug. She is anything but that, most lovable really. [to LB, 10 Nov 54, Church Farm, Aylesbury, England]

Or one with Princess Caetani[2]—

I am still rather seedy, feeling ill rather than well, with bed and a hot water bottle the desiderata—but there is Paris outside, meltingly gentle, the chestnut leaves falling and the formal parterres all aflame—today I went to the marché aux fleurs[3] and walked about among all the heavenly soft blue and purple primulas and the trays of amazing cactuses and the ferns and big bunches of asters and zinnias, and bought a pot of basil to take to Belgium. This was after having lunch with the Princess Caetani—she is really a very endearing person, who moves by instinct rather than perhaps a very developed taste, but I trust that sort of person. Also she laughs as my mother did till tears squeeze out of her eyes and I loved that. It was rather fun to go across to the Right Bank—she lives in a very shabby book-full, painting-full apartment on the second floor of a house which the Rothschilds own and are deliberately allowing to fall to pieces. When it has reached a state of ripe dilapidation, they will sell (or so she says). She took me to an Italian restaurant where I could have pasta and things good for my state. And I was pleased because there were no flowers at all in her apt. and I had brought three very fat bunches of really adorable roses, pale yellow, a soft pinkish-red and a deeper yellow like roses out of a garden. I have an idea that she is surrounded by poor poets and artists who exploit her rather. Oh dear, this is such a bad description because I am so queer and tired, darling. Two words do not go together. She spoke very warmly of you and longs for poems, by the way???? [to LB, 5 Oct 54, Hôtel Saint-Simon, Paris]

Or hearing Katherine Anne Porter at Wellesley—

But Katherine Anne Porter was a very strange apparition—she talked about herself nonstop, a monologue which began at the tea at four (I hear) and continued throughout the dinner which I did attend, and her speech was simply an egocentric ramble through her novel (no word showed that she was

[2]Princess Marguerite Caetani, editor of *Botteghe Oscura*. She was famous for nurturing young talent.
[3]"flower market."

addressing an audience of *students*)—she *says* that people criticize her characters as so awful but what she wanted to get across was that evil is caused by
"the damned" *plus* the good who are too indifferent to act. I can see that this
was a clear truth when Nazism began, but as a total view of life I still feel it is
too cynical. Her public personality (surely a mask) is, alas, a rather foolish
Southern belle, confiding in the audience as in a trusted friend. The attend-
ance was huge and we all applauded and stood to welcome her—a real
ovation. She wore what looked like two white gunny sacks (to the floor) and
long white gloves which hid the huge emerald ring which she bought for
$12,000 I hear! [to KD, 29 Sep 62, Nelson]

Or the death of Henry Copley Greene[4]—

Avant hier un très vieil ami à maman et à nous trois est mort. Il avait vers 85
ans et avait été dans une peine cruelle depuis des mois, alors c'est une bénison
pour lui de partir. Mais pour nous c'est un grand vide. Il était de ceux qui
partent vraiment, d'une génération noble et entière que nous ne voyons plus
sur cette pauvre terre. Il s'était épris d'une passion pour la France et deux fois
(dans la première guerre de 14 et après celui-ci bien qu'il était alors vieux et
malade) il s'est dévoué à la reconstruction. Un homme de moyens, mais dont
la vie était d'un pauvre car lui et sa femme avait littéralement *tout* donné sauf ce
qu'il fallait pour vivre très simplement. C'était pour moi tout ce qu'il y a de
plus noble dans l'espèce *Américain* (il venait d'une vieille famille de Boston
d'ailleurs). Pendant des années il a été dans la peine continuelle et atroce et à
cause de cela vivait par des drogues. Mais il ne voulait pas se coucher et même
après une opération qui a paralysé un côté il sortait *seul* avec une canne,
tombant plus d'une fois par terre, refusant tout aide. Quand il vous prenait la
main un tel amour sortait de lui dans la poignée que j'avais toujours les larmes
aux yeux. Et avec cela, d'une réserve extrême. Il s'appelait Harry Greene. Ses
trois filles sont comme des soeurs pour moi. Et sa femme une très grande
amie.[5] [to MC, 31 Dec 51, Myn Pl]

[4]Husband of Rosalind H. Greene, who with their daughters Ernesta, Francesca, Katrine, and Joy were
friends of the Sarton family. Ernesta died in 1939.
[5]"The day before yesterday a very old friend of mother's and of all of us died. He was about 85 and had
been in great pain for many months, so it is a blessing for him to be gone. But for us it is a great emptiness.

Like Virginia Woolf and Sylvia Townsend Warner, Sarton made use of her father's library, both its books and records. And Cambridge itself was for her a Byzantium of concerts, theaters, lectures, and libraries, which she devoured not only as a child but for all the years she lived there—

This weekend is just about perfect. I feel like a wanderer in Paradise. This afternoon E. St. V. Millay is reading from her poems, and tomorrow Eva Le Gallienne is coming up from New York to lecture at the Old South Church Forum. If I had been given three wishes those would undoubtedly have been two of them, and a letter from you a third, so really I think I must have a fairy godmother. [to AT, 8 Nov 28, Ray St]

On Thursday I spent some two hours writing a sonnet. It is fairly good for a first attempt. That and Chaliapin saved the week. After all I am one of the luckiest people on earth if I could only realize it. We went to Symphony Hall this afternoon to hear Chaliapin. He is a great singer and a great actor, full of life, of zest. He gives out of himself joyously and fully. He is never still, an eyebrow, a hand, a foot, a shoulder, he is always acting with something besides his splendidly changing voice. [HJ, 11 Mar 28, Ray St]

I went to the *Missa Solemnis* and Beethoven's first three symphonies with Daddy on Tuesday and Wednesday nights; I enjoyed them ever so much, especially the second movement of the third. I knew the first symphony quite well, as we had analyzed it in Miss Hancock's class; it was exquisitely played. During the third symphony Letty[6] and I went down to some vacant seats in the third row!

He belonged to those who come truly from a noble and whole generation which we don't see anymore on this poor earth. He was smitten with a passion for France and twice (in the first war of 1914 and the one after that even though he was then old and sick) he devoted himself to the reconstruction. A man of wealth, who lived the life of a poor man because he and his wife had literally given away everything except that which they needed to live on very simply. For me it was all that is most noble in the American nature (moreover he came from a very old Boston family). For many years he had been in continual and atrocious pain and because of that had had to live on drugs, but he did not want to stay in bed and even after an operation which paralyzed one side, he went out alone with a cane, falling more than once on the street, refusing any help. When he would take your hand, such a love came from his grasp that I always had tears in my eyes. And with that warmth, there was an extreme reserve. He was called Harry Greene. His three daughters are like sisters to me. And his wife is a very great friend."
[6]Letty Field, friend from Shady Hill; died in 1930.

It was extremely interesting to be so near Koussevitsky. [to EMS, ? Mar 27, Ray St]

On Saturday, a blessed oasis, I went to Hamlet for the fourth time. Again I have resolved to learn all those aching words, to say when I am in need of beauty. There is nothing more relaxing than to have all the atmosphere of one's doubt and dread put into music. It is a deeper experience each time. Each separate word has its particular flavor which I wait for eagerly.

As we came out I looked up at the grimy windows of the Arlington Street Hotel. In one a pale sad face looked down, leaning on a frail hand—my heart jumped "Fritz Leiber."[7] It may well have been. How terrible for him to see the bustling inconsequential crowd after such words. I was glad when he turned away. I realized how lonely a face it was and how aloof from most lives. I wondered if I too would ever look on such a crowd from a high window and regret. "Something too much of this."[8] . . . On Friday night I went to the opera with Bob Kennedy.[9] I was glad he asked me. It was Mozart's *Seraglio;* deliciously fresh, spring-y music. The American Opera Company is breezy, eager, intelligent, but chiefly radiantly young! Bob insisted on bringing me home in a taxi to my great delight. It gave us a nice time to talk. He too has loved *The Bridge of San Luis Rey* very much. I must read it. Next however I am going to read Tolstoy's *L'enfance, L'adolescence.* It will be good to roll French around my tongue again. I am fearfully out of practice. [HJ, 18 Mar 28, Ray St]

I am happy the minute I am in this room and working, and in Daddy's room full of music—he has the most wonderful collection of records—yesterday I played a Chausson trio. It is the only escape for me, because it is no escape but an abstraction, an essence. It *rests* the spirit and lifts it for a moment from bumping along on the earth. [to K, 21 Nov 37, Ch Pl]

[7]The Shakespearean actor.
[8]*Hamlet*, III, ii.
[9]Son of Edith Forbes Kennedy.

At present I am reading in small doses a short history of the drama, a book on the "Technique of Speech"; *Anna Karenina;* a history of ancient Europe; excerpts from L. da Vinci's sketchbooks, and a play a week for my modern drama. I find this plan of reading excellent and it keeps me fresh and with a broad outlook even though absorbing a great many facts. [HJ, 14 Jan 29, Ray St]

And this plan of reading and of self-education was there from the start and never ceases—

We are going to the village tonight and we are going to read on the way we have finished Pickwick papers, and are reading The Cloister and the hearth.[1] [to EMS, 16 Jul 21, Greensboro, Vt.]

Mother, I have found out something terrifically exciting. Mrs. Evans[2] gives writing courses in the winter. Just think! Don't you think I might be able to have one lesson a week with her to save me from the boredom of High & Latin.[3] It is $5.00 a lesson. Of course I could have it only every two weeks or even once a month if we couldn't afford it. [to EMS, ? Jul 28, GSLT]

The Cortina course[4] has come and looks very good. . . . But I can hardly wait to begin. I am buying *The Oxford Book of German Verse*—a secondhand copy in excellent condition for $3.00. You see it starts with very simple old lyrics which are easy and delightful to read and gets harder as it goes on. Then I wish if you have a German Bible and a dictionary you would send them because there doesn't seem to be a dic. with the course. [to EMS and GS, 10 Sep 29, 94 Macd]

About books—I wish you could make out for me a simple course of reading in philosophy which then I can follow because I really don't know where to

[1] *The Cloister and the Hearth* by Charles Reade (1814–84).
[2] Florence Evans.
[3] Cambridge High and Latin.
[4] A self-teaching German course which she sent for.

LEFT. May Sarton, portrait by Polly Thayer. Credit: Susan Sherman.

RIGHT. May Sarton, etching by Polly Thayer. Credit: Susan Sherman.

begin. This summer I read some Plato. Would it be a good idea to begin with a general book like Durant's *Story of Philosophy?* If so have you got such a book that I could borrow. [to EMS and GS, spring 1930, 94 Macd]

I'm reading a lot—and really getting educated even if there is no degree at the end. [to RWB and Polly, 9 Aug 42, Sudbury]

I couldn't agree more about the intellectual life—people who don't read really stop growing in one sense. Also it is the way out of the too personal to the universal, the point of comparison, that gives one a sense of proportion. I'm avid to get back to the Athenaeum. [to JM, 14 Aug 48, Oxon]

I have become rather religious you will be interested to hear and at the moment cannot get interested in reading much except *The Imitation of Christ* and philosophy. Also a fascinating journal of Charles Du Bos[5] with brilliant criticism of French literature in it. [to JM, 22 Aug 48, London (RP)]

J'ai finalment eu le courage d'aller chercher ma carte pour la grand bibliothèque de Harvard. J'ai le droit de me promener dans les rayons même des livres, humant cette odeur de vieux cuir, et tâchant de ne pas écouter tous les petit cris "Me voilà"—mais de chercher ce qu'il faut; ce matin des livres sur Thoreau, le cher homme que j'enseigne à partir du 5 fevrier. Je suis revenue avec un tas de livres dans lesquelles j'étais plongé quand le "chéri"[6] est venu.[7] [to MC, 22 Jan 51, Myn Pl]

I have been having an orgy of reading too because a batch of books came from England, Charlotte Mew's *Collected* (strange, tragic, not wholly "arrived" poems, perhaps), a perfectly wonderful book on Myth and Ritual in Christianity the first two paragraphs of which sent me into a trance of happiness that might turn into a poem, and "Mind You, I've Said Nothing," which is good for some chuckles, but perhaps overrated on the whole. And then I am still deep in Cather, Malraux's "Les Voix du Silence," which I absorb in small quantities. [to LB, 8 Apr 54, Wr St]

In one of your letters you asked whether I really knew English lit, the older poets I presume you meant. That is a good question. It is true that I missed out by not going to college on the kind of big survey courses which run through the gamut from Beowulf to Eliot. But I think I have made up for this lack by studying very deeply certain poets for whom I felt a particular affinity and some for whom I felt none, but from whom I could learn. I have really *studied* Donne, Wyatt, Herbert, Vaughan, Traherne, Shakespeare, Clare, Hardy (the poems especially), G. M. Hopkins, Yeats, Emily Dickinson,

---

[5]Charles Du Bos (1882–1939), French literary critic and man of letters, convert to Roman Catholicism.
[6]Marie Closset's name for the postman.
[7]"I finally had the courage to get my card for the great library at Harvard. Now I can walk in the light even of books, inhaling this smell of old leather, and trying not to hear all the little cries of "Here I am," but to look for what I need. This morning it was some books on Thoreau, the dear man I begin to teach as of February 5. I came back with a pile of books which I had already plunged into when the mailman arrived."

Frost, Milton (but long ago), Tennyson, Byron, Keats, Shelley, Wordsworth, and outside of English I have read very consistently and studied Leopardi, Ronsard, Scève (the French Donne), Valèry, Rilke, Goethe and among the modern French besides Valèry, Apollinaire, Saint-John Perse, Supervielle, Jammes. I forgot Eliot, whom I studied very hard in order to teach a course one summer in the roots of modern poetry: Hopkins, Yeats, Eliot. The modern poets in America are many of them my friends (John Holmes,[8] Eberhart, Wilbur, Louise Bogan, Marianne Moore, even John Ciardi are all or were once friends of mine). I do not know Chaucer at all well and it is one thing I plan to do. (Of course I have read him but not really studied him). [to KD, I Jan 62, Nelson]

Her insights into writers offer insights into herself, into what she values both as woman and writer, and chart pathways for her readers—

I have started Josephine Preston Peabody's[9] Diary and Letters as Aunt Agnes[1] advised me. They are wonderful, exquisite "things." It encourages me to keep on trying. [HJ, 27 Feb 28, Ray St]

I read a little of K.M.'s[2] journal, which like Josephine Preston Peabody's is full of arrows which I shall never be able to pluck out of my heart. [to EMS and GS, 29 Dec 29, 94 Macd]

Have been reading Angna Enters'[3] book *First Person Plural*—I wonder if it's come out in England. It's an extraordinary book because it is five hundred pages entirely about her work—the places, people, painters, music that have

[8]John Holmes (1904–1947), American poet, teacher, and critic. He was part of the poets' group which met at one another's houses in Cambridge, Lincoln, or Medford, Massachusetts, and in which Sarton participated along with Richard Eberhardt, Richard Wilbur, and John Ciardi for three winters during the late 1940s.
[9]American poet and playwright (1874–1922).
[1]Agnes Hocking.
[2]Katherine Mansfield's.
[3]American dancer, painter, and author (1907–49).

been built into it. The curious thing being that it is so much more personal than anything she could have said about herself qua self apart from her work. Have been rereading Bovary in a state of acute delight—those wonderful descriptions of her clothes, of the wedding cake with the first layer a Greek temple, the second a romantic garden and so on, the precision of detail in that pure flowing style—the kind of excitement that water creates in a landscape. And who is there to read now? I am fed up with the lack of standards, the sloppiness, the sentimentality and brutality of fiction today—or you get Hemingway whose virtuosity makes you gasp and lack of anything to say leaves you dissatisfied, angry. I do think *Fontamara* and *Bread and Wine*[4] great books, the only new ones I have read that seemed worth the time, and they are not so new. [to EB, 16 Jan 38, Ch Pl]

I have been reading the second volume of Monique St.-Hélier[5] and it is really very good stuff, full of matter and blood as well as the constant excitement of a style perfectly matched to the idea; nervous, perceptive, with a kind of tenseness and iron in it rare for a woman and bringing tears to one's eyes over and over again as she knows so perfectly when for a second to relax the tension. The first one is *Bois Mort.* Do get it. [to JH, 14 Aug 38, aboard *American Importer*]

For the present I am steeped in Rilke. Very few people dare go as far as he—very few people can surrender themselves far enough freely enough. It seems to me that he exists at the places where other people cease to exist, or cannot admit existence, because that is such a solitary place they cannot stand it. (I am one of those.) He is the only lyric poet who has seen what Eliot says somewhere: "Teach us to care *and not to care*" as a fundamental truth in love. He understood that one cannot ever become attached to life at its center, at its reality, without first having become painfully detached from it. [to K, 18 Dec 38, Ch Pl]

[4]Both by Ignazio Silone (1900–1978).
[5]French psychological humanist writer (1895–1955).

Paris was so quiet and *great* and beautiful—I had two lovely days by myself wandering about, buying books and sitting in the gardens not reading them. But I have decided that *Mauriac* is the great French writer—and this perhaps because he is Catholic (*not* in Eliot's peevish way) and his world is pivoted in good and evil—all his novels are *terrible*—all the stories of how souls are lost—but what a writer! [to K, 23 Aug 39, aboard *Normandie*]

I know that most writers are somewhere up the side of the mountain, some on little hills of their own, but Tolstoy is on the top of the mountain and the air there is quite different—it is so complete. He has solved once and for all *all* the problems—the going deep into character and still maintaining a large frame and idea, the infinite tasting of the moment without sacrifice to it (as in V. Woolf)—to read a page is nourishing as to read the whole and one can only think it miraculous. Also the *kind* of love he arouses in the reader is the great impersonal kind like Beethoven and Mozart, not the "I know all about you—that is just the way *I* feel" which the more personal lesser endearing poignant people like Chopin and Mansfield and even Tchekov do. It is so large and all-embracing. [to K, 17 Mar 40, Ch Pl]

Also K.M.'s[6] Scrapbook which has been O such a blessing and relief, such a *pain* of rediscovery like being suddenly planted into the center of someone's life whom one passionately loved long ago. As you say, parts are cruelly painful. One aches all over after reading them—but it is curious how she would never never in prose have done the bad things she does in poems (of course they were not meant to be published)— Over and over again it is the sheerest genius—who else could do what she does in "By Moonlight" when the mother is seen for an instant in the silent hall and then she goes dreamily over to the hall-stand and picks something up. "Why," she murmured aloud, "is there always an odd glove? Where does it come from?" One simply cries out, "Yes, there it is. That's how it is." [to K, 11 Feb 40, Ch Pl]

But the experience of the summer, what I have lived on, what has sustained me and cured me forever of impatience and ambition, have been Flaubert's letters.

[6]Katherine Mansfield's.

I cannot bear to have finished them. I have been living with him now for three months. He is a saint. And also of course a failure, a raging, unhappy, self-tormented, supersensitive gentle bear of a man whom one adores. It is a sad story with its culmination in three books while life was still in him powerfully and the critical sense had not overcome the creative sense, and the fearful concentration had not destroyed or warped the flow of life in him. O the balance, the balances between life and work. How can they be settled. Who can manage them. [to K, 24 Aug 41, Rockport]

I was interested in what you say of Mann—I love *Death in Venice.* Have you read it? It is maladif[7] of course but wonderful. But most of them have a dark and stuffy *smell* to me like red velvet sofas or the pantries of well-fed burghers. The *air* is very heavy in a Mann story and, as you say, one misses the French "clarté."[8] Did you see Janet Flanner's brilliant Profile of Mann in the *New Yorker* some weeks or months ago? It is curious how Mann has put himself over in America where, apparently, he is far more highly regarded than he ever was in Europe, even in Germany. [to BB, 9 Jul 42, Sudbury]

But I've buried myself in George Eliot's curious passionate egomanic and somehow *noble* life even though she did devour lovers like a female spider. And how glad it makes me that I am not a Victorian—that consuming longing for "respectability" which gnawed her always even though she had the courage to live her own life in spite of it—and the pathetic story of the party she and Lewes gave to celebrate his editorship of the *Fortnightly Review* (they had been living together for over ten years)—hiring musicians, ordering champagne and flowers, and butlers, and then *waiting* and *waiting* until 14 out of 140 guests showed up. [to MFH, 8 Aug 42, Sudbury]

I really hated the Huxley novel[9]—the sex in it seemed so 1920-ish and I really so despise books that talk about mysticism and are so wrapped up in the flesh at its most sordid and sensational. Give me a G.I. Joe looking for a female any

[7]"unhealthy."
[8]"clarity," "brightness."
[9]Probably Aldous Huxley's *Time Must Have a Stop,* 1944.

day—that at least has a certain indisputable *reality.* [to BB, 30 Mar 45, Santa Fe (ER)]

I'm glad you are with Dinesen—isn't she mysterious? Have you come to that beautiful short parable in the notebook section called "I will not let you go until you bless me"?[1] Her ability to get inside the skins of the natives and yet always to preserve the sense of mystery, aloofness and dignity in them is wonderful, I think. And the whole book has the clear atmosphere of plains high up, a mountain air. [to BB, 17 May 43, 5 E 10]

On the train I read most of the short novels of Henry James and it was pure delight, the perfect escape from the flat student minds I had to cope with most of the time. It is really all about a sense of values, isn't it? And how rare that is in literature, or anywhere for that matter. [to BB, 15 Mar 46, Oxf St]

I have read nothing that moved me deeply except one day a friend came and read the Spanish poems of Gabriela Mistral (she is the Chilean woman who won the Nobel Prize) and suddenly it seemed as if all our poetry was so sophisticated and self-conscious and afraid. She dares to be lonely, to be sad, to be happy, to be afraid—to be, in short, herself. A strong tender woman's voice. And I was ashamed— Everyone in Chile knows her as if she were their mother. The children learn her poems by heart. [to K, 2 Apr 46, Oxf St]

Have you read Kierkegaard? I am plunged into it up to my ears. Wonderful stuff that you have to mine for—for his tortuous style and fearful self-consciousness put off a natural animal like me, but under it all, it goes so deep. It is so absolute in this world of evasions and compromise, of appeasement on every side. He asks everything of the person and that is a tonic. One emerges glad to be human and to meet such a challenge, even though one fails. This for instance: "And now the Instant. It is short, indeed, and temporal, as every instant is, fleeting, as every instant is, gone like all instants, the following

[1] "I Will Not Let Thee Go Except Thou Bless Me," in Section 4, "From an Immigrant's Notebook," of Dinesen's *Out of Africa.*

instant, and yet it is decisive, and yet it is full of eternity. Such an instant must have a special name, let us call it *the fullness of time.*"[2] Your special genius it seems to me, darling, is to make every instant seem like the fullness of time. It is a very rare genius. [to JH, 13 Jul 46, Ch Pl]

Here is the beginning of Maritain's[3] introduction to a book of Léon Bloy[4] in translation I bought in the South. It made me think of you because you always believe you feel poor because you are poor but the fact is that you feel poor because you give so much: "We can give nothing we have not received, being in the likeness of Him who had received everything from His Father. That is why the more one gives, the more one needs to receive, the more one is a beggar." [to JH, 23 Mar 48, Oxf St]

But I am reading a wonderful book for the first time, Amiel's[5] Journals—full of real wisdom, though I think the translation I have is rather poor. There are some curiously reverberating sentences like "Reverie is the Sunday of thought" or "Which of us has not his promised land, his day of ecstasy and his death in exile!" and then more solid things like "Every day is a profession of faith, and exercises an inevitable and silent propaganda. As far as lies in its power, it tends to transform the universe and humanity into its own image. Thus we all have a cure of souls. Every man is the center of perpetual radiation like a luminous body"—well, enough. [to BB, n.d. (1950), Oxf St]

Je lis avec passion les lettres entières (non coupés ils viennents de paraître) de Mansfield à Murry. C'est un livre immense et déchirant et je m'endors dans une espèce d'angoisse chaude après avoir lu beaucoup trop longtemps chaque nuit. Ce qui est terrible c'est de comprendre comme il ne pouvait supporter qu'elle soit malade, qu'il lui fallait une femme sur laquelle il pouvait s'appuyer.

[2]from Walter Lowrie's *Kierkegaard* (Oxford Univ. Pr. 1938), p. 312.
[3]Jacques Maritain (1882–1973), French philosopher who came to America after the fall of France in 1940.
[4]French writer (1846–1917) whose work greatly influenced the twentieth-century revival of Catholic literature.
[5]Henri Frédéric Amiel (1821–81), Swiss philosopher and diarist.

Quand cela n'était plus possible le mariage n'était plus possible, mais quel déchirement pour elle—et puis quel courage inouï à se reprendre à tâcher de lui écrire des lettres amusantes, nourrissantes—on voit aussi si bien combien les lettres sont *dangeureuses* quand il s'agit de choses importantes entre deux-êtres qui tâchent de s'aimer bien à travers une impossibilité foncière de carac-tère et de tempérament. On voit clairement les lettres de l'un et de l'autre détruire leur amour. Tu t'imagines comme cela m'impressionne et me fait mal.[6] [to MC, 12 Dec 51, Myn Pl]

I celebrated by reading Gide's Journal about his wife, *Et nunc manet in te*,[7] a misquote, but you will know what I mean. His blindness to what he was doing to her really appalled me. It's a very sad story—and the fact that they never were able even to approach a conversation or clarification on the mute agony between them. He does appear here as a monster of egotism, I must say! What could be more cruel than to put someone on a pedestal not of their choosing and force them to stay there for a lifetime—[to BB, 5 Apr 53, Wr St]

I picked up the December *Encounter* and opened it to Robert Graves on Juana Inés de la Cruz and this is what I read:

"Every few centuries a woman of poetic genius appears, who may be distinguished by three clear secondary signs: learning, beauty, and loneliness. Though the burden of poetry is difficult enough for a man to bear, he can always humble himself before an incarnate muse and seek instruction from her— The case of a woman poet is a thousand times worse: since she is herself the Muse, a Goddess without an external power to guide or comfort her, if

---

[6]"I am reading with passion the complete letters (not cut it seems to appear) from Mansfield to Murry. It's an enormous book and tears one apart and I fall asleep in a kind of feverish anguish having read for much too long every night. What is terrible is to understand that he was unable to bear the fact that she was sick, that he needed a wife on whom he could lean. When that was no longer possible the marriage was no longer possible, but what torture for her—and then what extraordinary courage for her to begin again to try to write him refreshing and nourishing letters—one sees also so clearly how dangerous letters can be when it is a question of important matters between two people who are trying to love one another well across a profound conflict of character and temperament. One sees clearly how the letters from each to the other destroy their love. You can imagine how that affects me and makes me ill."

[7]*Madeleine (Et Nunc Manet in Te)*, Gide's "letter" to his dead wife in explanation of their relationship. The title is a Virgilian line that Gide used to mean "And now she remains in thee."

she strays even a finger's breadth from the path of divine instinct, she must take violent self-vengeance." [to LB, 26 Jan 54, Wr St]

All this makes me go back to Lavelle,[8] the French philosopher who really came to me like a revelation two or three years ago. It has to do I suppose with real freedom in love. "On aurait bien tort de ne voir dans l'influence qu'une sort d'éfficacité causale, produite par les paroles ou par les actions; les paroles ou les actions n'en sont que les instruments et les signes. L'influence vrai est celle de la *présence toute pure*; elle a une portée métaphysique; c'est une découverte de son être propre au contact d'un autre être."[9] And later on, "Car il n'y a pas pour la conscience de grâce plus parfaite que celle qui la met en état d'agir, c'est à dire de se donner. Ainsi, quand je suis le plus proche de vous, je sens votre être qui nait en moi, mais qui s'épanouit en vous; et il n'y a pas de communion plus étroite que celle qui, au même moment, vous donne le même sentiment à mon égard."[1] [to LB, 7 Feb 54, Wr St]

I'm glad you know Joubert[2]—he belongs in a Heaven for a few esprits délicats et surs,[3] doesn't he? with Mozart, certain discreet painters like Chardin, certain poets like you, where, though unworthy, I would feel at home on the smallest tussock at the bottom of the sacred grove. [to LB, 22 Jun 54, Wr St]

The whole Westcott[4] story is very fascinating. I used to hear about him and Munroe Wheeler[5] from Marion Dorn[6] and from Muriel Rukeyser who saw

[8]Louis Lavelle (1883–1951).

[9]"One would be very wrong to see power only as a kind of causal effectiveness produced by words or actions; words and actions are only tools and indications. Real power is *pure presence*, which has a metaphysical range; it is the discovery of one's real self in contact with another being."

[1]"For there is no more perfect awareness of grace than that which readies it to act, that is, to give of itself. Accordingly, when I am the closest to you, I feel your being as it is being born within me, even as it is unfolding within you; and there is no closer communion than that which, at the same moment, gives you the same feeling with respect to me."

[2]Joseph Joubert (1754–1824), French *pensée* writer.

[3]"delicate and dependable souls."

[4]Glenway Westcott (1901–87), American novelist, poet, and short story writer. Although he was for many years an expatriate, his most esteemed work is concerned with the puritanism and pioneering spirit of his native Wisconsin.

[5]Museum director, author (1900–?).

[6]Mrs. Ted McKnight Kauffer, friend, and subject of Sarton's poem "The Clavichord" in *The Lion and the Rose*.

them occasionally. But there is a kind of subtle poison that destroys the galaxy of corn-fed young westerners who come to N.Y. and suddenly acquire total sophistication. The Glenway Westcott of *The Grandmothers* is very far away and deep down now and over him there are a great many coats of lacquer. And whether it is good for talent to have "a patron" is another factor, isn't it? But I do not mean to sound (as Cummings would say) like an–New England non-ancestor of mine! [to LB, 3 Jul 55, Wr St]

Of course the simply amazing thing is to see the development in tension, in craft, that made it possible for Yeats as an old man to be at the forefront of *modern* poetry in his eighties. To me, it is a most inspiring vision. He kept his *intensity* to the end. It seems to me that there are two good ways of growing old, one is to keep that fire, intensity and conflict of youth, and the other is to achieve detached serenity. Somehow the former is more lovable to me, and also I believe makes for better art—though perhaps I am wrong there. [to KD, I Sep 57, Wr St]

Was also pleased that you are back with Yeats. I do not think that he was a great person, but I do think he was a great poet: as he himself says,

> The intellect of man is forced to choose
> Perfection of the life or of the work.[7]

[to KD, II Jan 59, Nelson]

My favorite of the great Russians is Turgenev—moderate, human, detached, yet idealistic, caring deeply—and such poetry! Of course Tolstoy is in a class apart like a giant mountain. But Dostoyevsky belongs to the self-intoxicated writers (Rimbaud for instance) whom I have never fallen for myself. Incidentally, Vladimir Nabokov, who is a distinguished critic as well as novelist, hates Dostoyevsky and thinks him very much overrated. Tchekov and Turgenev are my loves! [to KD, 2 Feb 59, Nelson]

[7]From "The Choice" in *The Winding Stair and Other Poems.*

For the sake of the novel[8] I have been rereading old journals—my journals are not "personal" but chiefly things I have read which hit me at the time, and I was rather comforted to find this the other day by Humphrey Trevelyan—"It seems that two qualities are necessary if a great artist is to continue creative to the end of a long life: he must on the one hand retain an abnormally keen awareness of the dangers and evils of life, must always demand the impossible and when he cannot have it, *must despair.* The burden of mystery must be with him day and night. He must be shaken by the naked truths that will not be comforted. This divine discontent, this disequilibrium, this state of inner tension is the source of artistic energy. . . . Wordsworth lost the courage to despair, and with it his poetic power." So here I am, really blest in every way, though sometimes the "way" is a little excruciating. . . . [to RG, 23 Feb 64, Nelson]

Yet at the same time I rather resent E. Bishop,[9] who never gives herself away at all and goes covered up in several expensive fur coats. And we come back to the very hard thing it is to be a woman and a poet. [to LB, 16 Sep 65, Nelson]

Last night I saw Le Gallienne in *The Madwoman of Chaillot* (next week I'll see their production of *The Trojan Women*) and that is such an exhilarating play in a good childish-sophisticated way. Giraudoux has so much tenderness and so much wit—it is a charming combination. Do you remember all the Madwoman's wisdom about how to *manage?* It reminded me of you and of myself. How fine to be mad enough to be sane. I laughed so much when the young man she rescues from suicide asks what he can do for her and she answers, "Lots of things. You can take the mouse out of the trap. I am tired of feeding it." The whole play is full of these tender paradoxes. Also when the wonderful King of the Sewers says, "They say we have orgies down here and the rats dance—it's ridiculous. The rats are not *allowed* to dance" etc. [to LB, 14 Nov 65, Lindenwood]

[8]*Mrs. Stevens Hears the Mermaids Singing.*
[9]Elizabeth Bishop (1911–79), American poet.

I have been plunged happily into the past which is a relief—my own with this book,[1] and also all the books about Woolf—I've just finished the early letters. In spite of the awful shocks (her mother's death when she was 13), her father's slow decline, what came through to me was how normal she was and what a marvelous thing to walk into a ready-made world of distinguished people, all related or friends—the kind of support that meant. You and I have never had anything like it. I'm reading the huge Edith Wharton biography[2] now—fascinating. And Evelyn Waugh waits in the wings. I feel like a bear with almost too many pots of honey. [to BB, 21 Nov 75, York]

And perhaps nowhere does she reveal more about her own sacramentalization of the ordinary and the power she effects for the common reader than in this observation of Virginia Woolf—

You started a long train of thought about Virginia Woolf when you called. I do understand the reaction now to an overestimate in some ways. But can you name a novelist today for whose next book one waits with such excitement *because* you will have no idea what it will be like? The daring of her experiments, *Orlando, The Waves, To the Lighthouse,* the fact that she never lets the mold stay to be used again . . . this is already a sign of genius. Some of these experiments were failures, but all were extremely interesting. People blame her for *not* being Joyce . . . why should she be? She was not experimenting with *language* so much as *form,* and there is a real distinction here. That is all what *critics* look for. But what about the common reader? I have yet to find a woman writer who can illuminate in just this way "ordinary life" or any one who has stated what women's lives are, the complexity they have to weave together, the harmony they have to make out of the emotional chaos and physical disorder of "family life," the *art* this takes. She has done far more in a real, unblinking coming to terms with the woman than all the Betty somethingorothers and their "feminine mystique." (It is *not* a sentimental view or a "feminist" view of the novels.) But for the common reader, perhaps her greatest gift (comparable

[1]Sarton was working on *A World of Light.*
[2]By R.W.B. Lewis.

to Emily Dickinson) was to make the ordinary things of life, a woman knitting a sock, a certain light on the grass, marvelously new and touching.

In one of the fan letters I have had recently, a woman writes, "I've found through the years as my family responsibilities have increased that I must put a ban on my reading or I become too restless to stick to duties. But two people I can always read. Virginia Woolf, because of all her awareness of small things, which is contagious and I then notice all the *small glories of my daily life.* And you" etc. (underlining mine). It is easy to be patronizing to this gift as it is easy to sneer at the saints, but I do not believe it is nothing to give back courage and to illuminate *daily life* for those (most of us) close to despair all the time. The word is "life-enhancing." [to LB, 31 Mar 68, Nelson]

Even sports, dancing, and singing have taken their places among the small glories of her daily life—

Did I tell you that we had a song competition. Mine got the prize which was 5 points! I was very surprized. [to EMS, ? Jul 25, DMC]

I had a peachy time at the Clarks. We acted plays and climbed on the rocks and did gimnastics. [to EMS, summer 1926, Ray St]

The smooth rhythm of beautiful skating literally makes me feel as if my heart were in my mouth. I am almost sick with the sheer curve of bodies. [HJ, 6 Feb 28, Ray St]

I hope you and all yours are out of it[3] now and somewhere high up on a dazzling snow-plain—I suppose you are expert on skis—I used to go up into the hills around here when I was a little girl at Christmas—knowing nothing about it—but oh how exciting! It is sheer magic, isn't it?— We used to ski a lot by moonlight, singing the Brahms *Requiem* in parts (in case of sudden death!)—but I was never any good. Do you jump? It must be the nearest thing to flying. [to JH, 31 Jan 37, Ch Pl]

[3]The flu.

In the middle of the week I went skiing—it was 25 below zero when we got there at night and I thought my nose was going to fall off like an icicle at any minute. But it seems to be firmly attached. The next day was dazzling and I went off by myself feeling wonderful. O Kot, if you could only see this country—the river streaming in the sun, and the pure trees almost touching the ground under the snow. I went over pastures where there was no mark, feeling as if I were the discoverer of the world. [to K, 23 Jan 38, Ch Pl]

The folk dance was just what I wanted after the exuberance accumulated at the lecture.[4] I almost wished I too could dance wildly for a virgin like Jean,[5] until I fainted—something heroic and terrible and sublime. [HJ, 11 Feb 28, Ray St]

I had Strawbridge[6] again yesterday—it really is marvelous. I feel absolutely relaxed and yet straight and free when we're through. He uses lovely images. For instance to get the feeling of holding one's head high, he said, "Pretend you have wings behind your ears like Hermes." And we did a thing of swinging our arms which he describes as "lassoing the earth, the universe" till we got terribly excited. [to EMS and GS, 13 Mar 30, 94 Macd]

After supper are the finals of the deck-tennis tournament we've been having—Eliot and I against Renée and David.[7] It is very thrilling as the whole company sits on the terrace and cheers and hoots. We each contributed $ .10 so the prize will be $1.65, which seems an immense sum. [to EMS and GS, 25 Aug 34, Rowley]

Daddy will be glad to hear that I have started to play tennis again—I played barefoot on a grass court and it was really delicious. [to EMS and GS, 28 Jun 37, London (Huxley)]

---

[4]She had just been to hear the Irish poet A.E.
[5]Probably Jean Tatlock, friend from Cambridge.
[6]A foremost dancer in New York at the time. Sarton took some classes with him as Le Gallienne thought it would be good for her posture.
[7]Eliot Cabot, theater director; Renée Orsell; David Marks, member of the Apprentice Theatre.

I danced and danced and got over my phobia about it. For years the idea of dancing was synonymous with agony because I did so little of it as a young girl (I was hard at work at 17)—I felt just like a person in a fairy story when a spell is broken. [to MFH, 6 May 41, Ch Pl]

And there is everywhere her vision of art, and music—

> I came upon it
> From long wandering
> In subdued tones of voices
> Subdued air,
> And old effaced tones of sienna reds.
> I had grown sick of the oval faces
> Of pale virgins.
> Then, O exquisite Fra Angelico
> I saw you like a very small dew drop
> Reflecting sky.
> I went home,
> Wondering that it was not May.

["A Little Fra Angelico," HJ, 6 Mar 28, Ray St]

Chinese music is like the language of strange birds, a sweetness within discord. Mei Lan-Fang[8] walks as if on clouds, effortlessly, with the most unbroken grace I have ever seen. His gestures enchanting, teasing. [HJ, 9 Mar 30, 94 Macd]

But now I think the problem for one living in this age is much more complex, that one must be able to create a still point in oneself, contain somewhere within this river and this timelessness, and learn to withdraw into it out of chaos, that to deny the chaos and refuse to live in it is simply not to face the issue. For two years I have been restlessly trying to arrive at this place in myself—but perhaps it takes five or ten—Le Gallienne I believe only reached it about five years ago—and yet an artist never comes to his full power until

---

[8]China's finest and most popular actor of the time.

he has managed to create it—Monet is an excellent example of this. [to GS, 29 Jan 33, NYC]

A wonderful Toulouse-Lautrec exhibition. I didn't realize what a great *painter* he was—the daring composition, the *personal* color, the sense again of a *created* world—the Toulouse-Lautrec world—so that when one comes out everything takes on his color, his personality, and for awhile one sees with a fresh, a *violent* eye. [to JH, 28 Nov 37, Ch Pl]

She[9] uses colors in a Stravinsky-ish sort of way—I mean the way he uses notes. They grate on your nerves and please you excessively at the same time if you know what I mean and it is really just a little off all the time and very physically exciting (that's why she's so good for musical comedy). [to MFH, 5 Sep 40, Rockport]

What I adore is that his[1] gaiety is the true kind, the kind that knows all about pain and suffering and dances to keep warm—[to BB, 8 Jan 42, Ch Pl]

But I love Rousseau because the strangeness is intrinsic and un-self-conscious and composed and refined to the point where it is not startling but only true. [to BB, 23 Apr 42, Ch Pl]

I'm sure you're right about the subject matter being of little importance, but the quality of vision and emotion being everything. A still life to be moving must have been seen and digested so completely—that is, I think, why the Cézannes hold up so well—and in another age some of Chardin's still lifes. [to BB, 26 Jan 47, Oxf St]

As I look back on these days the most significant moment was going to Battersea and seeing the outdoor sculpture show. There under two immense trees on a small rise pelouse,[2] stand Henry Moore's three figures—what

[9]Irene Sharaff (1910?–), costume designer; designed scenery and costumes for Le Gallienne's stage adaptation of *Alice in Wonderland*.
[1]Mozart's.
[2]"lawn."

presences they are, composing all the air around them, composing for an instant the world itself as if all were clear and calm now, forever. And how completely shabby and false the pseudo-classic or even purely realistic sculpture looked. Not as Brancusi said more and more like a corpse, but less and less like anything with meaning at all. [to JH, 25 Aug 48, London (RP)]

Then we have gone to various shows—Gauguin at the Orangerie. I was impressed at how beautiful some of the less famous paintings are—but it is all a little too fruity and pagan for me. We spent a morning in the Palais d'Art Moderne—especially a show of new tapestries, some lovely, some very ugly but all showing how much France is still inventing and creating. [to EMS and GS, 24 Jul 49, Hôtel Saint-Simon, Paris]

What a wonderful letter—of course I disagree rather violently with the tenets of nonobjective painting (which remind me of the discussions of "pure poetry" some time ago)—I would think that nonobjective painting was extremely valuable for the painter himself but only as the isolating of one part of a painting for analysis and study—the theory seems to be that "emotion" is something isolated and has nothing to do with "objects," yet surely this is just nonsense. Isn't it really that a good painting is nonobjective in the sense that it could be turned upside down and still hold together as composition, but this is just *one* element. Subject matter can, of course, get in the *way* if it is melodramatic as in Delacroix—who seems a great painter in spite of his subject. But does it get in the way in a Chinese painting of a flower or bird? or the Cézanne apples or landscapes? I do not see how one can bring any memories or associations to a completely abstract painting—it pleases as a *design* and has, to me, all the limitations of the decorative, however subtle and sophisticated. It is just the cutting out of association which seems to short-circuit this connection between the seer's experience and the painter's. One is left outside—and perhaps the proof of this is just the tendency to give complete abstractions fancy poetic titles. Surely the title should be absorbed into the painting and if it has to depend on a title for raising "associations" then it is a failure. However all this does not mean that as a step or discipline what you are doing may not be extremely valuable. [to BB, 15 Feb 53, Wr St]

In her work, as in her human relationships and uncompromising self-criticism,[3] Sarton's convictions, honesty, and transparency are as naked as her frog's[4]—

> One who above all is frank to his own self,
> Who dares to face his soul.
> One who gives generously,
> Is infinitely courteous,
> Who hates and loves with the whole force of his being,
> Who tries to see the Truth in all people,
> Has the power of perfect command over himself
> And is full of everlasting hope,
> He is my ideal.

> [HJ, ? Jan 27, Ray St]

She[5] said she thought I had character and (to my great delight) am temperamental. She defined temperamental as having a good engine and lots of gas but not always knowing when to put on the brakes. That's rather good I think. Afterwards I wanted terribly to tell her how much it had meant—[HJ, 25 Jul 29, Gloucester]

I am appalled at the lack of sincerity in the world. I try very hard to be honest and after all more than half I say is untrue. I blame Miss Cunningham[6] for not always criticizing honestly, but there is nothing harder. I suppose it is not her weakness but her lack of strength. If someone I disliked asked me why I disliked them I know I should lie. Yet why? It's disgusting. I suppose it's a kind of cowardice which I must learn to conquer like any other fear. And I will conquer it even if it means to be one man in a thousand. Deep down

---

[3]Self-criticism and understanding were important parts of her parents' legacy to her. In writing to her daughter of the power of a hurtful letter George Sarton had sent, Eleanor Mabel Sarton says: "Of course he does not mean to wound you, only to stimulate self-criticism."
[4]See "The Frog, That Naked Creature" in *In Time Like Air*.
[5]Florence Evans.
[6]Florence Cunningham, whom Sarton called Ariel, a teacher at the Gloucester School of the Little Theatre.

underneath I think most people are sincere, with themselves at least. I know that I'm not a genius though if someone told me I wasn't I would violently contradict them. [HJ, I Aug 29, Gloucester]

Isn't it funny that people always apologize for the truth—and never for a lie. [HJ, I Feb 30, 94 Macd]

Je déteste et hais les infirmières—dures commes des pierres avec cette voix tout à fait fausse et cette bonne humeur *sans coeur.*[7] [to MC, 14 Nov 50, Myn Pl]

The virtue of publication for the author (at least for me) is to make me see every flaw in a glaring light, but also to get rid of the poems, and so be able to go on. [to LB, 21 Oct 53, Wr St]

One darling old lady came up afterwards[8] and kissed me and said, "You are *just* the same little girl." (I must say this made me shudder for if true, I really would be a monster.) [to LB, 10 Feb 54, Wr St]

But Eugénie[9] is very helpful partly because she is ruthlessly honest. She told me, for instance, that as far as she has observed my angers *always* come out of vanity. This is a hard truth to accept but I think it is at least 80 per cent true, and I think it should help me to be more balanced and less on the defensive. [to JM, 12 Jul 57, Linkebeek]

Even in the smallest observations we find her philosophy, integrity, and sense of values and beauty—

[7]"I detest and hate the nurses—hard as stones with that entirely false tone and that cheerfulness *without heart.*" Written four days before her mother's death.
[8]After a lecture at the Lincoln School, Providence, R.I.
[9]Eugénie DuBois.

Eugénie DuBois with her class.

And what is life
If not the wingèd moment
In a butterfly's metamorphosis?

[From "What Is Beauty," HJ, 6 Sep 28, Ray St]

You said on November 21st that "no radical has ever wanted Beauty—their ideals are on too low a plane." Webster gives a definition of radical: "One who advocates extreme reform." Under this definition the following men were radicals, and in your opinion, had too low ideals to desire beauty.

Christ
Shelley
Byron
Tolstoy
Abraham Lincoln.   [to GS, after 21 Nov 30]

I'm afraid it is a hopelessly dated point of view but it still seems to me that human *hearts* are the most important things in the world. Triumphs in life can be summed up in the greatest joy and *cherishment* one has been able to give the heart of man. This is the extraordinary thing about any art that in this way one can reach, *touch*, so many people. [to EMS, 4 Jan 36, 245 E 37]

C'est drôle je crois que je dois mettre un forme humaine dans chaque paysage pour le voir en toute sa grandeur—une petite chose pathétique qui donne l'échelle à une montagne.[1] [to MC, 12 Jul 36, Austria]

Many people have taken the attitude that they must bear the world's pain and *never* be happy (a typically puritan idea) while I feel it is a betrayal of life and a *sin* not to appreciate doubly all that there is of joy and of luck in our lives here. It will not be for long. [to K, 22 Sep 39, Ch Pl]

I miss the bare grandness of Santa Fe—California has too much of everything. One violet under a rock, *secret,* to be found by exploring eyes is worth all the avenues of oleanders and roses and all the flowers mixed from all the seasons. [to RWB, 21 Feb 41, Pasadena, Calif.]

I am engaged in a furious controversy over Virginia Woolf with Haniel Long,[2] a poet friend in Santa Fe. I wonder if men can like her really. But he accuses her of having no maternal feeling and judges a woman I gather chiefly on her maternal feeling. This seems to me a comment on the present when all men want is a mother, and so have really neglected to bring women up at all, been content in fact to be brought up by them. When that happens it is a poor moment. In spite of all Elizabeth feels I do think women should root in men not men in women. And anyway Haniel's mad if he doesn't see that Mrs.

---

[1] "I find it odd that I must put a human form into every landscape in order to see its grandeur—a small vulnerable creature which gives proportion to a mountain."

[2] American poet, novelist, and publisher (1888–1956) who settled in Santa Fe and was responsible for Sarton's going there originally. Sarton wrote the preface to a posthumous collection of his poetry, *My Seasons.*

Eleanor Mabel Sarton and George Sarton, 1946. Credit: May Sarton.

Ramsey[3] is completely maternal as all wives of scholars have to be. [to MFH, 23 Jul 41, Rockport]

That is what I am dreaming of.[4] I can't tell you what it has meant to us these last months to sit quietly all three of us almost every evening in our small ragged autumnal garden together. It lays a quiet hand on one somehow to be out of doors, not as an Event like a picnic or walk which demands *response* but just every day taking it as it comes. And even if one has only *one* snowdrop, it is so exciting in the spring. [to JH, 19 Sep 42, Ch Pl]

I wonder if we in our time have not made some fatal mistake in believing that happiness was the most important end in individual life. Psychoanalysis with its emphasis on integration, on releasing the inner drives, badly understood no

---

[3]The central character in Woolf's *To the Lighthouse*, a personification of creative womanhood.

[4]For Juliette Huxley to have her own garden.

doubt by most of us, seems to me to have had a poor influence. And in seeking happiness above all, *of course* we never find it. It is a by-product and not the end of life surely. And all personal relations depend so much on patience, on living through the deep places, the dark places *together*. Women know this better than men I think. They are more rooted or perhaps the roots mean more to us. [to JH, 26 Nov 45, Oxf St]

I am more and more convinced that the art of criticism consists in *loving* a work of art sufficiently to take time really to consider it—and that is what you do for my poems. [to BB, 2 Sep 46, Martha's Vineyard, Mass.]

I'm convinced now that I've seen him[5] that he is a very great artist. He showed us a Leda which turned on a small table, a huge metal abstract object which went on turning slowly as we talked and much later seemed to me to come alive. One has to live with his things. After we had looked slowly at everything for about an hour we sat down and smoked and he talked wonderfully and gently about the life of an artist and about his work. I did so wish Agi[6] could have been there. She would have loved him and I must try to write to her about him. He said that he had for years lived on 10 sous a day "but I was never sad. I was never angry about this. I sang all the time—after all no one had asked me to be a sculptor. It was my own choice—there was no reason to be angry." And then he said, "We are diamonds and life does the polishing; it's hard but it has to be done, and we are far too lazy to do it for ourself, so hardship is not a bad thing." [to JM, 10 Jun 47, Paris (Huxley)]

As to what Hess[7] says—surely if anything literature is dwarfed at present by the immensity of the subject matter, not the lack of it. We are all stretched out to China, France, England, to absorb politics, art, Freud and Heaven knows what! It is time someone looked quietly at a stone or a bulb growing as far as I am concerned. [to BB, 26 Jan 47, Oxf St]

[5]Brancusi, to whose studio Sarton was taken by Juliette Huxley.
[6]Agi Sims.
[7]Probably Thomas Baer Hess (1920–), writer, former editor of *Art News*.

And things that grow slowly into whatever shape they must have are best. [to JH, 24 Jul 47, London (JS)]

Of course one is different selves for different people, a matter of response, but deep down inside *to oneself,* one is always somewhere it seems to me the *same.* In some people the buried real self never comes into action or into life and I think that's what *Demian*[8] is about maybe, and all life is about. [to JH, 16 Feb 48, Oxf St]

It makes me think of *The Death of the Heart* where Elisabeth says that when two innocents get together, the bodies lie strewn. I believe it is actually a sin to be as innocent as that at sixty. Somewhere or other one has failed as a human being. My mother, for instance, who has had little "experience," understands it all perfectly. . . . But there is enough in almost any relationship to teach one almost everything if one has an imaginative heart, don't you think? [to BB, 12 Dec 48, Oxf St]

I got quite cross with Kot today, though I did not tell him, because he seemed quite surprised that A.V. Hill[9] had been at my father's lecture. After all, G.S. is in his way a very great man and everyone who knows anything about his subject knows it. Why should it be surprising that some Englishman goes to the lecture? I sometimes think the abysses, the preconceptions, are so immense between peoples that there is no hope ever of their being bridged. One or two people can cross, but no more. We all have our treasured implacable prejudices. We are all snobs at heart, even the vulgarians. Even the pure in heart like Kot. [to JH, 14 Apr 48, London (JS)]

But then the only people who are interesting in this sad world are the people who keep their innocence (so much *deeper* than any other sort of wisdom). [to JH, 7 May 48, Chez Limbosch]

[8] By Hermann Hesse.
[9] Archibald Vivian Hill (1886–1977), English physiologist and biochemist.

Of course Montreux is just a lot of hotels and "foreigners." But the lake depressed me so much and the Wagnerian clouds, all too spectacular—I'm afraid I like understated landscapes. I do not like to be forced continually to gasp! [to HD, 19 Apr 49, Oxf St]

We had E. Bowen for 24 hours which totally threw me and I was only fit to lie down for a day afterwards. Of course it's because having no help, one is cook, chambermaid, secretary and host all in one. *Mademoiselle* sent photographers and a girl to interview Bowen and they turned the whole small house upside down like an invasion of the Gestapo. I felt my study had been violated and finally rudely put them out (after an hour and a half which took the only time E. and I would have had to talk in peace)—the more I see of celebrity the less I want it. In some awful way it destroys one's life and forces one to be "public" instead of "private." [to BB, 31 May 53, Wr St]

Yet the lives which move me the most are those like Marianne Moore and Yeats where the work goes on growing over a long time, and all comes to fruition like some marvelous tree in the end. I suppose they are Apollonian, creatures of light, lacking the roots in the dark of Dylan Thomas, or Rimbaud. [to BB, 22 Nov 53, Wr St]

How lovely it was to hear your voice—I had been thinking all this strange week that I would hear your voice at the end, if I got through it, and there it was—and I have hummed like a little tune "take life easy as the grass grows on the weirs,"[1] hearing you saying it in just that casual way like Mozart's music—not indifference or lack of love, but lifted out into some lovely spacious freedom of its own. [to LB, 7 Feb 54, Wr St]

I am regaining a little sense of what is possible, i.e. that all one can do is to go along like a little donkey from day to day and especially to pay no attention to

[1]Louise Bogan often quoted to Sarton from Yeats's "Down by the Salley Gardens":
    She bid me take life easy, as the grass grows on the weirs;
    But I was young and foolish, and now am full of tears.

what anyone says. I am prepared to listen very hard to donkeys and stones and trees and roses, but not very hard to any human voice for a long time, but that is because I suppose I am a donkey myself—rather stubborn and fond of thistles. [to LB, 4 Aug 59, Chez Limbosch]

Certainly one sees again here² that power does not so much corrupt (I was wrong to use that word) as cripple people as human beings. They have to be lonely and not *whole* if they are to be impartial, it would seem. But of course there are great exceptions—Roosevelt, Churchill . . . [to RG, 3 Jan 65, Nelson]

I wake up with joy in the morning and this in itself is so new after months of really severe depression, anxiety and exhaustion that I can hardly believe it. I am very cross with the *Times* for not reviewing *Mythology*—somehow I felt they owed me a break after giving *Selected* to Shapiro.³ But one of the things I have been battling through is an attempt to simply write off ambition once and for all. Just *give up,* and be happily and fruitfully my unfashionable, unsuccessful yet productive self. Let the bones shine in the dark after I am dead. For now it does not matter. It has been a hard stance for me to achieve but I think I am there at last. It was the last devil I had to conquer. For I now intend to have about twenty years of happy work, and not to worry as they say. [to LB, 16 Sep (n.y.; 1965?), Nelson]

Whatever my weaknesses as a writer, it is a respectable thing to be able to earn a living at it without ever having to compromise as to subject matter or with my resolve taken 20 years ago to do no reviewing. [to HW, 20 Aug 67, Greenings]

My hero is Martin Luther King—no amount of soft idealism will make a whole city of Blacks walk to work for a *year* to desegregate buses, for instance, as he did in Montgomery, without leadership. [to BB, 24 Jun 70, Nelson]

²In Dag Hammarskjöld's *Markings.*
³Karl Shapiro wrote a devastating review of *Cloud, Stone, Sun, Vine* in the *New York Times Book Review,* December 24, 1961.

My idea of life is to give all one can at top speed every day and then when one is spent, to die—so I think that I have no intention of sparing myself. [to KD, 28 Jul 65, Nelson]

The letters document what a reviewer called her "implacable core"[4]—

I suppose that the reason I am absolutely unafraid of giving myself away is that way down deep I have an implacable core that can't be given away or possessed; and that makes me in some way invulnerable. [to MFH, 15 Sep 40, Ch Pl]

I get frightened sometimes at how diamond hard I am somewhere very deep at the center. This disturbs other people, but I think you understand its necessity. To be as fluid and sensitive as possible on the surface but as hard as possible somewhere that can't be deflected or even, perhaps, touched. But it is rather frightening. [to LB, 7 Feb (n.y.)]

Rain, cold—and an awful struggle with the fires this morning—so I am late to work and it has made me feel so savage that I *know* that anything that threatened this job,[5] anything that in the end *can't* make permanent roots and be built into my life—that threatened it—would simply have to be cut out. [to JH, 20 Apr 37, Rye]

The letters and journals parallel her work—

Boulder Dam yesterday knocked me for a loop—it is absolutely thrilling—such implications for life in general this mastery and use of tremendous power, and the artificial lake it has made looks like a sapphire mirage in the middle of obviously *dry* red and crimson and orange bare mountains. I have written a poem about it.[6] The canyon is lonely— It was grey and I felt

---

[4]Frank Arthur Swinnerton (1884–1982) in his review of *The Single Hound* in the *Observer*, April 24, 1938.
[5]Rewriting *The Single Hound* after Marie Closset had made some suggestions.
[6]"Boulder Dam" in *The Lion and the Rose*.

overwhelmed by it and rather sad—the great endless life of stones and one feels flesh too frail for words. [to MFH, 25 Feb 41, Grand Canyon]

We had sad news that the boy[7] for whom "Navigator"[8] was written is reported missing in Tunisia. It came, that news, the day the Jewish Congress printed its really fearful report on what is happening to the Jews in Europe—5,000,000 will have been liquidated in six months' time. Putting these two events side by side I ached all over. The poem[9] came from them. [to RWB, 1 Mar 43, 5 E 10]

or give seeds of images that will come later—

There is the possibility everywhere of a sort of purification down to essentials—a feeling that certain values are *essential* and one will fight for them in one's private life just as they are being fought for by soldiers everywhere on a grand scale.[1] [to JH, 1 Jan 44, 22 E 10]

Bruges was such fun. We sat for a long time in the sun drinking coffee outside after lunch, tasting each other's smiles. Mother (who looks frightfully tired) said she felt like a butterfly opening and shutting its wings very softly on a flower. Then we saw the Memlings (how *vividly* it brought back to me the day when you and I saw them together in Paris!) and then took a slow put-putting boat and wandered lazily among the canals. We saw two swans gravely doing their courting dance, their long necks just *not* touching.[2] [to JH, 7 May 48, Chez Limbosch]

Chartres— Not only the presence of God but a renewed faith in man because he was capable of creating this formidable beauty "terribilità."

---

[7]Edmund Kennedy, son of Edith Forbes Kennedy.
[8]In *The Lion and the Rose.*
[9]"These Have No Dirge," written January 1943, unpublished.
[1]See "Innumerable Friend" in *The Land of Silence* and "To the Living" in *The Lion and the Rose.*
[2]See "The Swans" in *The Leaves of the Tree.*

The burst of sunlight so that it seemed as if the angel *spoke*.[3] [HJ, 26 Aug 54, Fontainebleau]

or add explanations and dimensions—

Then I have thought a great deal about swans—partly because I have been translating my swan poems for Elizabeth[4] for J.D.[5] and because it is only in England this year that I have fallen in love with swans. I think often of one Julian and I saw with her cygnets, the incredible furious majesty of the arched wing and then those absurd soft grey heads looking out from her back and sliding off and squeaking with distress—a sort of squeaking *gazouillement*,[6] and it seems so blessed that such things can be.[7] [to JH, 14 Aug 38, aboard *American Importer*]

So I have been writing quite a lot of new ones in a different sphere, meditative, though not personal. I enclose the latest[8] which is really against the Academics who always poison history and literature and might be dedicated to my father. It came also out of my passionately interested reading of Edmund Wilson's *To the Finland Station*, an analysis of historians from Michelet to Marx and of the makers of history from the Commune to Lenin. It is so clear and humane, a real work of art. And without Marxian bias so at last Marx emerges a real person and a great figure not a formula. [to RWB, 24 Aug 41, Rockport]

The poems always tell me where I have to go and when they come in form as these four sonnets have, I know that God is with me again. It has taken some doing. [to MH, 9 Oct 70, Nelson]

They give us insights into her theories on poetry and her methods of work—

[3] See "Chartres" and "Once More at Chartres" in *A Grain of Mustard Seed*.
[4] Elizabeth Bowen.
[5] Jean Dominique.
[6] "prattle."
[7] See "Memory of Swans" in *Inner Landscape*.
[8] "The Sacred Order" in *The Lion and the Rose*.

But I am not going to tell anyone about it[9] and I am going to wait awhile before beginning. It is just as with poetry—for some time one must ignore the feeling of having a bird in one's breast trying to get out, just pretend it isn't there and study the irregular German verbs. But there is a delicate moment, like a surgical operation, when as the bird flies, one must *seize* it, pounce like a hawk before it can escape. And perhaps novels are like that. They must be kept secret even from oneself for some time while they are given a chance to grow their wings. [to K, 28 Dec 37, Ch Pl]

I love reading my poems to anyone at all, especially old ones that I have almost forgotten and that suddenly seem quite good. I like to hear them *sounding.* [to K, 17 Feb 38, Ch Pl]

One of the deepest dangers for literature today as I see it is the same danger that is attacking us politically, the fact that if you are passionately one thing you are passionately *not* something else. The American writer born in a special part of America, in love with his corner of land, indignant at wrongs done, stupidity lived there, the infinite possibilities within it, and with tenderness for the people with whom he has grown up and nostalgia for the pattern he must break like a chicken in an egg to become a writer—he has his work cut out for him and his job is comparatively easy. Pearl Buck's article in the *Sat. Review* said a true word when she said that American literature today was regional, that when we read about a sharecropper, about a farm in Kansas, we say, "That is America," we feel good; we understand it. The country is being discovered by the people in it—everywhere due to the depression drought etc. people are beginning to think who before had only time to *do*—but that literature must be written by the people with a regional background. There is no point in trying to paste on such a background—it would be just as false for me as a writer, worse I think, to "go American" suddenly in a big way as for Jesse Stuart[1] to emulate Noel Coward. One's inner direction is another matter—one's inner truth slowly to be discovered. When I went into the

[9]The idea for a new, imaginative novel.
[1]Jesse Hilton Stuart (1907–84), American poet, novelist, and short story writer, wrote of adolescence in rural Kentucky between the wars.

theatre I remember saying that given ten years I could do something good. I feel it strongly about writing—I have been writing just three. I was until six months ago in a hurry. Now I am not. For there is another kind of literature, no better or worse but harder to create and impossible perhaps before one is thirty—the three books of the year as far as I am concerned are Malraux's *Man's Hope*, Ralph Bates'[2] *Sirocco*, and Elisabeth Bowen's *Death of the Heart*—the last of these might be what I could do. Whatever I say will come from *inside*, will in the sense perhaps that Thomas Mann's novels all are be autobiography, a series of allegories. I shall never write a great cross-section novel, or even one about a section of society or about any part of any country, but what I have to say will be about individuals and will be simply about the human heart. . . . Any American novel I might write would be phony—I am a stranger in Cambridge and in London and in Paris equally—and a stranger in N.Y. But here in this room I am not a stranger to something which could be written and which it is my job to write. If I ever say it it can wait three hundred years to sell and it may never sell, but that doesn't matter. I am not worried anymore about that. You cannot run against the mainstream and expect much from the public at first. But give me time and do not worry about me for now for I really believe I am on the right track. [to HS, 29 May 39, Ch Pl]

I am haunted and enchanted by Francis'[3] really magical lyric "Why Does the Drum Come Hither? Hamlet"—it seems to me to show that he is a true poet, with a sense of overtones of words, a remarkable ear (that lovely line "And straying of the leaves" with its slightly different stress). Well, he just seems to know all about it. Now I can only pray that he avoid cleverness and get to understand his own talent, not imitate what other people are doing, not be afraid to be simple and luminous, and himself. I am going to write to him but you can tell him the essence of this if you like. The poem was an event. I have sent it to several people—it is magic. It is poetry just as a pig is a pig. This is what I have not felt in Anthony,[4] who is trying of course to say more complicated things (but don't of course tell him that). With A. I have felt an

---

[2]English novelist (1899–) best known for his accounts of life in Spain and the Spanish Civil War.
[3]Francis John Heathorn Huxley (1923–), son of Juliette and Julian.
[4]Anthony Julian Huxley (1920–), son of Juliette and Julian.

intelligence and a sensitivity working together to *make* a poem, and the awful thing is that a true poem is born not made. One can never admit this to oneself because one has to struggle all the time but it is really true. One can only prepare oneself for the coming of a poem. And while it is being born do the right things, and work like an expert obstetrician (it is hard work I hear!). But it was conceived in the act of imagination long before. [to JH, 4 Mar 42, Ch Pl]

Do send the sonnet—I'd love to read it. Isn't it a tremendous satisfaction when it "Comes out"—a very superior form of solitaire! When one has really managed to contain one's whole idea in that form with nothing superfluous and nothing spilling over—[to BB, 24 Nov 42, Marietta College, O.]

I was interested to see somewhere that Matisse begins with a literal rendering of an object or person and then gradually reduces it to its essence, drawing by drawing. That is the way I write poems, but many people carry the changes in their heads and many painters I'm sure make the abstractions in their heads too. It is all fascinating. [to BB, 26 Jan 47, Oxf St]

When my poems are good, which is *very* rarely! it is because they are each time an act of the spirit. Something I put before me and try to achieve—very rarely of course can I be what the poem is. But that is the point. The poems are notes for an inner action; they make the direction. In that sense literature, as Kot calls it, is my life. There is nothing else that matters except friendship, except love. [to JH, 28 Jun 47, Chez Limbosch]

In Paris almost the most wonderful thing was an afternoon spent with Brancusi—did I tell you? And didn't you go there once when you were in Paris? It was a great time—he sat and talked for hours about his life and his work, a man who seems to be a mixture of a saint and a peasant—in white linen peasant clothes, sabots, going quietly from one hooded lump to another and taking off the hood on those extraordinary luminous and so sophisticated works of his. *The Bird in Space, Leda, The New Born,* and some of them turning slowly on turning tables so after a while I felt the room was full of living *presences.* Going into the studio one entered light and space and peace; it was very wonderful to be there after my impressions of the spiritual squalor of Paris—the greediness, lack of responsibility, desire to *get,* etc. etc. I really think the French are far worse than we are in their money-grubbing. But Brancusi is *pure*—what a relief it was! How good and I felt again so deeply the sanity, the healingness of art when it is great. [to BB, 13 Jun 48, VF]

And a book by the Abbé Brémond[5] called *Prière et Poésie,* less rewarding than the title. I don't know exactly what is meant by the inner current, but I think the writing of a poem presupposes at least a *temporary* solution of conflict, so that it must be at the end of the struggle which precedes it not the finding of oneself but the touching of the humanity in oneself, the place where one is universal just because one has gone down deep enough into oneself—and I suppose that might be the current for a poet: his humanness. It is the opposite of negative brooding of which alas I do far too much. [to JH, 14 Aug 48, Oxon]

I have been simply pouring myself out day by day into the difficult second part of my novel.[6] And today it is finished—175 pages in 6 weeks, the most concentrated effort I ever made, and now I feel so sad and empty. You know how it is—when you lay down the brushes and can't tell yet whether it is any good, but like the painter at the end of *To the Lighthouse* think I have had my vision.[7] Beside it real life seems like a dream. [to MFH, 17 Jun 49, Chez Limbosch]

And since I have come back I finished my novel[8] and sent it off to the publisher. Now I shall feel rather forlorn as one always does and wonder what they will think. It's all a great risk, really, these pieces of oneself one puts

[5]Abbé Henri Bremond (1855–1933), French literary critic and historian.

[6]*Shadow of a Man.*

[7]Lily Briscoe, the artist in Virginia Woolf's novel, captures eternally in her painting the beauty and creativity of Mrs. Ramsay, and the novel closes with the lines "It was done; it was finished. Yes, she thought, laying down her brush in extreme fatigue, I have had my vision."

[8]*Shadow of a Man.*

out—and I never know whether it is any good. With poems I do know, but prose is, I think, much more complex. One could go on revising a prose page forever whereas there is a point in a poem when one knows it is done forever. [to KD, 18 Sep 49, Oxf St]

The thing is that a novel exposes one's every lack—in maturity, style, under-standing etc.—and requires such a *large* imagination, whereas poetry only needs perhaps a certain depth and intensity in one area, the novel must encompass everything, all sexes, ages, etc. It is devilishly difficult. [to BB, 2 Oct 49, Oxf St]

I must say I am looking forward to talking and thinking about poetry. It is fun to go back to old lectures and find things I had forgotten—"Poetry is active, luminous and triumphant *always*—for it is the business of poetry to draw order out of chaos, to evaluate experience, to set us for an instant outside our works and furious blood and give us back a relationship with an Absolute." "A poem comes at a moment when thought and emotions are fused at a high pitch of intensity—and are married in an image." I suppose that the real problem for all of us is that so often it is passionate love that provides that sort of intensity and yet one does want to paint and talk about other things, and one's whole life may be a journey to find the purest intensity without such dependence of human meetings. [to BB, 16 Oct 49, Oxf St]

I do agree with what you say about Forster. It seems to me that there is a danger everywhere (in painting too) to formulate too much, to make too many intellectual statements about form, principles etc. and that the organic quality, the way a work of art grows, is really something quite different (though after it is done one may try to analyze it). So one does have to combine extreme passionate tension with almost a devil-may-care attitude at the same time—it's like the lightness and grief of the Shakespeare songs. The tension is somehow absorbed and then one is free—[to BB, 15 Aug 53, Bread Loaf]

I have always felt that I was writing for a very few people, the very few I trust, and if some others happen to overhear, that is just an extra. That is why when

V. Woolf died I felt for awhile "now there is no one whose opinion matters"—[to LB, 7 Feb 54, Wr St]

. . . if I had to choose between novels and poetry I would choose poetry
without batting an eyelash, without a *second's* hesitation, and would choose it
whether anyone ever read the poems or not—[to LB, 27 Apr 54, Wr St]

I am in entire agreement that psychiatry should not appear overly in a work of
art (unless it happens to deal with psychiatry and this might be possible in a
novel). I have always said "let the psychiatrists study the novelists and poets,
not vice versa." But one can tell no lies as a poet especially. [to KD, I Jan 62,
Nelson]

I have been ruminating about "personal poems"—I am inclined to agree that
one turns back to less personal poems yet you surely would not remove
Shakespeare's sonnets, all of Donne, much of Yeats, all of Emily Dickinson,
Sappho, Millay, Wylie (or most), Wyatt from the canon, would you? The
trouble is that one does not choose what one is to write about: poetry is a
seizure, and not done on will. The point is I think that a "personal" poem has
to go deep enough to touch the *universal:* the "I" is only a device like any other.
This is not to argue—as I agree that it would be better if the muse provided
more *less* personal poems. [to KD, 3 Apr 64, Sheraton Motor Inn, Philadel-
phia]

I do not believe that anyone who has not done it can imagine the creative
drain that a three-hour stint every day for a year on a novel means—it is a
marathon and just takes the guts out. I tell my students that it is like taking an
examination on which your whole future depends *every day* for a year. [to KD,
25 Jun 64, Nelson]

Meanwhile I have this last week been working at poems about Japan—the
problem is that they do not want to come in form and I find free verse
exhausting as one seems to be able to go on revising forever—there are no
walls and everything slides around. [to BdeS, 6 Dec 64, Yaddo, Saratoga
Springs, N.Y.]

Of course the thing about poetry is that one does not and *cannot* decide to write a certain kind of poetry or not to write it. It is not an art in which the will can operate *at all* as far as inspiration goes. [to KD, 4 Feb 65, Nelson]

The most interesting comment in your very interesting letter concerns revision and lyric poetry. As you no doubt know, a great deal of work has been done recently on this subject—and many libraries now collect the work sheets of single poems. Dylan Thomas, for instance, who *sounds* as if his poems spouted forth, revised a great deal. So did Keats. So did A. E. Housman (who worked for one year on the second stanza of a single lyric, the first stanza having come to him while shaving). So did Wordsworth—if you remember Dorothy's[9] journal she says, "William exhausted himself seeking an epithet for the cuckoo"(!) Frost revised in his head, not on paper—there are different ways to do it. Occasionally a lyric may come forth from the unconscious at the end of long work at something else—as if one got into gear— That is how Frost wrote "Stopping by Woods on a Snowy Evening"—[to KD, 29 Nov 65, Lindenwood]

On Monday I shall plunge like a salmon going upstream to lay an egg and *die,* into a children's book which I hope to finish before we go to Europe April 1st. [to LB, 11 Feb 66, Nelson]

The autobiographical book *Plant Dreaming Deep* will be out after Xmas and I'll see that you get a copy. Twayne is putting me into their series of books on American authors and that book is in the works now, I hear, though I presume it won't go to press for a year and so not be out for nearly two.[1] I saw the author's prospectus and was much impressed—at least she sees clearly that the whole work (poems and novels) belongs *together* as part of a total vision of life. [to HW, 20 Aug 67, Greenings]

[9]Dorothy Wordsworth (1771–1855), English writer and younger sister of William Wordsworth.
[1]Twayne Publishers brought out *May Sarton* by Agnes Sibley in 1972 as part of the Twayne United States Authors series.

I have even made a start at Inner Space[2]—a sort of journal of solitude, although my solitude is really an immense *crowd* and just that is, perhaps, the point. Anyway whatever happens at the moment it is a rest and a joy to lead a one-pointed life, where what I live each moment can be *used*—so different from the novel.[3] [to BB, 13 Feb 70, Nelson]

Why do I write? For two reasons. One is to communicate with myself—this is especially true of the poems. To find out what I really feel and think about something. *As We Are Now* came out of rage at that place (it was a real one, by the way) plus a traumatic experience I went through where true love was made dirty. I see it, the book, as a descent into Hell in which the last rung is that (Anna and Caro). The book was written at white heat and I suppose was a kind of exorcism for me of trauma. The second reason, closely intertwined with the first, is to communicate felt truths to others who might share. It is very important to hear from readers that a book or poem has *landed*, exists for someone else, in a word. These days I am quite overwhelmed by the response. I get 50 letters a week at least from readers all over the country, of both sexes, and of all ages and backgrounds. It is very exciting, but also very demanding. I try to answer as best I can. I talk a lot about all this in *Journal of a Solitude* (now in paperback, the Norton paperbacks) and probably answer your question better there. But I have not removed myself from life. I have lived alone for 20 years, first in Nelson, N.H., and for the last six years here on the Maine coast. People come to me—many, many people. [to Jack Simmons (a fan), 16 Jul 79, York]

And letters, themselves, are part both of the sacred order and the insolvable conflict of her life.

They can be beneficent—

Everything is good, even having to write letters, because there are things one can write that one can't say just as there are things one can say that one can't

[2]The book which became *Journal of a Solitude.*
[3]*Kinds of Love.*

write. Also one has the time to run away and bury one's delights like a squirrel with nuts. One must always get away to taste experience. One must always escape from people one loves in order to love them. Isn't it queer? [to MFH, 16 Aug 40, Ch Pl]

Tu vois en ce moment je suis providentiellement libre de toutes mes préoccupations et responsabilités ordinaires. J'ai une chose à faire, approfondir, pousser aussi loin que possible tout ce que je *deviens*, et de devenir tout le possible (autre chose peut-être qu'aimer)—car en t'écrivant je deviens moi-même. Et il me semble que le sens profond de cette aventure est justement qu'elle me rend à moi-même, qu'elle te rends à toi-même, pas autre chose. C'est déja beaucoup.[4] [to JH, n.d. (1948)]

They can be integral to the routine and discipline of work—

I feel self-conscious writing a regular notebook—I've tried it now and then for months at a time. It is helpful in times of crisis, in *evaluating*. But I suppose letters are my way of greasing the motor and perhaps one can't do both. [to LB, 24 Oct (n.y.)]

Yet, they are also a huge burden. Just before leaving on her trip around the world—

Herewith you shall find the horrendous schedule—I can hardly believe I shall ever be in all those fabulous places—and I do look forward to the time, the space, the utter freedom from daily cares and anxieties—and especially from the albatross of correspondence I carry round my neck. I suppose I have written between three and four hundred letters since just after Christmas. I have got to find some way OUT and travel at present seems to be the only

---

[4]"You see at this moment I am providentially free of all my ordinary preoccupations and responsibilities. I have one thing to do, to deepen, to push as far as possible all that I become, and to become all that is possible (other than doing, other than creating a poem, other perhaps than loving)—because in writing to you I become myself. And it seems to me that the profound sense of this adventure is precisely that it gives me to myself, it gives you to yourself, nothing else. That is already a great deal."

possible one—so you must be patient and know (as I'm sure you do) that my best gift to my real friends will be the poems I write, if I manage to write any. [to KD, 25 Feb 62, Wr St]

But their burden notwithstanding, letters always have been central to Sarton's need for communion—

ô Juliette, I have just come home from standing in Max Gordon's[5] office in a *herd* of actresses only to be told, "You're not the type"—and found a nice fat letter from Julian—how wonderful letters are—how unexpected—especially across an ocean. One has no idea what time of day, what mood, what event they are going to meet. And this was a perfect spar to a drowning man! [to JH, 27 Oct 36, 239 E 17]

I saw Jean-Do yesterday and we laughed a great deal about the boat[6]—she is furious about it and makes all sorts of plans to get me off, or to prevent its happening (like bribing the captain!). We agreed that if it were we we would simply tether it near a post office and stay there, writing poems and drinking wine like Chinese philosophers. [to JM, 14 Jan 47, Chez Limbosch]

And of the essential value of correspondence in general, as letters too are journeys[7]—

The excitement, the delight of the mind is one thing—passion is another. And in letters one is so free of the *mortal* part. [to JH, 28 Nov 37, Ch Pl]

But you labor under a delusion if you imagine that I write good letters to *anyone* but you. You are my joy and writing to you is just necessary for my own inner équilibre, setting everything in its place. And sometimes I imagine that I

[5]theatrical and film producer (1892–1989), owner of the Village Vanguard from 1934 on. He was holding auditions for *The Women*.

[6]The Limbosches had arranged for a week's boat trip to Holland for all of them on a small, primitive sailboat with no comforts.

[7]See "Of Friendship at Christmas," Christmas broadside, 1952, published as "Of Friendship" in *The Land of Silence*.

hardly experience my life until I have sent pieces of it off to you in a letter—
[to JH, 20 Jan 48, Oxf St]

It is very good now that we are in a letter writing place (not a meeting place)
because letters are so much easier than living. One can give one's best. [to JH,
20 Aug 48, London (RP)]

And they serve as a conduit toward the work—

But actually I am feeling very cheerful as I have at last begun to get into the
first of the N.H. novels since I arrived here 6 days ago, and to begin what
always comes first, a series of letters to myself which gradually define what is
vaguely stirring, and from which the characters slowly emerge as living people.
[to HW, 20 Aug 67, Greenings]

And the same element of mystery she is drawn to in silence, in art, and in nature
has its place also in letters—

I began this letter in bed with the kitten asleep beside me with one paw curled
over his face—I began it with a pen which gives one a chance of drawing as
well as writing a letter—yours is wonderful for its spaces between paragraphs
in which one's thoughts go on the journey you begin. A typewritten letter
leaves no deliberate spaces, no elisions, no sous-entendus[8] possible. [to JH, 12
Mar 37, Ch Pl]

For ultimately letters are Sarton's invisible bridge from mind to mind[9]—

If personal isolation doesn't compensate for itself by some sort of communion, religious or simply human—if one cannot feel something like companionship somewhere, somehow, there would be nothing but an end to make of
it. [to JH, 12 Aug 39, Chez Limbosch]

[8]"innuendo."
[9]See "Innumerable Friend" in *The Land of Silence.*

And, like her poetry, they are sent out to transcend and heal—

> In this nightmare world where we are all working—and not *believing* (as one doesn't believe a nightmare while it is going on)—there are still some things that seem clear and simple like the sun, poetry, the love of friends—that is more difficult I know because if I do not talk about the war *you* may perhaps think again that I am indifferent or that we here feel safe and apart. And *I* must all the time look for words that will *not* be tarnished, lose their value, if London is bombed before you get this. [to JH, 10 Sep 39, Rockport]

Indeed transcending is basic both in her work and in her life—

> You must, according to your nature, bring everything down to the most rational level possible. I must, according to mine, transcend and sublimate as much as possible. [to CD, 19 Aug 58, Greenings]

And Sarton hears from others of what her letters mean—

From Elizabeth Bowen—

> I love your letters altogether. I know I don't deserve them, but do write more. Your life sounds lyrical, darling, or at least you have the power of giving it that quality. [EB to MS, 2 Nov 37]

From H.D.—

> This is not much of a note, but just to thank you as always for writing, it is such a joy, you can't know what a joy—to hear of just the ordinary things of life, people, lights, walks, work etc. [HD to MS, Easter Saturday 1944]

And shares that news—

H.D.

H.D. sent me a wonderful book about the Blitz called *Front Line*[1] and touched me very much by writing in it "To May with gratitude for help and sympathy in our ordeal." It makes all the time I took writing letters and not poems suddenly flower—I am happy. [to EMS and GS, 2 Nov 43, 22 E 10]

Last night when I came back from Jean-Do's I found a letter from Marjorie Wells (H.G.'s daughter-in-law and Kot's faithful friend) to tell me that Kot had tried to cut his throat on June 7th, not succeeded, and now was in a deep depression in a sanitorium and that they were trying to get him back with shock treatments. He is over 70 and very ill and I really think it utter sadism not to let him die in peace. Marjorie wrote a very dear letter and said he had asked to have my last letters read to him several times and once for a fleeting moment smiled—I have wondered sometimes if I didn't waste time writing so many letters but then when something like this happens, what balm to know at least that in so far as it was possible I didn't fail him. [to JM, 4 Jul 47, Chez Limbosch]

While in the late years Sarton has not sustained as many correspondences of primary intensity as she did earlier, her journals of those years[2] have become her letters to the world.

And as the journals document, so it is that moments of pure joy shine out like fairy gold from the pages of her life—

I have been absolutely light-headed for two days like the birds qui n'ont pas de cerveau qui n'ont que de l'âme.[3] [to JH, 6 Aug 37, Austria]

And always there are celebrations of the moments, events, places, and friends from among the usual days—

---

[1] *Frontline 1940–41: The Official Story of the Civil Defence of Britain,* issued for the Ministry of Home Security by the Ministry of Information (London: His Majesty's Stationery Office, 1942).
[2] *Recovering, At Seventy, After the Stroke, Endgame, Encore.*
[3] "who have no mind, who have only soul."

I am so excited at having Ruth Pitter to own.[4] Nothing could please me more, in fact. I saw a perfect beauty of hers in the Nov. *Mercury* about a wood dove.[5] The technical perfection makes a shiver of excitement go down my spine— like watching a perfect swan dive, or a figure skater. Let us all praise and love each other in the new year. It is so curious how people resent the ones different from themselves—and this, it seems to me, is the whole wonder and delight of man—his infinite variety—and that Ruth Pitter and I can both be alive at the same time and write poetry almost proves the existence of a genius called God. [to K, 28 Dec 37, Ch Pl]

Such lovely things happen here partly because the tempo is less fierce than in the East. Three women friends and I drove out one spring day to a little town in the mountains where a family has carried on the tradition of carving saints for three generations. I found there a little white wooden tree with fat formal leaves on each of which sits a bird or a squirrel or a beaver, a tree alive with animals, and I got it for Daddy. Then we came back through the ancient land, watching young boys plough (the men were all at war) and old women sow, and the fruit trees all in flower and the marvelous running brooks, miraculous always in this arid landscape. After that day we all wrote poems and now there is a little book to celebrate the day for which I have painted a cover with a phoenix on it.[6] These are precious things. [to JH, 3 Jun 45, Santa Fe (ER)]

I had such a heavenly dear time reading my poems to Jean-Do's little class—et elles en étaient éblouies, parce qu'elles ne s'attendaient pas peut-être au vrai souffle, mais pensaient que j'étais la petite amie de Marie et voilà tout.[7] They had brought flowers and a huge box of chocolates and after all the greetings I sat in Jean-Do's chair on the platform in that familiar classroom where I sat as

[4]*A Trophy of Arms, Poems 1926–1935* by Ruth Pitter, with a preface by James Stephens (Cresset, n.d.). Still in Sarton's library in York, inscribed "For May, affectionately, Kot, Christmas, 1937."
[5]"Early Rising."
[6]A booklet called "Garland for a Day," still in Sarton's possession, with poems by her, Judith Matlack, Dorothy S. McKibbon, and Edith B. Ricketson. It contains "In a Dry Land," later published in *The Land of Silence*.
[7]"and they were dazzled by it because they were not expecting perhaps real inspiration, but only thinking that I was just a friend of Marie's and that was all."

a child, and read first a French translation of each poem and then the poem in English. Jean-Do herself has never heard me read publicly and of course it is much stronger and better when one can use a louder voice—so she was very moved. I ended with "Chartres"[8] and when I had finished she went over to the wall and unpinned a large photograph of the angel of Chartres and gave it to me. All of this was just formal enough to seem like music and I was awfully happy. [to JH, 20 May 48, Chez Limbosch]

We have had a really splendid Christmas, the first one in this blessed place. It was much quieter than our usual ones in Cambridge, more intimate, and really I think better—Judy is in splendid spirits, enjoying her year at Douglass College and the "boys" (for she is housemother in a nonregistered Fraternity!) as well as teaching English; the pussies respond to voices in the house and come alive and play wildly when we are here together (otherwise they behave more like hibernating bears than cats)—and you can imagine all the beauties of the tree, the cards and all against these white walls. The great glory has been a bright pink cyclamen, a perfect tower of winged flowers which look like stained glass when the sun touches them, that and lots of paper-whites in flower here and there. I invited families of neighbors in for cider and cookies—it was wonderful to see toothless Grace Warner, in her heavy boots and overalls, sitting in your mother's chair and so delicately and shyly *peeping* while we talked at the big colored pictures on the Swiss calendar I gave them, as if she couldn't wait to see the next—she is a great woman, looks 80, is probably about my age—the matriarch of a great clan up the hill at that tumbledown "Farm of Contented Animals" and contented people! Mildred came with her darling granddaughter Randy, a very bright little girl indeed who, at three, was far more delighted by a picture book than by a toy rabbit (much to my delight); on Xmas Eve that wonderful Lotte Jacobi, the photographer, wise old woman who has become one of my closest friends around here. [to RG, 3 Jan 65, Nelson]

I had forgotten our birthdays were so close—two tauruses, a fierce animal, full of guts and fight with his feet firmly on the ground and an occasional

---

[8]"Return to Chartres" from *The Lion and the Rose.*

heroic moment! Bless you, 84, and may I even faintly resemble you in large vision, implemented caring, and sheer beauty, darling! when I get there if I ever do—[to RG, 28 May 69, Nelson]

If, as Sarton says, we must make myths of our lives,[9] certainly letting anger out has been a great part of the myth and gestalt of hers. Anger has been her demon, and yet also her *feu sacré*, her sacred fire, without which there would have been no poetry. And so, another conflict—that between staying vulnerable and keeping the poet alive, and yet also keeping the demons at bay. She understood herself at fifteen—

I am honest with myself but have been dishonest with other people several times. Strangely enough it has never been of any importance to myself, it has never been to shield myself. I am very proud but not self-satisfied. I am naturally selfish. I have a hot resentful temper which I am slowly learning to control. I am foolishly sensitive and self-conscious (that is partly my age). I think too much. In work I am of average intelligence and can concentrate well. I have no presence of mind whatever. I have an impossible memory. I have a strong will. I am impetuous, very. I love a few people intensely. If I grow in soul and understanding I shall be a poet. ["Ego," HJ, I Jun 27, Ray St]

Having grown in soul and understanding and become that poet, she has firmly taken a stance on letting anger out, and always on examining it, for anger, too, fuels growth just as it fuels poetry, if it is understood—

And I might further say that no milk in my life is spilt. Everything has to be faced, probed, gotten down to essence and *understood.* [to MH, 17 Jun 72, Nelson]

It has been a week of good work and much inner stress, which is why I haven't written. I was consoled by a letter from Janet Flanner saying that it worries her that she is so violent "without warning," as that has been my state, to the point that I decided that in future I really had better go into a burrow and

[9]See *I Knew a Phoenix,* pp. 104, III–II3.

never see another human soul. It had been hard going to get through into the poems, but that is no excuse and I wonder how in Hell I shall ever learn both to be vulnerable enough, yet controlled. It seems to be one or the other. It does not help (yes, it does—what a lie) that people here are so understand-ing—I am never blamed, which makes me feel even more like a criminal. Well, enough of this. I have written 8 poems in the last 10 days or so and maybe one or two of them are good, better anyway than those you have seen. But I shall not know of course till much later. [to LB, 30 Oct 54, Chez Limbosch]

I did smile about The Fight with the Dragon[1]—yes, I am on the side of the dragon for creative purposes at least! It is borne in on one here over and over again that people do not let the dragon out enough. You do, though—I am not worried! I do trust that victory (in the book by Neuman)[2] will prove worth it, only the dragon *must* be allowed out for there to be any battle. No? [to LB, 26 Aug 55, Bread Loaf]

And in these stanzas from one of several drafts of a poem—

Come to me with your anger
For well I recognize
Its anguish and its danger
The wound behind the eyes.
It is my way and yours
To break down the closed doors.

It is my long held guilt
The source of so much woe
I bear it like a curse or fault
But I will tell you what I know
Cold anger is a greater curse
Cold anger's punishment is worse.

[1]The fight for control between the ego and the dragon of the unconscious, an image used by Louise Bogan in a letter to Sarton dated August 22, 1955.
[2]Erich Neumann (1905–), German analytical psychologist, student of Carl Jung, and author of *The Great Mother* and *The Origins and History of Consciousness.*

How anger leaps up from the throat
A seizure very close to tears
I cannot daunt or shut it out
It has been with me all my years
Cold anger comes from the cold mind
And is as furious and blind.

Come to me with your anger
I know it all too well
To rages am no stranger
Can share your lonely hell
Cold anger cannot share
It feels superior.

[from "Anger," n.d. (1980s)]

It was so good to get your frail page in the mail. It is splendid that you trust your doctor there, and he does sound as if he were "getting at" things. I am consoled to hear that "anger" is a problem, for it is surely mine. But I could not read the second word—was it "reviewing"? For me depression is *always* suppressed anger I have discovered—and if the anger has not been suppressed, then guilt and shame because it is such a bad thing, except an occasional, very occasional "holy anger" I suppose. In order to keep an even keel, no doubt you have buried a lot of stress and strain in these last years—and maybe later on some of it can find its way into poems. Give your genius into the paws of the tiger he will not rend. [to LB, 14 Nov 65, Lindenwood]

And Sarton has done just that with her genius. But anger is inextricably bound to her integrity and sense of values—

I suppose it is the perogative of youth to be *indignant*—"the cry against corruption"—that Katherine Mansfield speaks of as one of the primary things that made her write: the other was joy. [to GS, 31 Mar 36, 23 Taviton St., London]

The full horror is beginning to dawn on people—and I suppose a general *rage* will be a good thing. We have been far too tolerant *inwardly* and the war won't be won until the sacred anger really takes hold. [to Polly and RWB, 9 Aug 42, Sudbury]

And here her indefatigable indignation over "a poverty-stricken sheaf of reviews" she sends to H.D. about that poet's latest book, and even more, over the state of criticism in general[3] and the problems of the woman poet in particular—

I had several seizures of imaginative apoplexy as I read these over—Muriel's book too has simply not been *read*. Louise Bogan, who was once a fine poet, has not survived menopause, I take it, and has become a rabid anti-feminist and self-hater in consequence—her review is simply pathological. I hear that she drinks a great deal. But nothing excuses this sort of thing to my mind. Not content with treating fine poets with the condescension of a Bishop whose ring is being kissed, she must cast ashes at the Comtesse de Noailles[4] (whom she has evidently seen photographs of but never read). God knows, Anna de Noailles has faults but she was *The* romantic par excellence, and I do not think that her apotheosis of gardens smelled of the Casino. And, for God's sake, are we still in the dark ages that "female poets" are considered a race apart, a sport of monsters to be reviewed as such? There is not a spark of generosity in Bogan apparently. She is unable any longer to *rejoice,* poor woman!

We now come to our little friend Oscar Williams[5] gravely presenting his synthetic bouquets and brickbats, and unable to resist his own cheaply clever little monkey mind. Yes, I am angry. [to HD, 29 Oct 44, Ch Pl]

[3]Sarton certainly shared the sentiments of her father, who wrote: "The *Transcript* article was excellent too. You are very lucky in having such good interpreters of your thought: even when a man has obtained all the success he could desire—he is misinterpreted more often than not, by his friends as well as by his enemies." [GS to MS, 12 Sep 34, London]

[4]Comtesse Mathieu de Noailles, *née* Princess Anna-Élisabeth de Brancovan (1876–1933), Paris-born poet of Rumanian and Greek ancestry. See epigraph to "My Sisters, O My Sisters" in *The Lion and the Rose.*

[5]Poet, critic, anthologist (1900–), known for his *A Little Treasury of Modern Poetry,* from which Sarton was omitted.

Indeed her values and sense of justice are frequent causes for indignation and always come first, even when friendship is at stake—

It is the most fair day, with light snow on all the branches and a pervenche[6] and rose sky—in the dark before all these wonders were visible I lay awake for an hour or two this morning considering the business of Nellie.[7] None of these things are small or light or don't matter. They do matter awfully. That is the Hell of this world. But I am sorry that I caused you trouble—that I hurt someone whom you love and who has taken such good care of you for so many years. (I am really tremendously grateful to Nellie when I think of all that.) I never believed that the opinion of any single human being was unimportant or not to be taken seriously, so when Nellie started talking about Germany I talked with her as I would with any other friend of yours, man to man. If I remember accurately it began quite calmly in a friendly way. But I do remember well that I was by the end really angry and no doubt showed it. I suppose that most people would say what a waste of emotion and why bother? Why not let it slide? What you or Nellie believes is not going to change the world. But Margaret, my whole belief is centered in the fact that what Nellie and I believe *does* change the world. If she only knew how much I love Germany, how I have fought for and helped Germans in exile from Hitler's Germany—how much more faith I have than most people that there can be a strong free Germany and that indeed the welfare of Europe depends on it. But I also believe that until the Germans recognize the evil they have done there is no hope whatever. Punishment seems to me totally unimportant compared to that recognition (have we not poured ashes on our heads *for years* over the injustice of the Versailles treaty—but I have yet to meet a German who will take full responsibility for what Germany has done).

The German has a wonderful way of twisting things so that he always gets the pity of the world wherever he is. Perhaps in the argument with Nellie I too am to be pitied. After all I was in the house of a friend and at that and this very moment my dearest friends are being starved slowly if not killed *for the*

[6]"periwinkle."
[7]Margaret Foote Hawley's housekeeper.

second time in my life by the Germans. I did not expect to be attacked in your house because as a Belgian I cannot admit that the Germans are all good and sweet as angels. Everything we owned was destroyed once. We were driven out with nothing. It all came out right in the end—but it might not have. My mother is frail now because of the ravage of those years when we lived on $30 a month (for two years). Not to mention the radical uprooting for her—the loss of her dearest friends—

Nellie refused to admit that this or anything else ever had happened by any fault of the Germans.

Once more it will be said, "What does it matter that a few Germans in Yorkville, impregnated with loyalty for a good Germany that they remember, will not recognize the present evil?" But I believe it does matter. Twenty years ago Hitler's gang was a small fanatic minority whom nobody took seriously. If the Wheelers and Smiths and Mrs. Dillings ever got control of this country, it might be because we did not take the opinions of the Nellies seriously enough. We did not fight them with every arm we possess while there was still time.

Well, enough of this. But I felt attacked the other night and this is my defense. It was not an aberration. I would behave exactly as I did then if I was talked to in the same way by anyone whatever their race, color or social position. Therefore perhaps it's for me to say—and not for Nellie—that I would rather not stay in your house. [to MFH, 23 Jan 45, Ch Pl]

If Goldwater is elected President I shall leave the country and be repatriated as a human being. That is how strongly *I* feel—so perhaps we had better drop that subject for good. I do not believe that he is even intelligent or he could not have said the idiotic things he has said. As for the Civil Rights Bill, I (thank God) am not responsible for your ancestors having been in the slave trade and all those old Anglo-Saxons you admire so much who had a Bible in one hand and a thousand human beings treated like animals below the decks—from *whom* (the sale of whom) they made their fortunes. But if I *had* this crime in my blood, believe me I would feel it my duty now to make amends. The Civil Rights Bill is too late— But at least *at last* it is on the books. I am astounded that you believe *JUSTICE* to have a race (White!)

which it exclusively protects. Well, much love anyway. [to KD, 12 Aug 64, Chez Limbosch]

And her values always come first when poetry or art is threatened—

O yes, one must talk straight from the shoulder, there isn't time to beat around bushes anymore. And as you say a few socks make them sit up! One day in a girls' college, South Ca., I was infuriated by some girls yawning in the back row and finally lost my temper and asked them to leave, not for my sake but for the sake of poetry. Afterwards I thought I'd be frowned upon but everyone from students to teachers thanked me with tears in their eyes. None had *dared* do that. There should be some *fierce* teaching and some awe of learning. Everything is made so easy and is so second-rate. They are so easily satisfied with themselves. [to GdeS, 24 Nov 40, New Orleans]

Since I heard from you I have had something of a contretemps with Froman,[8] who was much heartened to hear the faculty doesn't like him! He had the insouciance, rudeness, or simple crudity to ask me if I would be "good enough" to "stand by" and give the commencement address in case Marguerite Higgins[9] cannot come at the last minute. The idea of making poetry "stand by" for journalism irritated me, and also he asked it as if it were the most natural thing in the world. It would take me a week to write the commencement address, which I might not even give! Well, to make a long story short I phoned him person-to-person. The poor innocent creature said immediately, "Were you scared by my letter?" I think he imagined I must be a very shy poet and he evidently had no idea that I am a professional lecturer and that my fee would be $300 for a commencement address. Anyway he was much startled when I said, "Not scared, *furious!*" Then he was ready to climb down and decide to have *me* do it, but that is not at all the point—and I said finally that I would "stand by" if he gave me a month's notice. If I do have to do it I think I shall make rather an aggressive address about what really "puts

[8]President of Russell Sage College, Troy, N.Y.
[9]Chinese-born American journalist, author, reporter for *New York Herald Tribune.*

a girdle around the earth in forty minutes" and that it is *not* journalism! Anyway I wrote him a brief note after our conversation to confirm it and added that I hoped M.H. would be able to give the address, "and then we shall all be happy." So much for that.[1] [to KD, I Mar 59, Wr St]

I am very fond of her[2] but we will always fight about certain things which I do perhaps take too seriously. I really wince when people call Mozart superficial, for instance, and it is quite silly to care so much. Also she hates modern poetry such as Edith Sitwell, Eliot, calls Yeats superficial and rubbishy etc. And I too have made violent attacks because these things matter far too much to me. [to JH, 28 Oct 48, Oxf St]

But perhaps anger is most sacredly and inviolably entwined with the vulnerabilities of staying open as poet to the very end—

Anger is not withdrawal. It is pain. Try to imagine just for a second that bad behavior on my part is always the signal of acute pain—a person who swears when his finger is caught in a door. I felt this so very much when *you* got angry (and with so much justification) on the phone. In a funny way I didn't mind at all. You minded because bad behavior is a key matter with you, a point of honor. It is not with me because I have to forgive myself to keep on creating and being what I can be—and if I dwell too much on my lacks I simply become useless to myself and others. That they are immense and terribly destructive I need not be told. But I believe truly that God has forgiven me a long time ago because He knows what He has laid upon me and that to remain as transparent and vulnerable as I must, and to go on creating forever, is all that He can ask. [to MH, 5 Jun 70, Nelson]

And then there is detachment, which Sarton greatly values—

In art—

[1]Sarton received an honorary degree at the forty-second commencement of Russell Sage College on Sunday, May 31, 1959, and was the graduation speaker.
[2]Lady Beatrice Glenavy.

The three big experiences for me in Europe this time, at least of a visual kind, were picnicking over and over again in olive groves, the Matisse Chapel at Vence (pure radiance and joy, a truly religious place and so exciting that a contemporary achieved this) and finally the great Piero della Francesca frescos at Arezzo, which opened up and made clear to me a whole new conception in art: why the impersonal is more moving than the personal, often. One is moved to tears here by the use of space and silence, by something quite beyond the subject which is close to mysticism. It is that that I am after in the new poems. [to KD, 15 Dec 54, Wr St]

In work—

It is very wicked and adorable to take time from sleep, but don't do it again—and we will talk about the poems. Your criticisms are never brutal and even if they were, you must know by now that a poem is a thing in itself, not me, and I am very detached about them. I want to know *all* the criticisms, all the shades and nuances of hesitations you may have. [to JH, n.d. (1948), Chez Limbosch]

In love—

I begin to think one cannot be too introspective if at the same time one can detach oneself from events and people and become objective. [HJ, 4 Aug 29, GSLT]

There is (don't you agree?) a point of detachment in any attachment which is the saving grace, and all the intensities can be balanced if one can just lay a finger on it somehow. [to LB, 20 Feb (n.y.)]

. . . finally I came to see that my loneliness (acute and awful) was really a loneliness for *myself* and what I had to do was get back to my blessed solitude. My motto, the opposite of dear Forster's, has become "only *disconnect*." It has to be done, at least for the present, or I shall not survive. [to BB, 24 Jun 70, Nelson]

Yet too much detachment is something she rails against—

Whether it be detachment from love—

Well, I shall practice detachment this spring from all save the cat. He can be loved madly and unreasonably and it doesn't matter, does it? He can purr of course which makes him superior—especially as his purrs have subtle differences which may be analyzed; and range from "affection" to "love" and even (rarely and when he is hungry) "passion." Give me time and *perhaps* I'll learn. It is really I suppose that I have no wish to learn this particular thing. Surely it is when one is out of love that detachment seems a blessing? How is one to be inside it and *wish* to be anywhere else? [to LB, 20 Apr (n.y.)]

"Detachment" has not very much meaning unless it is detachment *from* something, has it? It is the getting away, the better to understand or observe. In itself it would seem to me rather a negative than a positive. [to CD, 4 Feb 59, Nelson]

Or detachment from commitment—

There was a very good man here called Ulich[3]—professor of Education, ex-German, who said that he thought one of the problems was how to keep disenchantment out of disillusion—and also that we must find the other side of the coin of detachment—an *attachment.* How one misses it everywhere. There is no faith in us to bind the dragon with. [to JH, 15 Dec 39, Ch Pl]

But the great changes which happened to England at Dunquerque (and only *after* Dunquerque, remember) have still to happen here. The same half-baked pacifism, objections to conscription, etc. are still there. They will have to be blown away. I talk myself blue in the face and have made a small dent in the "detachment" so carefully cultivated by students here and planted by liberalism at its most unrealistic and dangerous. [to K, 1 Nov 40, Black Mt]

[3]Robert Ulich, professor at Harvard University.

Or the detachment of critics as when Ruth Pitter's book is not reviewed well—

It would have been such a chance for the clique people— Spender for instance—to prove that they have a standard. What a petty passionless age it is. People crawl about like reptiles talking about *detachment*.

> The best lack all conviction while the worst
> Are full of passionate intensity.[4]

[to K, 13 Jan 40, Ch Pl]

Ruth Pitter, 1972.

And certainly any detachment from one's primary responsibility to growth and change is anathema to her—

But I stayed with an old friend from Saint-Jean de Luz, an English girl who is now a refugee—she was part of a gay gang of us who spent one summer (the only one of my life) in Lido style, drinking etc. She is *absolutely* the same while the whole world has changed around her and every one of us except her has grown up and really amounting to something—so it was very shocking and saddening and hopeless. I had forgotten that there were people who only thought about bridge, drink, flirting, clothes, gambling, literally *nothing* else! And she is being supported by a rich couple who are even worse. I went there for dinner and literally for three solid hours the conversation consisted of horse racing, bridge, gossip, and so on. I was, needless to say, silent as I could only gossip and we don't know the same people. Marjorie,[5] this girl, is quite intelligent too but rotten now I expect and beyond hope. She doesn't even know how empty her life is. [to MFH, 25 Feb 41, Grand Canyon]

The problem of detachment is something she tussles out in *Faithful Are the Wounds*—

---

[4]From Yeats's "The Second Coming."
[5]Marjorie Terry.

The whole question of the passionate being, *passionate* because his dearly held beliefs are in danger as against the cool, calm detached person who is cool and calm *because* they are detached.

In the novel Damon Phillips, Grace Kimlock, Edward Cavan are brought together by this *passionate* concern—Goldberg cares very passionately but has deliberately chosen not to involve himself. Isabel: what price have you paid for *not* being involved? [HJ, 19 Mar 54, Wr St]

For throughout the letters is the passion of her political conscience, which was there very young—

The camp is very excited about Sacco and Vanzetti—I was wondering what Daddy thought about it. It seems to me that if four such intelligent men who have examined the case so thoroughly believe them to be guilty, they must be. Fuller certainly is brave. I have heard rumors that he may be a presidential candidate—I think he'd make an excellent president, don't you?[6] [to EMS and GS, 13 Aug 27, DMC]

Russia and Germany fight with a disregard of human life no democracy would tolerate. No democracy would have taken Sevastopol at that cost and any democracy would have surrendered earlier. [to BB, 9 Jul 42, Sudbury]

I am working now on writing a lecture on the poets of the last war and this and it is quite inspiring. When the illusions of the holy war fell for the young men of 1914 in the horrors of the trenches there was nothing left but hatred and pity—pity for the men, English and German, and hatred for the civilians. The *fact* of horror possessed them, the utter futility of trench warfare. This we have not yet had—even at Stalingrad they are dying in thousands for a city, not for yards of mud. And we have been forced to understand this war so thoroughly before fighting it, because until it was understood in its final implications no one *would* fight. It is really just the opposite—we knew the

[6]In July 1927, Governor Fuller of Massachusetts appointed a committee headed by President Lowell of Harvard to review the conviction of Sacco and Vanzetti; the committee upheld the original verdict, and the two were executed the following month.

horrors of war so well, they loomed so large and definite, that it was *only* when the reasons became implacably clear that we could fight. So all the emphasis now is on what we are driving at and what changes must happen in us and in the world *afterwards.* That is a great advance. That, the great war poets like Wilfred Owen helped to bring about, by making us pacifists *first* not *afterwards.* We have been lifted up by their pity and helped to understand and warned by their hatred. Poetry is a help. [to JH, 19 Sep 42, Ch Pl]

I went to a great gathering of poets the other night—the Gregorys,[7] John Holmes, Robert Frost, and a lot of aged women who apparently come to sit at Frost's feet. He held forth in a charming way, being much the "homely philosopher." But he made me very sore by intimating that the war didn't interest him "now we knew who would win." As if it were a baseball game and as if there weren't hundreds of men dying every day to see that we do win. The worst of it is that he is listened to as a God. I was the only person who dared talk back at all and I didn't really say what I felt, only suggesting that every day the war was prolonged it meant oceans of human suffering. Then he answered that he didn't need to be told about suffering, that he had lived with death all his life! Somewhat off the point and what arrogance anyway. He has not lived in a concentration camp, that is one sure thing. It is a terrible sign of weakness not to be able to face other people's suffering and I fear it is an American weakness. We do not want to believe the worst. I have been writing bitter poems about that very thing—[to BB, 22 May 44, Ch Pl]

Meanwhile there is work to do. I am hoping to work at the Negro Settlement in Cambridge—perhaps start a writing class there. The racial tensions are very serious now and I would like to do what I can, in a small way, to help solve that problem. It is a profoundly Christian one. [to JH, 25 Sep 44, 22 E 10]

I was perfectly infuriated by a snide article on England by Koestler in *Partisan Review.* He is a destructive bloke, isn't he? I'm afraid it's all rot that rootless people make better internationalists than rooted people. The opposite is

[7]Horace Gregory and his wife, Marya Zaturenska.

actually true. You have got to have some deep root to spread out from. Loyalty begins at home. How beautifully Gandhi illustrates this. It was sad about old Tom Lamont[8] and I thought it would be a shock to you as you had seen him so recently—and what an amazing contrast between Gandhi and Lamont! In one editorial it said that Lamont had been at times the most powerful single influence in the Western hemisphere—and yet he will be forgotten in three or four years. And Gandhi will never be forgotten. Because perhaps Lamont's power was almost accidental, whereas Gandhi's was personally created, a real creation, something which has never been seen before and never will be again. Even Christ did not combine politics and sainthood, and that is what makes G. so fascinating. He was a great politician, and I use the word deliberately rather than statesman. But he was also of course a saint. One would have thought the combination impossible. [to JH, 8 Feb 48, Oxf St]

Then I have to race over to the State House to speak for the Civil Liberties at a hearing on four very dangerous bills that are coming up, ostensibly to keep commies out of gov. jobs, from voting or running for office but actually so worded that they would affect all liberals. Anyway you cannot fight ideas by repressing them and that is what I am going to say, by flattering the ignorant Irish Congressmen to the best of my ability. I put great faith in a great-great-grandfather whose name was Tims.[9] What could be more persuasive than Tims. [to JH, 20 Jan 48, Oxf St]

I *enraged* the students at the last college (in a remote mountain valley) by saying that one's way of judging the degree of civilization of a country was whether the police carried guns or not. However several students told me that I had done good and at least made them think. Some said I was a wolf in sheep's clothing, i.e. a politician in poet's clothing. [to EMS and GS, 14 Mar 48, Bridgewater, Va.]

[8]Thomas William Lamont (1870–1948), American banker. Julian Huxley had stayed at Lamont's NYC home on his U.S. lecture tour in 1930. Corliss Lamont (1902–), the youngest son, had been a paying guest of the Huxleys while attending New College, Oxford University, 1924–25.
[9]John Timms Hervey Elwes (1771–1829), of Stoke College, Suffolk. Born Timms but took name Elwes in 1793.

Meanwhile I have also got myself involved in a local fight to try to do something about the *growing* police brutality in Boston and here—it is perfectly incredible. A negro child was picked up by a p. wagon the other day, kept in it two hours and so beaten that she had to go to hospital. A few weeks ago a boy was shot dead on very slight provocation. As this goes on always in slum areas where the people don't dare complain and we others don't know about it—and also it's very hard to prosecute as it is always a bum's word against a cop's—it is a very interesting problem. The meetings are amazing—some violent young kids, black and white, who want to take everything by storm, some patient aged negros and wiser people (like me!) who realize that we must go slow, some Reverends (the way Negros taste the word Reverend is wonderful!) and other odd representatives of various Social Action groups. It takes an hour to decide the simplest piece of business and is altogether a fascinating example of democracy in action. I'm sure it's good for me to get out and do something useful as I am not really working at poems. [to BB, 20 Mar 50, Oxf St]

I think if we could talk we would discover many points of agreement, and fewer of disagreement. But I must add just one more word. You make a large generality about Europe owing us everything. But we owe England our very lives. She stood *alone* against the Nazis for a *full year* while we slowly got ready. Without that year we might have lost. As for France, what we give her is a drop in the bucket to what she is spending in both blood and money in the Indo-Chinese war. And this war would have stopped long ago except for the pressure from us. They have nothing to gain by it as they have promised the Indo-Chinese their freedom. We are unpopular in France today for this chief reason. Then we are at a low ebb in everyone's esteem because of McCarthy.[1]

You have no idea what an effect this sort of thing has on the democracies of Europe. We have given up without a fight a man's right to a fair trial, to a lawyer, to be *heard* in fact. No amount of talk about idealism can counteract such things. They speak for themselves. This is the really serious issue to my

---

[1]Senator Joseph McCarthy (1908–57), whose charges of a large-scale Communist infiltration into the State Department and careless accusations brought great hardships to many people.

mind. White[2] is a case in point. He was never convicted, yet people talk as if he had been. There was not enough evidence. It is in times of fear and hysteria that a nation's soul is tried. How is ours doing? Very badly to my way of thinking. My god how safe we are compared to France or England—but have they gone berserk and given an innocent man no chance to defend himself? We are indulging in trial by *hearsay,* and on the evidence of confessed renegades and Commies! [to KD, 20 Dec 53, Wr St]

You just don't like the poems where I come closest to being political ("Who Wakes"[3] for example) but these in the whole view, all-sides-to-a-man, are crucially important. I know how "Who Wakes" moves audiences. The same is true of "The Tortured,"[4] which took me two months to write because of the horrible suffering in the concentration camps; to have found a form for that, to transcend (without mawkish consoling), is one of my real triumphs and I must have it. [to KD, 9 Nov 60, Wr St]

It was a fortunate time for her[5] to come, as we had Town Meeting yesterday and she could witness this illuminating piece of democracy. It was my first, also, and I made a maiden speech—and was grateful to see my side win. We have had a very bitter battle about hard-topping a small stretch of road which abuts on the town green—and has for years sent down tons of mud and silt into Mildred Quigley's cellar and yard. I love the dirt roads, but not when they are so active and destructive—I am on the side of the people who live here all year, the poor and independent "natives." But what is fascinating is to see how we vote $15,000 without anyone asking how it is to be spent (on roads) and then there is a battle royal about $27.00 for a single street lamp by the firehouse. [to BdeS, 12 Mar 63, Nelson]

Inherent in her vision of life is her sense of religion. It seems fitting that her first recorded impressions of "church" at nine are of its flowers—

[2]Probably Henry Dexter White, an assistant secretary of the Treasury who was accused of disloyalty in 1948; he died soon after, but there were efforts to reopen the investigation as late as 1953.
[3]In *The Lion and the Rose.*
[4]In *The Lion and the Rose.*
[5]Kyoko.

I went to church with the Spragues last Sunday. There were beautiful flowers at church. [to EMS and GS, 20 Jul 21, Greensboro, Vt.]

And as early as fifteen she had already formed her credo. After a discussion on religion at camp—

I believe that there is a wide beautiful strength in the universe. I should like to call it Truth; for Truth is my ideal—I have consecrated my life to the search of it. I believe in the immortality of the soul. I believe in Christ as a great personality who has come the nearest to Truth of any man; who has loved men most purely and most beautifully. I do not try to be like him—that would be against my whole philosophy of life; that each man must work out his own salvation in his own way. [HJ, 19 Jul 27, DMC]

And a few months later her search for something mysterious beyond her knowledge finds expression in these images—

> Come out into the night; the moon is fair.
> The quiet and the cold will scrape distrust
> From our sick eyes, perhaps, and make robust
> Hearts of this seeking and despair.
> Come, dearest friend, come let us go to stare
> At multitudes of stars till we have thrust
> To highest heaven these thoughts of flame and dust.
> If there is truth, surely it will be there.
> Such beauty, keen, sad, piercing and strong
> Enough to freeze our very eyes into four
> Moons reflecting starlight, wide for more,
> Will steep souls in God, if God be.
> Come from far singing a mighty song,
> Giver of light and love, Oh let us see.

> ["The Search," HJ, 8 Mar 28, Ray St]

And then continual reflections on her sense of religion and her reverence for life—

I find it very comforting and dear to be in a part of the world where religion is a natural and important part of life—a continual reality. I myself do not quite believe but I am comforted that others have this comfort. The churches are so gay and at the same time full of a simple acceptance of agony and human suffering. The stiff primitive Christs hanging on wooden crosses and then the so human saints. There is one favorite here called Santiago,[6] always dressed in Spanish clothes (which the women make) and on horseback. He has to have many pairs of new shoes as he wears them out going out at night on errands of mercy. Today, Corpus Christi,[7] there is a great procession in which the Archbishop carries the Host through the streets and everyone kneels.

And then going along beside this new religion, hand in hand with it, for there are missions and chapels in all the Pueblos and Franciscan priests, streams the ancient Indian religion, out in the open air, drenched in sunlight with its beautiful sense of the relation between man and the elements, man and the earth and sun. It is extraordinary after one of the Indian dances to see the Indians go to kneel in full costume before their patron saint, and to bear him back into the church. (They bring him out to watch the dances.) Even more strange when the Indian chant changes suddenly to a liturgical one. [to JH, 3 Jun 45, Santa Fe (ER)]

I am delighted to have the Du Bos. Here I have been reading von Hügel.[8] I think myself that it is a great insult to God to turn to him out of suffering because it is not a matter of being *found* by God (comforted in) but of being lost *in* Him. One should only praise God and only look to him in joy and for the sake of purifying joy and feeling its true human proportions perhaps, but *not* out of despair. Von Hügel says, "The great rule is, variety up to the verge of dissipation; recollection up to the verge of emptiness; each alternating with the other and making a rich fruitful tension." [to JH, 14 Aug 48, Oxon]

---

[6]The apostle St. James, brother of St. John the Evangelist; patron saint of Spain and many Spanish-speaking countries.
[7]A festival of the church, kept on the Thursday after Trinity Sunday, in honor of the Eucharist.
[8]Baron Friedrich von Hügel (1852–1925), Roman Catholic theologian born in Italy, naturalized British subject 1914. The quote that follows is probably from his *Letters to His Niece*.

I was enormously helped by the von Hügel letters these last days and at its best the Catholic mind seems to me much wiser than the Protestant, wholer and saner and also more gentle, more human. But I also think it is almost impossible to be a converted Catholic. The strain of belief is too great and one has to accept too many impossibles. Basil says that he becomes less and less Christian as time goes on. He teased me very much because I steeped myself in all this, but it did help. The essential Christian wisdom is after all a beautiful wisdom and in the end it all comes back to what one can dig out of oneself, call it God or the soul or whatever it may be, the dying to self, the renunciation and the being reborn. "Teach us to care and not to care" as Eliot says in "Ash Wednesday." I said it many times and also just two words, "Dieu seul."[9] All the love came back and the meaning and all the bitterness was washed away. [to JH, 17 Aug 48, London (JS)]

I am now quite sure that denial never works—one must go on and love more, not less, more purely and deeply but not less. "God indeed is not the Cosmos, but far less is he Being *minus* Cosmos. He is not to be found by subtraction and not to be loved by reduction." I was helped by a book by a German philosopher called Buber, *Between Man and Man*—it helped me to see that denial and shutting out was not the way, and one did not find God by giving up human love but only through it. [to BB, I Sep 48, Dublin]

Hier soir nous avons conduit dans la petite auto Daddy à l'université juif de Brandeis où il devait faire un discours sur la science et la religion—j'étais triste car à cause du jour de congé, les étudiantes étaient en grande partie pas là, et c'était dommage d'avoir une si petite salle pour un si beau discours. Toute la bonté et la pureté de mon père et sa vision de la vie était là—et j'étais éblouie. Ce qu'il a dit c'était surtout que la religion et la science ont besoin l'un à l'autre et même ne peuvent vivre l'un sans l'autre—la religion a besoin de la science. C'est à dire la religion *pure,* pour lutter contre superstitions et les dogmas qui obscurent la lumière. La science a besoin de la religion pour se rendre compte toujours qu'elle touche à des mystères profondes—et Daddy a

[9]"God alone."

très bien montré que plus la science avance plus il découvre de mystères, et non moins. Daddy a parlé une heure et demi avec fougue et tout le monde était ravi.[1] [to ML, 22 Nov 51, Myn Pl]

Someone sent me a wonderful line from *Religio Medici,* "I have been shipwreckt, but am no enemy to sea and wind." Isn't that fine? [to KD, 27 Dec 59, Nelson]

I have never *seen* such a variety of faces—and have an overwhelming sense of God's creation, of the *human* multiple variety—indescribable. [to JM, 9 Apr 62, Puri, Bay of Bengal]

My theory is that the greatest people of all creeds have much in common— they are *humanity's*—and that great spiritual leaders also have something in common with great artists. [to KD, 27 Aug 63, Nelson]

I really have read the New Test. several times, dear Basil, but must have chosen to forget the horrendous passages you quote. Is not the great mistake to have made Christ into God? If he is taken as one of the leaders—flawed like every human—but with certain insights we still have to come to terms with—*then?* [to BdeS, 7 Mar 64, Nelson]

The Greek was unmystical and it seems to me that the *value* (from the point of view of joy and/or happiness) of the mystic view is that it sees the universe as suffused by a beneficent power—as endlessly *creative,* as never finished. When you make man the measure of the universe, it stops something. [to BdeS, 3 Nov 64, Nelson]

---

[1]"Last evening we drove Daddy in the little car to the Jewish university Brandeis where he had to make a speech on science and religion—I was sad that due to a holiday students were largely not there, and it was a shame to have such a small room for such a beautiful talk. All the beauty and purity of my father and his vision of life were evident—I was dazzled. What he said was that above all religion and science need one another and even cannot exist without the other—religion needs science, that is to say *pure* religion, in order to combat superstitions and dogmas which obscure the light. Science needs religion in order always to realize that it is dealing with profound mysteries—and Daddy showed very well that the more science advances the more it discovers such mysteries, not the less. Daddy spoke an hour and a half with ardor and everyone was enthralled."

On Wed. I make my last (thank God) speech in Chapel and am taking as theme Hopkins' poem "The world is charged with the grandeur of God" and talking about how the only way we can praise Him, know Him, is to *look* at his creation, which is not necessarily visible in churches, alas. A simple flower growing out of an infinitesimal seed being so much more miraculous as poetry, chemistry, mathematics, physics than any flight of two astronauts into space can possibly be—you get the gist. [to BdeS, 5 Dec 65, Lindenwood]

I think I see love as action, rather than as contemplation—"what ye have done unto the least of these ye have done unto me" is the only thing I truly can say I *believe* of Christ. I mean this is the one *command* I truly understand. [to MH, 4 Mar 70, Nelson]

The answer would be religion but I really have no sense of a *personal* God and have never felt Christ as a living presence in my life—I envy those who do. [to JM, 22 Oct 71, Nelson]

For Sarton the mystical is essential not only to her sense of religion but also to poetry, to communion within love and friendship, and to experience in general—

In these lectures every year I take a theme which is not literary but about life itself and then build a group of poems into it for the purpose of making the children see that poetry has a lot to do with life and says the most complex things so simply that one can understand them. So I am not thinking about the poet especially in relation to the moment of possible communication, but that this moment *in life* itself is the crucial moment, in teaching for instance, in friendship of course, in religion also, it is the moment the mystic spends his life hoping for and sometimes gets. I think I may end with St. John of the Cross, the famous lyric which begins

> In darkness on a night
> Inflamed with love and sweet anxiety
> O daring! O delight!
> I left—none noticed me—
> My house was yielded to tranquillity.

And which ends of course with the mystical union of the soul with Christ. The Chapman sonnet[2] is good because we can get this moment or actually have it, every time we open a great book with our real attention—then also the moment of real communication often happens *after* the event (hence Frost's "Tuft of Flowers" where he and the man who left the tuft for the butterflies commune with each other though the man has left the field). I hope this makes what I am after more clear. These lectures are always, in a way, sermons. They are an attempt to define the essential spiritual experience of the year for myself—and have often dealt with problems in relationships. Last year I did a more simple one called "The Delights of the Poet." The poems are simply illustrations of a central theme which is philosophical or mystical. [to KD, 30 Sep 51, Myn Pl]

And as all her work, the letters and journals are full of thoughts on aging—

I sat beside a darling old Polish countess, the Châtelaine of Mon Trésor (one of the loveliest of the Loire chateaux). She has asked me to lunch there tomorrow as we are going into town this afternoon to have our hair done and I am taking her my book.[3] She says, though she was anxious to read it and very warm in her interest, that she has no time for anything but the papers as she must advise the grandchildren what to do—she is passionately interested in politics, altogether very alive with a cold gleaming eye that I found most attractive. She told G.[4] that I was obviously very remarkable—with such eyes. I do like old ladies—it is a passion. [to EMS and GS, 22 May 38, VF]

It is always for Sarton the inner radiance which comes from suffering that holds it all—

It's only the faces that have been created from *inside*—like facility in art, pure beauty doesn't somehow *touch* my marrow—except in very rare cases—and

---

[2]Keats's "On First Looking into Chapman's Homer."
[3]*The Single Hound.*
[4]Grace Dudley.

even then, as I think, it was some *shadow* of thought across the beauty, some pain, some mortal anguish that set it in relief. [to MFH, 21 Aug 40, Ch Pl]

Middle age is a great test of peoples faces—and everything depends on what goes on inside, don't you think? The delicate bones, the tension of experience all come into their own if the person is exceptional. But O the pudding faces, the sullen, pasty faces people grow usually! You are right about New Englanders. They grow old well. They make marvelous old ladies! They make awkward young girls or cheap young girls. [to BB, 23 Apr 42, Ch Pl]

> I saw an old woman with a face like a queen
> Stamped on a gold coin, such fire was within,
> So proud and so tender the flash of her eye
> And this was her wisdom and this was her cry:
> "Give away your heart, child, give away your bone
> For the world as we knew it is crumbling and gone,
> Be prodigal, my ardent child, and never fear the cost
> Now is the time for love, my child—or we are lost."

> [from "Song," unpublished, written for Rosalind Green, Oct 42]

. . . but you are so right about the New England faces. I hope I shall have the sense not to wear any makeup as time goes on. Virginia Woolf for instance was so perfectly transparently beautiful later on—but that is achieved from *within*, as you say. [to BB, 14 Jan 45, Ch Pl]

The old Spanish women in their long black shawls look so beautiful—they have ancient El Greco faces—they are so much more beautiful than the younger generation it is sad. [to EMS and GS, 5 Jun 45, Santa Fe (DMcK)]

I know for myself that everything will happen to me about work and life in about fifteen or twenty years—one only begins to hold one's life in one's hands if it is a deep life, a life of your kind of genius, at about your age.[5] [to LB, 26 Jan 54, Wr St]

[5]Bogan was then fifty-seven, Sarton forty-one.

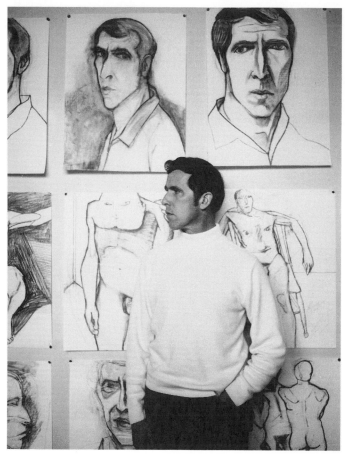

Bill Brown, 1970.

I sometimes imagine that as one grows older one comes to *live* a role which as a young person one merely "played"—[to LB, 3 Jul 55, Wr St]

The photo is a great valentine. I am impressed by the *strong* face you have created. I am sure that at 50 and from then on in, the face we have is what we have made, not what we were given. Also the drawings are somehow redefined and even more impressive in conjunction with the *real* face. [to BB, 13 Feb 70, Nelson]

She loves the richness of age in others and has longed for it also in herself—

My feeling about growing older is that every age has its particular value and beauty—in fact I can hardly wait to be 60 when ripeness is all. What worries me is that people seem not to realize this and, as you say, wish to remain young, which is just a waste of the next experience, equally valuable. But of course one's powers grow and grow if one has anything at all inside. [to KD, 13 Apr 49, Oxf St]

Et, Mon Dieu, j'ai soif de cette *vieillesse* qui vient si lentement. C'est vrai qu'on est malade de jeunesse. Peut-être faudrait-il s'enfermer dans une bibliothèque, tout apprendre, tout *savoir* et ne rien *sentir*—et ne commencer à vivre qu'à trent ans![6] [to JH, 13 Jan 38, Ch Pl]

[6]"And my God I thirst for *age* which comes so slowly. It is true that one becomes sick of youth. Perhaps one must lock oneself up in a library, learn everything, *know* everything and *feel* nothing—and not begin to live until one is thirty."

And then there is memory with which she steals from the past rich store, and brings it home[7]—

Just at present I think my idea of perfect bliss would be to climb the big red maple at old Shady Hill with an enormous peppermint in one pocket—and sit on the very top—you remember the sort of stump there was—and the wind blew your hair into your eyes and made you quite dizzy or the trunk swayed, then slowly, O very slowly to eat the peppermint, licking out its middle first through a hole in the chocolate. [to JC, 15 Mar 30, 94 Macd]

In the afternoon I doze until tea, lying in my upper bunk and watching the sea rise and fall through the porthole with an occasional haze of foam falling across and sometimes making a rainbow. It is then that I think of earth and of you so happily. How wonderful a thing memory is—how terrible to *lose* one's memory, to possess no longer these endless perfections, perfect because they are inalterable, the past, and can be looked at like paintings for what they *are*, not for what they might or should be. Demanding nothing of will, nor of conscience. [to JH, 14 Aug 38, aboard *American Importer*]

> Ah, what is memory but this holy gift:
> To keep the whole heart open, where
> Split and to hold death in the rift:
> So in all living still to die with her.
>
> And in all dying still with her to live.
> Wherever the pure absolute of pain
> Leaps unarmed from the heart, you give
> Hers back to earth, as mercy in the rain.

[from "For Nadia Boulanger," unpublished, 16 Mar 39, Ch Pl]

Do you remember how we ordered a little red cat for Jeannie[8] from Sears Roebuck? Did it ever come? I remember the waiting and the planning and

---

[7] See "Death and the Turtle" in *A Private Mythology*.
[8] A goat. The "cat" is puzzling.

how meanwhile she always escaped into the marsh—also the fearful effect that *Stalky & Co.*[9] had on our view of life at that age! I had a letter from Belgium, a dear courageous letter telling all the things the students are doing, silly things to keep up courage like parading with macaroni on a stick tied with black crepe to celebrate the Italian defeats. They are completely pro-British and at least united. That was a virtue in Leopold's[1] staying. But anyway Aunty Lino said that those summers we were together gardening and discussing seem now like an eternal spring. Ernesta[2] is part of that spring. I often think of her. [to RG, 27 Mar 41, Springfield, Mo.]

How long has it been, six years, since I have seen you in a vermilion cap, or eaten a cucumber sandwich under a tree with you and Julian and the boys. Dear dear times. Often and often they come back like a song. [to JH, 3 Jun 45, Santa Fe (ER)]

What images of you I have, what a treasure—the blue dress, the pink hat and you all gold and shining at the station the first time; you kneeling before Janet[3] and looking about fifteen; you sewing the lace on your slip having an awful time threading a needle with an obstinate look which I loved; and running away from the car on Ave. Kléber in a black suit and your legs like a deer's so nervous and delicate—and you asleep, a secret child; and you with a brilliant scarf at your throat in a black dress in the restaurant, and once looking down into the table as if you were for once really pleased with yourself. I who forget everything remember these things precisely. [to JH, 6 Jun 48, VF]

As you know, being a guest is not an ideal life and five months of it is long. I think I shall not do this again quite like this, but there were many factors involved. And meanwhile I do work and much is wonderful—I know I shall

[9]A collection of boys' stories by Rudyard Kipling; largely autobiographical, they narrate the pranks and adventures of three schoolboys.
[1]Leopold III, who in 1934 succeeded his father, Albert I, as King of Belgium.
[2]Ernesta Greene, who commited suicide in 1939.
[3]Janet Flanner.

remember these two weeks afterwards in all their rich detail of vine and sun and wild poppies and wheat and wonder how it was that I was not happier. [to JM, 14 Jun 48, VF]

Our two weeks in Montreux open in my memory like a Japanese flower in water—all the joys—and the great joy of being together. [to EMS and GS, 20 Jul 48, Paris (Huxley)]

But part of me swings back to Paris for a last look at you, at the river, at the lights on the ceiling; part of me stays in Belgium in the little chair opposite Jean-Do's; part of me remembers with tender gratefulness the fun at Glenavy's and dear Beatrice with her childlike *joie de vivre* which nothing in her hellish life has touched or tainted; part of me seems to be here—and a large part looks forward to the great leap back into small human responsibilities, lectures, work etc. [to JH, 9 Sep 48, Ireland]

How I think of you all these days. And somehow or other it is all a parting for me too.[4] I think of your room and the great blue curtains that opened to the moon, and through which once the night I slept there alone a large cat suddenly appeared, rather like the devil. And of the waves of light on the ceiling, and the delicate light wool blankets (those at least will go with you) and the little desk covered with invites from ambassadors, and roses. And I think of all the music we listened to in the other room and all the lights over Paris, and the fireworks at 2:00 A.M. and the sunrise once or twice, and the olive-green river. I think of the mantelpiece which will never see again the fat crystal candlesticks and the red candles and the Mexican death's head—and of all the leaves which used to come in with you so it was an arbor, pointed pale green beech leaves against the wall and their shadows. And of the little plants in the big window. I think of you looking down at yourself once in the glass table like Narcissus. I think of the dear little birds on my wall. . . . Never, never will there be such a place, such a time again, such a spring. O, how I hate

[4]The Huxleys were about to leave their apartment in Paris for a conference in Beirut, Lebanon, and then on to Italy.

your leaving. How I hate it all to be packed and foreigners to live there (I hope they are haunted).

And Edward Lear said, "All things have suffered change. All is packed. All is empty. All is odious. All is anger. All is sorrow. All is bother."[5] [to JH, I Nov 48, Oxf St]

I too have never felt the "presence" of anyone dead—I think we keep them alive in our memory—no other way. We *invoke* them to help us through bad times, too. [to KD, 17 Feb 63, Nelson]

It was very moving to hear from Shady Hill that music on a good piano will be heard for Eve[6] in three classes at Shady Hill forever and ever—what a splendid gift, as well as the tape recorder *and* a small instrument (a tiny 'cello is a delightful thought). As I write I see Eve's face so clearly and a look of shining delight which sometimes crossed it—and it makes me think of Johnson's so moving tribute to Stevenson about "when that day comes, he will not be there, but it will still be his day." And it will be Eve's day for years to come whenever a child has that rapt expression of delight at music. Oh Rosalind, what heartbreak. [to RG, 29 Jul 65, Nelson]

And although some memories take time to build inward—

Those memories[7] have not been distilled into essences and are a bit too painful. [to LB, n.d. (1954?)]

Eventually they fill her bin[8]—

But my premise that true memory is the key to creating works of art is proving very valuable. [to KD, 13 Mar 60, Wr St]

[5] In his letters to Lord Cromer, edited by Evelyn Baring.
[6] Francesca Greene Morgan's daughter, who died.
[7] Concerning the death of Sarton's mother.
[8] See "In Suffolk" in *Halfway to Silence*.

As they have done unceasingly since childhood—

> Thus are our moments
> Not to be wholly lost
> Or wholly found
> Ever again.
> In melting snow,
> Wood-smoke,
> Or birch-bark
> We shall think to have them all,
> Forgetting that on earth
> Such hours are comets
> Across the infinite
> Which even memory
> Cannot recall.

["Great Time," HJ, 13 Jan 29, Ray St]

But everything passes with time, and memory I think forgets the pain and remembers the joy and the beauty of which there has been so much in this strange and terrible summer. [to JM, 11 Aug 48, London (K)]

It has been an earthquake to go back to that dazzling time in the thirties when I knew Bowen and everyone else—I dream a lot and feel quite harrowed. But I think maybe the portrait is quite good—I hope so.[9] [to BB, 15 Jan 75, York]

And then there is death—

It is quite terrifying to think of seeing you both so soon—I always suffer unreasonably from the "mal du départ"[1]—and the horrible cheerfulness of tenderness that *hides* has already descended on Mummy and me. I hate leaving her. It makes me feel that I am getting old, that I am now constantly

[9]Sarton was then working on "Elizabeth Bowen" in *A World of Light*.
[1]"sickness of departure."

somewhere deep down preparing myself for the time when she will die. It is absurd of course. The things one prepares oneself for and are armed against never happen, do they? It's always the unexpected things. [to JH, 3 Mar 37, Ch Pl]

It is true that one can be an orphan suddenly at any age—and it is terrible to think that every human being must lose his mother sooner or later—all one's life is preparing for it so that one will be able to sustain it when it comes. I think of KM's letters when her mother died—and of waking up when I was a child sobbing because I had dreamed that mother was dead, with a sense of desolation that even her presence did nothing to help, because I knew it *would* happen someday. [to K, 21 May 39, Ch Pl]

I have been feeling a little mad, like a leaf being blown down a long tunnel—strange cities and loneliness and the really awful news of Virginia Woolf's suicide,[2] which a girl at a college told me quite casually just before lunch, and I suppose because I couldn't cry then I have had fits of crying ever since. I knew her quite well and I had always hoped to do something someday that she would like—that doesn't matter—I don't know why I even say it, but her death matters a great deal. It leaves a hole in literature and her living presence in the world was an assurance that there was someone putting the pieces together and looking at them always rather tenderly and maliciously at the same time—no matter how often they were broken apart. She had a tender regard for life, and just now that is so needed. [to MFH, 10 Apr 41, Allerton Hotel, Chicago]

It's not her[3] *dying* now that matters—she has been desperately ill for months and I expect it will be a release. It's the years and years ahead when she will not be there that I do not face. She can die but we cannot do without her. There is the enormous human egotism. I felt it once before, when Virginia Woolf

[2]At about 11:30 on the morning of Friday, March 28, 1941, leaving one letter for Leonard Woolf and one for Vanessa Bell, Virginia Woolf, tormented by mental illness, crossed the meadows to the river and with a large stone in the pocket of her coat went to her death. See "Letter from Chicago" in *The Land of Silence.*
[3]Edith Forbes Kennedy's.

died, a sort of *rage*. Virginia Woolf, Edith, Lugné-Poë, Jean Dominique, Kot, you. These, in absence of God, were my gods and three are dead, one lost in the hell of silence. And perhaps it is a sin to say she is dead. Perhaps she will live but the doctors say not. Could faith do it I wonder? And would it be better for her if she lived? That is what one doesn't know. I do not mean to be so mournful. There should be nothing but *praises*. [to JH, 19 Sep 42, 22 E 10]

You speak of Roosevelt's death. It seemed unbelievable here. And his greatness shone out of those days and on many people's faces. It laid the responsibility squarely on all our shoulders where it belongs. I liked what a Merchant Marine boy wrote, "All the men write me the same thing—'We've lost our leader, but there is more of him in each of us. We have to finish his work.'" [to JH, 3 Jun 45, Santa Fe (ER)]

Last winter he[4] was very near death—and he said, "C'était si doux, si doux,"[5] and he wanted to die, but at the foot of his bed was a large piece of chestnut wood, standing, that he had meant to work on and suddenly it began to put forth leaves and stems, and he said, "It was a presage and so I knew I must live. Oh it was agony to live. It was horrible, but I did." Then he smiled his wonderful delighted smile. Really a *saint*, the point where the artist meets the saint. [to JM, 10 Jun 47, Paris (Huxley)]

I hope you go to a dr. now and then for a thorough checkup. I have become quite terrified for all I love. So many of our friends are dying horribly of cancer. Three people on Channing Pl. this year. Now I have just heard that Elsa Ulich[6] (that living angel of strength, Elsa Brandstrom she was, and known as the White Angel in the last war) is dying in horrible tortures and nothing to be done. And so many useless people live. How hard it is to accept, to understand. *Why?* Why she of all people, why have to suffer so much when her whole life has been a gift, a warm, large happy spending of herself for

---

[4]Brancusi.

[5]"It's so peaceful, so peaceful."

[6]Lecturer in the U.S. from 1921 on. Human suffering and the hardships and dislocations of war were her subjects; author of *Among War Prisoners in Siberia* (1921). Wife of Harvard professor Robert Ulich.

others? I cannot resign myself to it and tremble for my mother, for you, for Judy. Who next? It is terrifying. Please be sure you are all right if you have the slightest shadow of pain *anywhere*. [to JH, 20 Jan 48, Oxf St]

I think what it is to leave this continent once more, the great moving skies over Belgium, the forest to which I said goodbye yesterday when it was shot through with sunlight, full of mystery. I think of Jean-Do. She is greatly diminished in strength these last months and I feel now the almost imperceptible lifting of the anchor, as if she were altogether lighter and more fragile and the wind of that final parting already rising. Shall I see her once more before she dies? I think of Edith,[7] of Lugné-Poë, the anchors of faith. When Jean-Do dies, when Kot dies, then I shall have to begin to try to be for other people what they have been for me. Very slowly one's life tilts towards giving and not taking. [to JH, 8 Aug 48, Chez Limbosch]

Mother died on Sat. very peacefully in her sleep—thank God it is over. The last three weeks were so awful and at the end one felt the slow difficult uprooting, that letting go, so painful and terrible. She just wanted to die and was so frightfully tired and weak. The funeral is tomorrow and I wish you could be there as it will be all Bach on the organ with just that little chapter from Paul on Charity read, and that is all. What is awful is how much there is to do, and all I wish is to sit for a long time silent and alone and just be still and try to be reborn again, for I have been dying with mother for so long. [to BB, 20 Nov 50, Myn Pl]

The month when Jean-Do hovered between life and death very gently, not in pain, quite lucid—was for me a sort of balm. I was there and could help and it was almost as if I had mother again, but this time not in agony. I do not know how to explain this but the relief it was to make little meals and that Jean-Do could enjoy them (every meal for months had been an ordeal for mother)—it would have been beautiful and right if she could have slipped away while I was there. But one cannot, alas, choose one's death. And now she must try to live

[7]Edith Forbes Kennedy.

and perhaps for some reason we do not yet know. [to RG, 21 Aug 51, Bread Loaf]

It was strange that your letter came the same day as one from my Chilean friend, Eugenia,[8] all about Kathleen Ferrier.[9] It does seem such a cruel death—and somehow that loss of a voice, like a bird who will never be heard again on earth, is poignant in the extreme, and she gave the purest joy, that joy so near to grief that poetry sometimes can too. [to BB, 27 Oct 53, Bryn Mawr, Pa.]

It was a shock about Dylan Thomas. I shall always remember the flood of relief I felt when I first read "October Morning" and "Fern Hill" and "Do not go gentle into that good night," as if a long starvation were at an end. It is cruel that he should go, but it is, I suspect, the Dionysian fate, the exalted feverish climb that cannot make a natural end. How mysterious—these angels and self-destroyers who appear now and then. But something has gone out of our world now forever and it does chill one to the bone. Also I get scared because such deaths make one feel responsible, I mean responsible for one's own future—to have more time is such a responsibility. To use it well, to keep on growing, to be implacably self-demanding and self-critical. Given less to begin with, we must become more (but I am talking of myself, not of you, of course)— What if Yeats had died at forty? Or Marianne Moore? I like best to think of poetry as a long life with the best at the end. [to LB, 13 Nov 53, Wr St]

It was very helpful what you said about *we* not *they* mourning. They are finally ready to die and we are not ready for them to go, ever, though at the very end I was ready for mother to go. Yes, I really was. [to LB, 2 Apr (n.y.)]

I am reading an enchanting book of autobiog. sketches by André Chamson, *Le Chiffre de Nos Jours.*[1] I read it drop by drop as hummingbirds sip honey. Once

[8]Eugenia Huneeus.
[9]British singer (1912–53); died at forty-one after several years' illness.
[1]*The Measure of Our Days.* A French Protestant novelist and essayist, Chamson wrote of life in the Cévennes and of the Resistance.

he tells about an uncle who at 80 finished harvesting his grapes and then at noon, sat down under an olive tree and said "Thy Will Be Done" and died. Isn't it a wonderful death? [to LB, 18 Apr 55, Mt. Pleasant, Mich.]

Je ne peux m'accoutumer ni comprendre du tout le moment de la mort—ce moment où tout à coup la personne n'est pas *là*. Quelle infinie séparation dans un instant où toute la vie est renversée et nous ne pouvons voir l'autre côté et nous ne savons rien. Nous vivons dans l'ignorance.[2] [to MC, 18 Jan 51, Myn Pl]

Je sais trop bien comme on revit et revit ces choses et que le trou reste béant, et que le temps n'a absolument rien à faire avec cela. On ne guérit pas des vrais pertes. On apprend à vivre avec—c'est tout.[3] [to MC, 25 Mar 52, Ch Pl]

It's a supreme photograph[4]—my heart turned over when I opened it—what an angel you are to part with such a treasure (are the other two as good? I hope so or I would feel like a thief). If only we can look like that two days before we die—the transparency, the ineffable smile, the wall so very thin between flesh and ghost. I feel that it is going to speak to me when I get started on Inner Space—which I am longing to do. [to BB, 20 Nov 69, Nelson]

I just heard that Stravinsky has died in his sleep—it will be a blow for you—another of the "elders" leaving for ports unknown while we struggle on, more and more isolated. But how splendid that you had that wonderful dinner with him last year when the will was signed! One cannot grieve for him—it was such a fulfilled life and such a long one. [to BB, 6 Apr 71, Nelson]

[2]"I cannot accustom myself to nor understand the moment of death—that moment when suddenly the person is not there anymore. What endless separation in a second when life is ended and we cannot see where it has gone, we know nothing, we live in ignorance."
[3]"I know too well how one relives and relives these things and that there remains a gaping hole, and that time has absolutely nothing to do with that. One does not heal from true losses. One learns to live with—that is all."
[4]Cecil Beaton's photograph of Baroness Karen Blixen (Isak Dinesen).

With Céline Limbosch, Belgium, 1956.

Isak Dinesen photograph by Cecil Beaton. Credit: Susan Sherman.

Also I haven't written because I have been staggering under a series of deaths that have really shaken me. The first, Céline, taking with her my infancy really and childhood—the only person then alive who knew me all the way through and knew even my English grandfather (who died when mother was 19); then Helen Howe[5] (I read the obit in the *Times*, always a shock), a very old Boston friend and one of the funniest people I have ever known; then one evening I was watching the news and saw Julian's face on the screen, and knew what *that* meant; finally day before yesterday Rosalind Greene. All were very old, except Helen, so one does not mourn for them, released at last, but for oneself. So many memories well up—I feel *overcharged.* [to BB, 5 Mar 75, York]

Death does frame a person and somehow it is the good that stays. [ibid.]

And as part of that good, and at the center of her own salvation, is her courage and self-healing, those wings of the phoenix which are always pushing out.[6]

From the beginning she has started again, remade herself, created her own luck in a dirty time[7]—

We had a puncture and also got stuck on several hills and had to walk up. Luckily we always seem to strike a raspberry patch and ate as we walked along. [to EMS and GS, 2 Aug 27, DMC]

As usual *Poetry* sent back my poems "Monday," "A Friend" and "The Doll's House," but just think, Harriet Monroe[8] herself wrote the refusal, "Not yet—but these show promise." If she could only know how that warmed my heart. Well, we'll try again in a month or two. Meanwhile I'm going to send these to the *Atlantic.* [HJ, 13 Feb 28, Ray St]

[5]Helen Huntington Howe (1905–75), American novelist, biographer, and monologist who performed throughout the United States and England. She makes mention of May Sarton in *The Gentle Americans,* her literary and social chronicle of Boston.
[6]See "The Phoenix Again" in *The Silence Now.*
[7]See "A Recognition for Perley Cole" in *A Private Mythology.*
[8]Harriet Monroe (1860–1936), American editor and poet, is known chiefly as the editor of *Poetry,* which she founded in Chicago in 1921.

The swift prophetic wind,
The eager rain,
The fever of rebirth
Swept through my dizzy brain
And stung.

[from "Reaction," HJ, 31 Mar 28, Ray St]

And her love of gardening has planted images of rebirth throughout her life—

One begins to imagine the possible renascence of the bulbs which one planted
so hopefully and despaired of at every frost— The spring *exists* now in the
mind—that is why January is such a hard month—one is already in a state of
expectation of what can't begin actually for months. We have planted single
white tulips—I can't wait for them. Never has there been a year when one
needed more to be born again. [to VW, 15 Jan 39, Ch Pl]

If this[9] is not good I will write another until there is a whole chest full of
rubbish for a phoenix to be born out of. [to K, 22 Nov 39, Ch Pl]

And I'm sure you're dead right that an illness now and then (when one is
convalescent at least) is a good thing for the super-tensions of people like us.
One has to be born again. [to MFH, 26 Jan 42, Ch Pl]

Spring has the effect of making me extremely earthy and interested in sensa-
tions such as food, drink, love, poetry, paintings, music—one is really born
again. This year I thought it wasn't going to happen. I have been really dull
and empty for such a long time. But it did, in New York, and now I am so full
of zest about writing I should turn out a masterpiece. [to BB, 9 Apr 42, Ch Pl]

I came out the day after the funeral,[1] a brilliant soft crystal day—and at last
was alone and could cry and then pick myself up and play the *Emperor Concerto,*

[9]"Fire in a Mirror," unpublished manuscript.
[1]Of Edith Forbes Kennedy, one of Sarton's dearest friends in Boston.

*Edith Forbes
Kennedy. Portrait by
Paul Child.*

and get back to work. Poems have suddenly spouted and it seems like a miracle. *Now* I know how awful it was to be separated from poetry. That was the illness, nothing else. And now I am well. [to MFH, 27 Jul 42, Sudbury]

And as someone wrote to me once in a similar situation, "I believe in phoenixes"—there is a worm stage first, you know, but then the great fiery bird flies off! [to BB, 11 Dec 42, Ch Pl]

I am more cheerful and have discovered that there are *two* words for hope in French, so I hope in French. [to GS, 24 Mar 47, Oxf St]

And you *are* a phoenix of course so it is all right.

To this urn let those repair
That are either true or fair;
For these dead birds sigh a prayer

says W.S.[2] of the phoenix and the turtle, if you remember. [to BB, 2 Feb 49, Oxf St]

All you can be is yourself and trust in life. My own experience has been that it's always when one has lost hope that suddenly someone appears on the horizon—[to BB, 23 Sep 50, Myn Pl]

And after a drought in Nelson—

We are back on the well now and have had some rain, so the garden begins to perk up—and I expect to myself, soon. [to KD, 18 Aug 63, Nelson]

[2]Shakespeare.

*Sunrise at York.
Credit: Susan
Sherman.*

So I go up and down—have been lonely here for the first time. But I have just had to make back the good *solitude* from the inside out, or from the outside in (right now autumn is in its glory and one can't feel depressed when looking up at the great shout of maples against the blue sky)—[to RG, 4 Oct 64, Nelson]

Well, I am rambling on. Tomorrow I begin a *Vita Nuova,* and attack the new book,[3] also give up smoking and try to lose ten pounds! I think I probably will not teach again—not anyway unless someone comes to me. I think I can manage as a lecturer and writer and everything looks a great deal more cheerful than when I wrote you. [to RG, 3 Jan 65, Nelson]

[3] *Miss Pickthorn and Mr. Hare.*

Or regarding a bad review—

Never mind—maybe the climate of adversity is in the long run more fruitful and possible for us than the horrendous and consuming climate of success. I am over it now—tears are a purge and I cried for 48 hours and couldn't stop. Now I feel very clear and whole and myself again. [to BB, 3 Dec 70, Nelson]

In response to depression—

Your letter was a most extraordinary relief and somehow blessing to me—but oh darling, I am so sorry about the depression. I guess we have to die over and over again and be reborn over and over again—and it is so *exhausting* a process that I wonder that either you or I is still alive and working well, as we are. [to BB, 16 Feb 71, Nelson]

Well, dear heart, rest now and begin again, like a fountain. [to BB, 10 Jul 71, Nelson]

During the final days of her mother's illness—

. . . et ne sois pas trop anxieuse. Au fond de moi j'ai encore un puit de forces et je le trouverai—sans doute demain matin.[4] [to MC, 8 Nov 50, Myn Pl]

It was a very marvelous summer and I feel alive again, like Antaeus, the very root which I now see was starving has been nourished. This the faces in Europe do for me, the trees—I don't know what it is. All I know is that I begin to feel transparent to life again instead of opaque. [to RG, 21 Aug 51, Bread Loaf]

Just one more thing about my poems: there are two ways to take the fact that the critics have never been interested in the poems. One is to blame the critics,

[4]"Do not be too anxious. Deep down I always have a source of strength and I will find it without doubt tomorrow morning."

but surely, Louise, it is healthier and more positive in every way to blame myself and learn and try to do better? The real crux of it is that I must find the way out of battering my head against that wall. And the only creative way is dissatisfaction, relentless self-criticism and a new start each time. This is not really a matter of will as much as what an old friend of mine once said, "Il faut rinser l'oeil."[5] [to LB, 25 Mar 55, Wr St]

And so it is with a rinsed eye that she sees each loss and change—

I am getting ready to tear up my roots, deeply embedded here. I hate leaving. I hate partings. But I *love* the new life ahead whatever it is, and I feel *ready*. [to MFH, 26 Oct 42, Sudbury]

And with each bout of disappointment, despair, or illness, true to her symbol of the phoenix and obeying nature's laws,[6] she recalls what she said one Easter during the war—

It is a good Easter—because in spite of the destruction the end is in sight and the rebirth. I feel it deeply. And I myself feel reborn with all this work going on inside me. [to EMS and GS, 30 Mar 45, Santa Fe (ER)]

[5]"One must rinse the eye."
[6]See "The Phoenix Again" in *The Silence Now.*

Endpiece. Credit:
Susan Sherman.

INDEX

Page numbers in *italics* refer to photographs.